DIY

(Do It Yourself)

Portfolio
Management

Yes, with a little independent thinking and discipline, you can beat the returns of popular indexes, and of fund managers

Lyle Wilkinson

Selact Publishing, Kahului, Maui

Do it Yourself Portfolio Management! With a little independent thinking and discipline, you can beat the returns of popular indexes, and fund managers

by Lyle Wilkinson

Published by:
Selact Publishing
Post Office Box 3182
Wailuku, HI 96793-3182
orders@diyportfoliomanagement.com
http://diyportfoliomanagement.com

Copyright © 2003

International Standard Book Numbers (ISBN)

ISBN, print ed.   0-9728395-0-X
ISBN, PDF ed.   0-9728395-1-8

Library of Congress Control Number: 2003101312

Publisher's Cataloging in Publication Data
(Prepared by The Donohue Group, Inc.)

Wilkinson, Lyle.
   DIY (Do it yourself) portfolio management / Lyle Wilkinson.

   p. : ill. ; cm.

   Cover title: DIY portfolio management

   Includes bibliographical references and index.

   ISBN: 0-9728395-0-X

1. Portfolio management. 2. Investments--Decision making. I. Title. II. Title: DIY portfolio management III. Title: Portfolio management

HG4529.5 .W55 2003
332.6

                                                      2003101312

Printed in China

Contents

Special thanks go to Charlotte Wilkinson for relaxing other deadlines to give me book time, to Bailey Wilkinson for helping with marketing research, to Harry Eagar for putting the manuscript into readable English, and to Victor Pellegrino for guiding me to print.

Preface

For most of my 30 years of investing, my formal education in the theories of perfect knowledge and rational man guided my financial life. I diversified retirement assets across the Fidelity mutual funds available to my 401k account, keeping 10% of my assets in each of the 10 funds in order to attain average wealth growth with minimum risk. It wasn't that I didn't want to get rich quick; it was more that I didn't want to lose equity. Fear conquered greed.

My conservative 401K strategy kept my mutual fund holdings growing nicely, averagely, through the late 1990's. My life was consumed by career, kids, and getting my MBA. At the same time, my discretionary trading was bad enough that I hadn't found a reason to doubt my formal education.

Then in the fall of 1998, a career event gave me more time to study the market. My dabbling in equities over the years had never been very successful or disciplined. Other than my 401k diversification strategy, I had no plan. I was mostly a discretionary investor. Trades came from hot tips, a little fundamental analysis, a little gut feel, and lots of optimism. Some refer to this as the religious approach to investing. Buy a stock; pray the price doesn't fall.

BBA and MBA Finance Professors over the years convinced me of the existence of the rational man and of the validity of the efficient market hypothesis (EMH). Although the exact details of the theory might escape me, the theory shaped my deeply held beliefs about the market:

- Equity prices move randomly, and the only way to beat the market is to have inside information.

- Equity prices reflect all the knowledge available about the market and the only way to beat the market is to have inside information.
- Most individual investors, traders and day-traders fail to beat the indexes.
- Most professional fund managers fail to deliver to investors a return better than market indexes. Some beat the indexes each year, but few beat the indexes consistently.
- Return realized is proportional to risk assumed

Now, after reading a few books and losing a few dollars, the beliefs left over from a formal education seem too much of a generalization, too simple.

It is now clear that certain investors/traders consistently win (beat the market). Examples of winning investor/traders come from books and from conferences, such as the annual Online Investor Expo. Other examples come from brokerage house clerks who only remember 2 classes of clients, those that win and those that lose.

Book Organization

This book has three parts. The first part is background that explains the origins of ideas about portfolio strategy and portfolio management. The second part details the logic and back-testing of *Trend Regression Portfolio Strategy*. The third part contains investment and money management ideas peripheral to *Trend Regression Portfolio Strategy*.

The ideas for *Trend Regression Portfolio Strategy* come from statistics and from studying books and periodicals. Most of the statistical theory is from *Theory and Problems of Statistics* by Murray R. Spiegel published as part of the Schaum's Outline Series in 1961. The books with the most impact on *Trend Regression*

Portfolio Strategy were *Against the Gods* by Peter L. Bernstein published by John Wiley & Sons in 1996, and the part of *High-Return Low-Risk Investment* written by Robert F. Drach published by Putnam Publishing Group in 1981. Other publications also influenced the *Trend Regression Portfolio Strategy* in direct or subtle ways.

The details of the *Trend Regression Portfolio Strategy* are explained through the construction of models, the back-testing of models on historical data, the paper-trading of portfolios and the tracking of actual trading results. The meat of Portfolio Strategy is in the second half, but for many people the second half alone is too much like a black box. Here I am defining black box as something that provides a solution to a user based on a process the details of which are hidden from the user.[1] A trading black box issues trade recommendations based on analysis not clear to the trader. For a trading black box to be useful, the trader has to have faith that the black box works. It is very hard to trade a system that you do not understand or trust. Regardless of how well the system should work, or how well it works for someone else it won't work for you unless you believe in it. You don't necessarily have to understand how a black box works to use it successfully, but you do have to trust it with your money.

Disclaimer

Any statements about future expectations, including statements about anticipated levels of financial return, are suspect. Actual results may differ materially from those indicated by back-tests and paper-trading. History is history. Tomorrow is tomorrow. The laws of physics do not bound financial evolution, and past performance is no guarantee of future results.

What worked in the past, doesn't necessarily work in the future. Back-test and paper-trading successes don't guarantee real dollar trading success. An optimization process can find the best fit on historic data. However, future data may or may not follow patterns of historic data, and the models that worked before may or may not work again. Optimization finds the best fit for past data, which we hope is also a reasonable fit for the future.

Be especially careful with back-tests that have exceptional results not confirmed by closely related models or by back-tests in other time-periods. Try to see why the optimized model works. Seeing why, how the model works, doesn't necessarily make the model work better in the future, but it makes it more tradable. It is easier to trade when you understand and trust what the model is doing.

The purpose of this book is to educate and inform the reader in portfolio management. Its goal is to get you started, rather than explore every conceivable nuance. Its goal is to complement, rather than replace, other books on portfolio management, investing, trading, and personal finance. The author and publisher shall have no liability or responsibility for loss or damage caused by any person or entity's use of information in this book.

If you cannot agree to the terms of the last paragraph, you may return print copies of this book for a refund of your purchase price.

Part I — Background

Investing your money in security instruments can be an expensive way to gain a portfolio management education. Studying investing/trading books can help reduce the time and cost of your education. Reducing the cost of your education gives you more money to invest and reducing the time to acquire your education will give you more time to compound your return.

Jack Schwager's *Market Wizard* books describe traders who consistently win.[2] The most surprising aspect of his series is not just that there are winners, but that many winning strategies or methods exist. Each of the traders described by Schwager has a unique way of taking profit from the market.

Based on interviewing and studying traders and on his own trading experiences Schwager developed the following beliefs about the market:[3]

- The markets are not random, regardless of the large number of academicians who have argued the efficient market hypothesis; they are simply wrong.
- The markets are not random, because they are based on human behavior, and human behavior, especially mass behavior, is not random.
- There is no "holy grail" or grand secret to the markets, but there are patterns that can lead to profits.
- There are a million ways to make money in markets. The irony is that they are all difficult to find.
- The markets are always changing, and they are always the same.
- The secret to success in the markets lies not in discovering some incredible indicator or elaborate theory; rather, it lies within each individual.

- To excel in trading requires a combination of talent and extremely hard work (surprise!) -- The same combination required for excellence in any field. Those seeking success by buying the latest $300 or even $3,000 system, or by following the latest hot tip, will never find the answer because they haven't yet understood the question.
- Success in trading is a worthy goal, but it will be worthless if not accompanied by success in your life (not just financial success).

These are the insights of a man who has not only traded, but also studied both the markets and the market masters. Maybe Schwager overstates the number of ways to make money, and maybe he understates the amount of work needed to uncover patterns that will work in the future, but he is definitely right on target about individual responsibility. To make profits, the individual trader must take the responsibility for uncovering patterns and for building confidence in the pattern to the degree needed to stick with the trading plan.

I'm still on the fence about the "holy grail," incredible indicator, elaborate theory idea. Sure, the trader/investor has to have talent, perseverance, and discipline to find and trade a system. However, the system has to be one that works, one that creates profitable trades. Whether it is the latest $3,000 system or your best ever homegrown system, it has to be a system that you understand and trust. The system needs to inspire confidence to be tradable, and it needs to generate winning trades or the trader will run out of money.

At first reading, I didn't genuinely buy into the idea that the markets are not random. At the time, I thought the markets were mostly random with a few isolated situations where some pattern or logic prevailed. Probably it was and still is just a complexity issue. Prices move for reasons, but we are not consistently smart enough to make the connections between price change and cause. Cause and effect is at work in the markets and price changes do happen for reasons. However, the number of variables (causes), and interactions between variables, affecting prices are too great to be simultaneously evaluated in a useful way. Because of the complexity, being greater than our comprehension, the market seems random.

> " The failure of the rational model is not in its logic but in the human brain it requires. Who could design a brain that could perform the way this model mandates? Every single one of us would have to know and understand everything, completely and at once."[4]

After the fact, it is always easier to make the connections between price changes and their causes. The analyst can see a price change, and then search for an event that preceded the change. Much harder is to witness the event, then predicting the price change. If the market jumps up after the Federal Open Market Committee (FMOC) of the Federal Reserve Board of Governors lowers interest rates, it is easy to say the reduction in financing costs had a simulative effect. However, even if you are 95% sure there will be a rate reduction, you wonder: do stock prices go up because of the simulative effect of lower finance costs or do stock prices go down because the FMOC is signaling a weakening of the economy?

1. Specific Recommendations

Have you lost faith in the experts?

Do It Yourself (DIY)! Direct Invest Yourself (DIY)! Take charge of managing your portfolio. You, with a little independent thinking, can beat the returns of indexes and fund managers.

Do you want some easy-to-implement tips on how to increase your wealth?

These specific recommendations are included here, early in the book, for those who want to "Do It Yourself" to improve their investment returns, but don't have the time or energy to read this whole book before they take action.

What makes me think you can Direct Invest Yourself? You can read and you have some keyboarding skills. You have the desire, you want a better return than you are getting.

What makes me think you will do better direct investing versus hiring a portfolio manager? I believe the Vanguard Group's John Bogle put his finger on it; most actively managed funds don't beat the averages. I believe you will manage your portfolio, your life savings, with more care and diligence than a professional manager whose income is probably uncorrelated with increases in your net worth, and may be in some cases inversely correlated with increases your net worth. You have fewer restrictions on how you can manage your portfolio, than a mutual fund manager.

What makes me think you have the courage to Direct Invest Yourself? You are willing to take responsibility for your investing life. You don't need to blame someone else for the decline in your net worth. You want to feel the risk and enjoy the gain. Even if you don't Direct

Invest Yourself, it's your net worth that goes up and down. You can delegate authority for investing decisions, but cannot delegate the results of those decisions.

What makes me think you have the time to Do It Yourself? Managing your portfolio can take as little time as you want. A simple market-matching portfolio can include SPY shares alone, that you buy and hold. You pre-retirement individuals should find a broker where you can buy a set dollar amount of SPY each pay period, to maximize the time each dollar is invested and to take advantage of dollar cost averaging. Once you establish your account and set up automatic payroll deduction, you're done. No maintenance required. Of course, if you want to beat the market, it will take more investment of time.

What makes me think you will enjoy Doing It Yourself? It's not only potentially more entertaining than gambling, it lacks commercial gambling's inherent negative expectation. Negative expectation is rooted in aggregate balance: gamblers' pay out dollars equals gamblers' pay in dollars less house operating cost dollars (including house profits). The house has to have a positive expectation or it cannot cover its operating expense and profit costs.

What makes me think you will enjoy Doing It Yourself? It's more entertaining than playing games on your computer, and it is a more socially acceptable use of your time, at least in some circles.

What makes me think you will enjoy Doing It Yourself? You understand compound interest. You know that if you pay your financial advisor, or mutual fund manger, 1½% of account value each year, you are transferring a large amount of your nest egg to your advisor. Assuming the average nest egg will grow at the 11% rate the S&P 500 has averaged, a dollar invested today will grow to $2.84 in 10 years, you will have $2.48, and your broker will have $0.36. Not a big deal? What if you invest $100,000 for 30 years? Your $100,000 grows to $2,289,000, you will have $1,522,000, and your broker will have $767,000.

What makes me think you will be capable of handling the emotional roller coaster of Doing It Yourself? Get used to it; your nest egg is going to fluctuate in value, whether or not you direct invest. You must face your fears and learn to accept drawdown as an inevitable component of having your nest egg in anything other than a savings account, or you must leave your money in the savings account.

Individually, we have many goals. Often we can state at least some of our financial goals in relationship to the market. We can state some lifestyle goals as to how much time and effort we want to commit to managing our finances. I have some specific recommendations for you, based on your goals. The recommendations step up from least aggressive, least effort to most aggressive, most effort.

If the goal is to match the return of the market with minimum effort, the best plan is to "buy and hold" index funds tied to the market you are trying to match. This is a little boring. However, as John Bogle said during a recent CNN Pinnacle interview "Do you want to be interested or rich?"[5] Mr. Bogle is founder, CEO of the Vanguard Group, one of the world's largest mutual fund companies. Bogle created the first index fund in 1974 on the premise that "mutual funds can make no superior claims to the market." In other words, he believed no fund manager has consistently outperformed the market on a cost-adjusted basis. Average long-term gross mutual fund returns might be close to market average returns, but net returns are lower due to management fees and income tax impact. Peter L.

Bernstein reported in *Against the Gods* that, during the decade from the mid 1980s to the mid 1990s, 78% of actively managed equity funds underperformed the Vanguard Index 500 fund designed to track the S&P Composite.[6] Filling your portfolio with a broad index trust such as the S&P 500 SPY and holding it forever is a good strategy. Holding SPY doesn't take any maintenance, is broadly diversified by holding 500 large USA companies, and gives you cocktail party bragging rights of being amused by the latest schemes to beat the market return.

If the goal is to beat the market with minimum effort and risk, the best plan is to subscribe to Robert F. Drach's weekly newsletter. There maybe other systems that work, but Mr. Drach's system is clearly explained in his books and has a quarter century of documented success. I'd like to stress the importance of the books and the documented performance through different economic cycles to the usability of Drach's system. The tangible hardcover book and long documented history of trade success make it much easier to commit the money and actually place the trades. More on Drach later.

> Apparently, the newest way for big investors to get index fund results is to sue mutual fund managers. A 12/6/2001 Forbes newsletter says Merrill Lynch agreed to pay Unilever an undisclosed sum and claims it is a moral victory for advocates of low-cost index funds like John Bogle.
>
> "NEW YORK - The epic case of **Unilever** vs. **Merrill Lynch** finally is over, and the winner is ... **John C. Bogle**.
> ...
> Which brings us back to Bogle, who invented the passively managed index fund and remains its best-known champion. Why, he asks, should people pay higher fees to traditional fund managers when the active approach cannot beat the market? "
>
> Mark Lewis, *Merrill Settlement A Boost For Index Funds*, Forbes.com, 12.06.01, 12:08 PM ET

If the goal is to beat the market by more, while accepting a little more risk and responsibility, and doing some work, read on.

If your goal is to get rich quick, I recommend you try day trading. Day trading isn't for everyone. Detractors say it is gambling, with the complication that neither the odds nor the payoffs are known. A few people through intellect, skill, concentration, work, perseverance, and/or luck get very rich quickly. Quite a few people make enough money day trading to stick with it as their means of livelihood. Many people lose their nest egg and find a new line of work. Although some of the best day traders are discretionary traders, most popular writers recommend disciplined adherence to a system that works. "The proper mind set that I'm speaking of is the result of self discipline and habit. Without exception, all consistently profitable traders have it."[7] The portfolio ideas in this book may have some application for day traders, although the application of these ideas to less than daily time periods has not been tested .

If your goal is to get rich quick, without any work, I recommend you continue to buy Powerball or Lotto tickets.

If your goal is to satisfy your need for living on the edge, I recommend you keep increasing your bet size and the speculative nature of your trades. Wrong! Actually if you are treating trading as entertainment or a source of excitement, I recommend Kiplinger's Personal Finance magazine August 2001 issue. It has alarming information about the progression from a few impulsive stock trades to becoming a problem or compulsive gambler.[8]

Although managing a portfolio is not entertainment, managing your portfolio should not be onerous. Don't lose track of your main objective, which is to grow your nest egg without subjecting it to excessive risk. You can get enjoyment from seeing your nest egg grow, rather than from a brilliant individual stock trades risking your life savings. Doing It Yourself, while beating market returns, is a very satisfying combination. Beating the market is a difficult but reachable goal. Every year many direct investors and professional portfolio managers beat the market. Fewer beat the market consistently. Our goal is nest egg growth consistently better than market growth.

2. Regression to the Mean

Averages are measures of the central tendency of a set of numerical data. The most popular of averages is the mean or arithmetic mean. The mean of a set of numbers "$\overline{X}$" is equal to the sum of the numbers "X" divided by the number of numbers "N" in the set.

$$\overline{X} = \frac{X_1+X_2+X_3+...+X_N}{N} = \frac{\sum X}{N}$$

The degree to which numerical data tend to spread about an average value is the dispersion of the data. Standard deviation is a common and useful measure of dispersion. Deviation "d" is the difference between each number "X" in the data set and the mean of the set "$\overline{X}$."

$$d = X - \overline{X}$$

The standard deviation "s" of a set of numbers is equal to the square root of the mean of deviations squared.

$$s = \sqrt{\frac{\sum (d)^2}{N}}$$

The standard deviation is the amount you might expect any value in the data set to be different from the mean of the data set. The amount you might expect a value to differ from the mean is further described by continuous probability distributions. The most often used probability distribution is the normal curve, the bell shaped curve. Most readers likely recognize the graph of the standardized normal curve shown below.

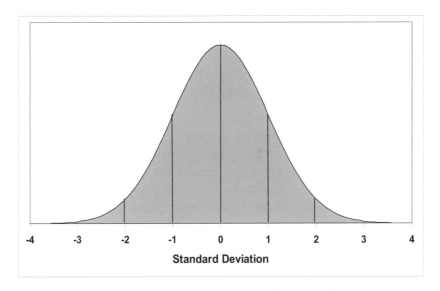

Standard Deviation

The centerline labeled "0" on the graph represents the mean. The area under the curve represents the probability of data points falling at a certain point relative to the mean. Fifty percent of the area is above, to the right of the mean. Fifty percent of the data points fall above the mean. Fifty percent of the area is below, to the left of the mean. Fifty percent of the data points fall below the mean. The area under the curve between -1 standard deviation and +1 standard deviation is 68.27 %. The probability that any data point from the data set will be between -1 and +1 standard deviation from the mean is therefore 68.27%. The area under the curve between -2 standard deviations and +2 standard deviations is 95.45 %. The probability that any data point from the data set will be between -2 and +2 standard deviation from the mean is therefore 95.45%. The area under the curve between -3 standard deviations and +3 standard deviations is 99.73 %. The probability that any data point from the data set will be between -3 and +3 standard deviation from the mean is therefore 99.73%.

The probability that any data point is above the mean is 50%. The probability that any data point will be between the mean and +1 standard deviation is 34.13%, half the probability that the data point will be between -1 and +1 standard deviation of the mean (50% times 68.27%).

What does *regression to the mean* mean? For the human population *regression to the mean* predicts that the babies of short parents are likely to grow taller than their parents, and the babies of tall parents are likely to be shorter at maturity than their parents.[9] For sweet peas *regression to the mean* predicts that the offspring of small diameter parents are likely to grow larger than their parents, and that the offspring of large diameter parents are likely to be smaller at maturity than their parents.

While the offspring are closer to mean than the parents, the offspring of parents from one extreme are closer to that extreme than the offspring of parents at the other extreme. In his 1886 "Regression toward Mediocrity in Hereditary Stature" article Francis Galton detailed his analysis of the heights of mature children to their parents.[10] He showed:

- Offspring of tall parents are shorter than their parents and offspring of short parents are taller than their parents.
- Offspring of tall parents are taller than average offspring and offspring of short parents are shorter than average offspring.
- Heights of offspring from each parental height group were normally distributed.

Bernstein thinks a lot of Galton's impact on the story of risk.

"regression to the mean is dynamite. Galton transformed the notion of probability from a static concept based on randomness and the Law of Large Numbers into a dynamic process in which the successors to the outliers are predestined to join the crowd at the center. Change and motion from the outer limits toward the center are constant, inevitable, foreseeable. Given the imperatives of this process, no outcome other than the normal distribution is conceivable. The driving force is always toward the average, toward the restoration of normality, ...

Regression to the mean motivates almost every variety of risk-taking and forecasting. It is at the root of homilies like "What goes up must come down," "Pride goeth before a fall," and "From shirtsleeves to shirtsleeves in three generations." ... It is the credo to which so-called contrarian investors pay obeisance: when they say that a certain stock is "overvalued" or "undervalued," they mean that fear or greed has encouraged the crowd to drive the stocks' price away from an intrinsic value to which it is certain to return. It is what motivates the gambler's dream that a long string of losses is bound to give way to a long string of winnings. ...."

What, if anything, does it mean for financial instruments? What mean is of interest? The price mean? The moving price mean, trend? An indicator's mean?

Many investors and traders quote rules based on regression to the mean:

- "Buy low and sell high"
- "You never get poor taking a profit"
- "Bulls win and bears win, but hogs get slaughtered"
- "It can't go much lower"
- "Sell when everybody else is buying and buy when everybody else is selling"

Many investors and traders repeat these rules, and strongly believe them. Unfortunately, many more believe them than trade them. It seems these rules have a broader intellectual appeal than emotional appeal. It is hard to sell when everybody else is buying and pushing up the price. It is hard to buy when everybody else is selling and pushing down the price. The emotions of greed and fear cloud logic.

In the late '90s the regression to the mean moved to the back burner for a large group of investors and traders as momentum trading gained favor with 'new' rules:

- "Buy high and sell higher"
- "The trend is your friend"
- "Go with the flow"
- "Don't fight the market"
- "Never average down"
- "Never meet a margin call"
- "If you must lighten up, liquidate your worst position"
- "TOPS COLA – Take out profit slowly, cut off losses at once"

After the NASDAQ peaked over 5,000, in early 2000, and fell below 1,700 by mid 2001, the frequency and volume of these trend following momentum mantras have dropped off.

There are 2 competing ideas about making money in financial markets. One is look for prices that are far from their mean and "buy low, sell high." The other is find a price trend and buy, or sell into it. Although it may seem that these ideas can't possibly both be right, both have their champions.

Drach

I promised we would get back to Robert F. Drach. In November of 2000, I read his 20-year-old *High-Return Low-Risk Investment*.[11] The theory advanced in this book made sense to me, the theory seemed to work in paper-trading, and also in back-testing models I tried in late 2000. Testing of Drach models worked well enough that I subscribed to the Drach Market Research weekly letter and started trading Drach's recommendations, on 1/02/2001. As of 11/19/2001, my Drach Market Research account was up 19%.[12] During the same 10.5 months the Dow was down 6%, the S&P500 was down 11%, and the NASDAQ was down 28%. My appreciation for Drach's methodology grew.

As he explains in *High-Return Low-Risk Investment*, Drach believes the 2 main drivers of equity price are fundamentals and emotion. His approach is to screen for solid fundamentals, then trade on emotion, not on his emotion, but on the emotion, sentiment, of the market.

Master List

Drach limits his master list using criteria designed to select stocks that are expected to be least affected by changing fundamentals, thus making emotion more predictive of their short term price moves. Drach screens for:

- Earnings Predictability: Eliminating equities without demonstrated predictability, as to earnings, eliminates surprise. Drach estimates 80 percent of equity candidates disappear in this first step.
- Earnings Growth: Past and future earnings growth make stocks attractive to a large number of investors. This step halves the number of stocks surviving from the predictability test.
- Dividend Protection and Growth: Important in the same way, but to a lesser extent than earnings is dividend predictability and growth.
- Concern for image, in investment community.
- Primary and secondary issues: More stock

to share pie.
- Institutional Following: Interest from both institutional and individual interest facilitates selling.
- Stock Classes: Stay away from corporations with large non-voting stock, as it hints of pomposity and hypocrisy.
- Family Held—Publicly Traded: Can be problem especially at generation change-overs
- Listed versus Over-the Counter: Listed preferred because more transparent, more liquid

At the beginning of 2002, Drach's master list had 81 equities. Fifty-eight equities were NYSE listed, 17 were NASDAQ listed, 4 were Toronto listed and 2 were American Stock Exchange listed. Of the 17 NASDAQ stocks, none is a technology company.

The master list determines which equities Drach follows. The market determines when to place buy and sell orders, and which master list equities to trade.

Market Timing

Buy and sell signals are based on factors affecting the entire master list. Buy soon before, or in conjunction with, the last period in which the sellers are dominant. Once sellers get out, buyers can get in, then dominate, and start to advance prices. Sellers are dominating when the market is declining. As they sell, their influence is diminishing. Stock must be purchased when sufficient sellers are available, which is usually as prices are declining, not after they decline. Sell soon before, or in conjunction with, the last period in which the buyers are dominant. Once buyers commit their equity, sellers can start to dominate and depress prices. Buyers are dominating when the mar-

depress prices. Buyers are dominating when the market is advancing. As they buy, their buying influence is diminishing, because their equity is committed. Buyers become holders or sellers, their focus shifts to selling; when, at what price is the question.

Sellers control supply. Buyers control demand. When supply exceeds demand prices fall, sellers are dominating. When demand exceeds supply prices climb, buyers are dominating.

The Buy Indication

P/Es are falling. At least 75 percent of the stocks monitored are lower in P/E than a month earlier. Cannot substitute index for 75% rule, must be 75% of stocks in master list. When historical weekly P/E are not available, substitute price change for P/E change raising required percentage of issues that must be down in price to 80 percent.

Price Volatility is increasing. Compare price change (current - 4 wks ago) measured this week to last week's measure.

The Press is negative: Look for Doom and Gloom in headlines of local paper.

Beta factors: If the percentage change of the high betas is the same or lower than the rest, this ancillary criterion has been met. If the high betas are not declining faster than the average, it is an indication that most of the selling pressure of beta followers has already been felt.

Trend Analysis: This criterion is met when prices go below the 180-day moving average.

Believed Cause and Effect. Interest rates and gold prices rising.

The Buy Indication

Volume: Criterion met if market volume increases by 15 % or greater.

The Sell Indication

P/Es are climbing. 75 percent of P/Es have shifted higher.

Price Volatility increasing.

Press is positive, reporting how wonderful the market is.

High Betas: price change no greater than other stocks.

Trend: Majority of stocks over 180-day moving average.

Cause and Effect: Interest Rates and Gold Prices both declining.

Overall Market Volume up by 15% or greater.

Drach's basic buy and sell signals assume regression to the mean. Buy when P/Es are falling and sell when P/Es are climbing. Buy when press is negative and sell when press is positive. Buy when stocks are under their 180-day moving average and sell when stocks are over their 180-day moving average.

Entries and Exits

When a buy indication is received from the market timing method 5 stocks with the lowest P/E's, lowest prices (relative to 4 weeks ago), or highest dividends (relative to price) are purchased. Sell indications generated from market timing trigger selling of profitable long positions. If not profitable, positions are reviewed to see if the original purchase criteria (lowest P/E's, lowest relative prices, or highest dividends) are still met.

Again, as with the basic buy and sell signals, entries and exits assume regression to the mean. Buy lowest P/Es or prices and sell highest P/Es or prices. Basing buys on highest dividend rate, at first glance, appears to deviate from the basic regression to the mean strategy. However, with stable dividends, relative dividend (dividend as percent of price) moves opposite price. Therefore, high dividend rate correlates with low prices.

In summary, Drach's three-step methodology is:

1. Select a group of stocks to track (master list).
2. Determine market emotion (market timing).
3. Determine relative emotion of individual equities (entries and exits).

Does a mean reversion strategy really work?

Drach's book, *High-Return Low-Risk Investment*, was co-authored by Thomas J. Herzfeld. Mr. Herzfeld's part of the book focused on closed-end funds, which led me to www.cefa.com the web site of the Closed-End Fund Association (CEFA).

> "**Closed-end funds** have a fixed number of shares outstanding. Following an initial public offering, their shares are traded on an exchange between investors. Transactions in shares of closed-end funds are based on their market price as determined by the forces of supply and demand in the marketplace. Interestingly, the price of a CEF may be above (at a premium to) or below (at a discount to) it's NAV. The transaction price will also include a customary brokerage charge. The invested capital in a closed-end fund is fixed and will change only at the direction of management. Capital can be increased through the issuance of shares in conjunction with a rights offering or through the reinvestment of certain dividend payments. Capital can be reduced when shares of the fund

are repurchased in conjunction with a stock repurchase program or tender offer."

Within the CEFA web site, I found *Does A Mean Reversion Strategy Really Work?* produced by Flemings Research.[13]

Yes! According to author Peter Juhl, mean reversion does work.

Some closed fund basics before we get into Mr. Juhl's work. From the overview of closed-end funds above, we know closed-end funds trade at premiums or discounts to their Net Asset Value (NAV). NAV is the value of all equity held in the fund divided by the number of fund shares issued. Market price is NAV times (1 minus discount) or NAV times (1 plus premium).

First, Juhl found that closed-end fund premium/discount reverts to its mean. Premium/discount for individual closed-end funds reverts to the historical mean premium/discount for the individual closed-end fund. The premium/discount of both large discount and large premium reverts to its mean in correspondence to the degree of the funds' premium/discount distance from its mean. The bigger the discount in relation to its historic mean the more the discount will shrink. The bigger the premium in relation to its historic mean, the more the premium will shrink.

Then, he found that the market value prices of closed-end funds increase as discounts are reduced and as premiums are increased toward their historic means. Juhl confirmed Herzfeld, the co-author of *High-Return Low-Risk Investment,* who believed that as the equities of a fund moved out of favor and NAV dropped, the discount for the fund grew, and that as equities moved into favor and NAV increased, the discount decreased. That is, falling NAV and increasing discount are complementary bearish signals, as increasing NAV and decreasing discount are complementary bullish signals. Herzfeld used discount/premium as a market-timing indicator.

Paper-trading and funded account *reversion to the mean* tests run through 2001 confirmed that there is validity to Thomas J. Herzfeld and Peter Juhl's works. In the graph below, blue lines are paper trading results for long only positions and hedged long/short positions. The green line is for a funded account, following the long only strategy.

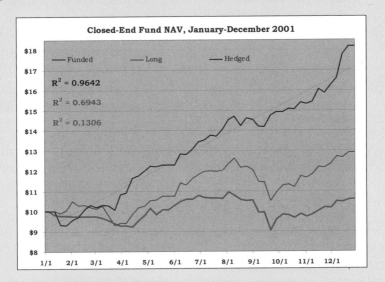

The underlying strategy was a little different from Juhl's, with long and shorts pulled from a group of 46 funds based on discount/premium farthest from their historic norms. The 50/50 hedge strategy looks good (50/50 has long positions matched with equal dollar amount of short positions). The funded account was small, leading to high transaction costs, and the account couldn't go short. The closed-end funds market sometimes lacks liquidity, so slippage was a problem. However, year-end Net Asset Value for the funded account was a respectable $10.60 compared to $9.65 for the 46-fund index, starting from $10 on 1/1/01.

Juhl is probably right in judging the efficacy of mean reversion strategies will depend on when the reversion strategy is tried and which funds are traded.

Along the way, Juhl also discovered that a reversion to the mean strategy does not work for all funds, and that the funds for which it works best, change continually. Juhl recommends four closed-end fund strategies, based on his reversion to the mean research.

Strategy 1.   Buy funds at a discount of 2 standard deviations or more below their 52-week average. Sell after 3 months.

Strategy 2.   Buy funds at a discount of 1 standard deviation or more below their 52-week average. Sell after 3 months.

Strategy 3.   Buy equity funds which have been trading at a discount of 35% or more for at least 6 months. Sell after 18 months.

Strategy 4.   Buy equity funds which have traded for at least 6 months at discounts between 30% and 35%. Sell after 1 year.

CEFA tracks about 500 closed-end funds, has discount/premium statistics, and has other useful information, including research articles like Juhl's *Does a mean reversion strategy really work?*

Tversky and Kahneman found security prices tended to regress to the mean. They speculated that this tendency comes from recent news taking up a larger portion of investors' consciousness than fundamentals and driving prices away from fundamental, intrinsic value. They postulated that cool-headed investors could profit from the *regression to the mean* phenomenon.[14]

Balvers and Wu took it as a given that security prices tended to regress to the mean and attempted to prove that a combination momentum/mean reversion strategy is better than either strategy alone.[15] Based on the research of others[16] Balvers and Wu believed contrarian strategies work for sorting periods ranging from 3 to 5 years matched with subsequent holding period of 3 to 5 years, while momentum strategies work with sorting periods of 1 to 12 months with subsequent holding periods of 1 to 12 months. This implies that trends of 1 to 12 months continue for 1 to 12 months, and that trends of 3 to 5 years break down and reverse.

Balvers and Wu used a database of 18 equity market indexes: Australia, Austria, Belgium, Canada, Denmark, France, Germany, Hong Kong, Italy, Japan, the Netherlands, Norway, Singapore, Spain, Sweden, Switzerland, the United Kingdom, and the United States. Balvers and Wu back-tested combining potential for mean reversion and momentum for each country employing a strategy of buying highest expected return and shorting lowest expected return. They used prior price data only, from Morgan Stanley Capital International (MSCI) index returns 1970-1999.

For momentum only strategy, they found return declined when sorting period or holding period went beyond 12 months. For reversion only strategy, keeping sorting period maxed to available data, they found return peaked at a holding period of 6 to 15 months. Interestingly, they found pure momentum and pure reversion strategies were profitable at the same holding periods. Their results generally confirm the earlier research, except for lack of separation between optimal holding periods for pure momentum and pure mean reversion strategies.

Balvers and Wu tested a "random walk" strategy with the same data. Their strategy was to buy the country with the highest return on the theory that high returns come from high risk. Countries with highest average return are riskiest. Assuming when risk stays high return will follow, then countries with highest risk should have highest return. The random walk strategy produced unexpected, negative returns for all holding periods. Return and risk were not inversely correlated.

The table below summarizes their most telling combined momentum/reversion strategy results:

Strategy Annual Return		
	1 position	3 positions
pure momentum	9.5%	11.2%
pure reversion	8.5%	3.4%
combination	16.7%	11.9%
12 month sorting, 1 month holding		

The 1 month holding assumes models are updated monthly. The same long and/or short positions might be taken in subsequent months. Their research, as summarized above, shows that momentum may be a bigger contributor to profits than reversion.

Balvers and Wu summarize their research:

> "we find that strategies combining momentum and mean reversion typically yield …(more than)… pure momentum and mean reversion strategies, which in turn outperform a random-walk-based strategy. The results cannot easily be explained as a reward for taking on systematic risk, but readily support a behavioral overreaction perspective. … these observations suggest a mispricing rather than risk-compensation explanation of returns …"

Trend

"The trend is your friend!" This is a rule of investing/trading books and of financial commentators. But! Is it true? Is it a rule you can count on to make you money? Or, is it one of those rules that only works for other people?

Trend introduces the element of time to the idea of regression to the mean. What if the average height of humans changes over time? Is time a predictor of offspring height? Is time a better predictor of offspring height than parent height?

In the earlier discussion of regression to the mean only one variable was considered, equity price. Regression to the mean implies that equities priced lower than their mean will increase in price and equities priced higher than their mean will decrease in price. If the price is at -2 standard deviations, 97.7% of future prices will be above the current price, or the mean will change.

Trend adds to regression the idea that the mean that the price will regress to changes over time.

The simplest trend is a straight line drawn through a plot of equity prices plotted against time. The straight trendline is drawn to minimize the area between the trendline and a line connecting individual data points. The areas above and below the trendline are equal, just as the areas of the normal curve on either side of the center highest point are equal. The sum of the squares of the vertical distances of individual data points from the trendline is at a minimum. The straight line having this property fits the data in the least square sense and is often called a least square line, instead of the trendline. The equation for the trendline is:

$$Trend = Slope * Time + Origin$$

where Trend is the trendline price at a point in time, Slope is the amount of change in price per time-period, Time is the number of time-periods since the first time-period and Origin is the trendline price at the first time-period (origin is trendline price at time 0). The calculated Trend is dependent on, determined from, time.

Conceptually the trendline comes from trying different lines and calculating the sum of the squares of the distances from the data points until you find the line that has the smallest sum of squares. The trendline can be calculated from these equations:

$$Slope = \frac{N \sum XY - (\sum X)(\sum Y)}{N \sum X^2 - (\sum X)^2}$$

$$Origin = \frac{(\sum Y)(\sum X^2) - (\sum X)(\sum XY)}{N \sum X^2 - (\sum X)^2}$$

where "N" is the number of time-period samples, "X" is individual time-period value, and "Y" is individual equity price from the individual time-periods. The trendline produced is the least squares line, or least squares trendline. The sum of the squares of the positive differences from the trendline equals the sum of the squares of the negative differences from the trendline. The areas, between the curve connecting the data points and the trendline, above and below the trendline are equal.

Excel and other spreadsheets have these equations built into functions; you just click on the trend function, and select the time values and prices of interest. Also, in Excel Chart, a trendline can be easily added for a line series by selecting the series, clicking the right mouse button, and selecting add trendline from the popup menu.

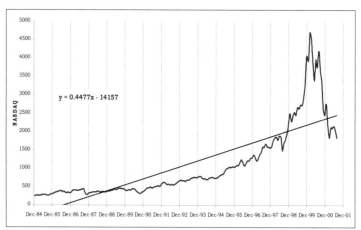

The Excel Chart above shows the NASDAQ composite index plotted against time, with the calculated equation Trend(y) equals 0.4477 times the time-period(x) minus 14,157. Half the area between the line connecting actual data points and the trendline is below the trendline and half is above the trendline. This is always true because of the formula for calculating the trendline. Half the area is on either side of the trend-line, but not necessarily half the data points. If the data-points are far from the trendline, it takes fewer of them to create the same area, and vice versa.

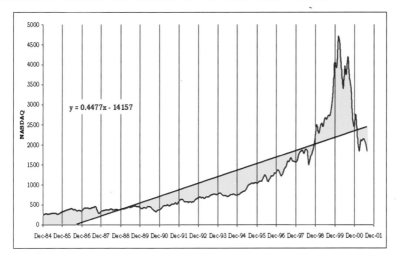

Because some of the positive variances from the trendline are so large, the NASDAQ graph has fewer data-points above the trendline than below it.

Regardless of how far the trendline is extended into the future half the area will still be on either side of a new trendline through all the data, because that is how the trendline is calculated.

What happens if all future data points are above the trendline? The trendline keeps rising until vertical. Not likely, as it implies that price is moving to infinity. Some future data points must be below the trendline, or the trendline keeps rising. What happens if all future data points are below the trendline? The trendline keeps falling until price drops to Ø. Possible, companies go out of business and suffer stock price declines to Ø.

Remember cause and effect. The trendline is where it is because of the data. Future data-points don't fall where they fall because of the trendline. The trendline comes from the data. The data don't come from the trendline.

If the current trendline is extended into the future, it is not a forgone conclusion that future data points will produce equal area on either side of an extended historic trendline. It is highly probable that the trendline will change. The future trendline is calculated from future data. The future data are not calculated from the historic trendline.

"The trend is your Friend," like a train is your friend; only when you can jump on it and move in the direction you want to go. If you jumped on the NASDAQ train any time in the '90s you were going where you wanted. If you waited until early 2000, because by then the upward trend was clearly established, you probably didn't go in the direction you wanted. Trends go in both directions up and down. Statistically sideways is a trend too, a flat trend. Usually periods of flat trend are called ranging, range bound, flat or channeling. Those who recognized the NASDAQ trend had changed in late March 2000 went short to get where they wanted.

Clayton M. Christensen explains why some jump on the train too late. "In our teaching we have so exalted the virtues of data-driven decision making that in many ways we condemn managers only to be able to take action after the data is clear and the game is over."[17]

There are 2 approaches to getting on the trend. The trend or momentum approach waits until the trend is clear then jumps in. The danger is that the trend fades as soon as you enter. The reversal approach anticipates the end of the current trend, and subsequent start of a new trend. The danger is that the current trend may continue, failing to reverse. This comes back to the competing ideas about making money in the market (page 21); reversion to mean or trend following. Now we see the competing ideas as really just different approaches to timing entries.

Correlation

Correlation measures how closely 2 variables move relative to one another. Correlation can measure how closely the height of offspring is related to the height of parents. Correlation can measure how closely the price of General Motors is related to the Dow Industrial Index.

Correlation is important to portfolio diversification. A primary reason for diversification is to limit risk, and portfolio diversification only limits risk to the degree the price movements of the equities in the portfolio are not correlated. If the equities all move together then holding a little of each will probably be as risky as holding a lot of one, and incur more transaction cost.

I have used the term risk loosely, somewhat generically, to this point. One of the dictionary definitions of risk is "the possibility of investment loss."[18] Another dictionary definition of risk is "the variability of returns from investment."[19] In most finance literature, the second definition dominates with "risk" used synonymously with variability of returns. Through much of this book 'risk' is used the same way and measured by SEE (Standard Error of Estimate). Therefore, "risk" is the chance of a different from expected output, whether it is positive or negative, rather than the possibility of loss. Part of the logic for using measures of variability like standard deviation and standard error of estimate is that if variability is normally distributed relative risk comparisons will produce the same result whether or not both sides of variability are included. Risk concepts and risk calculations are a recurring theme of this book.

Correlation is the degree of relationship between variables, how well an equation or trendline describes or explains the relationship between variables. Variables perfectly correlate if the variation in one explains all the variation in the other. A financial example: Future Value (value at the end of a period) equals Interest Rate for the period times Present Value (value at the beginning of a period) plus Present Value.

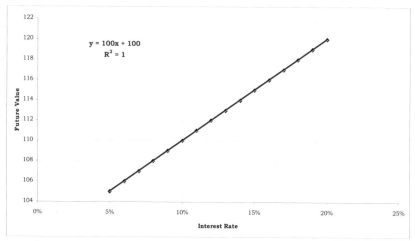

The trendline lies directly on top of the data points. The increase in present value to future value is solely dependent on and 100% explained by the interest rate the present value investment earns over the period to which the interest rate applies. Future value positively correlates to interest rate, future value increases as interest rate increases.

For equity price data sets, a straight line cannot explain all the variation in the dependent variable. Total variation for the equity price over time is the sum of the squares of the deviations of prices from the mean price.

The unexplained variation is the sum of the squares of the differences between prices and trendline values. The explained variation is the sum of the squares of difference between trendline values.

> Total   Variation   Unexplained Variation
>   + Explained Variation

$$\sum (Y - \overline{Y})^2 = \sum (Y - Y_{est,})^2 + \sum (Y_{est.} - \overline{Y})^2$$

$$\sum (\mathrm{Pr}\,ice - mean.\mathrm{Pr}\,ice)^2 = \sum (\mathrm{Pr}\,ice - Trend)^2 + \sum (Trend - mean.\mathrm{Pr}\,ice)^2$$

How well an equation or trendline describes or explains the relationship between variables is quantified by the ratio of explained variation to total variation. This ratio, R^2, is the coefficient of determination. R^2 varies between Ø and 1. If there is no explained variation, the ratio is Ø. If there is no unexplained variation, the ratio is 1. Notice the $R^2 = 1$ in the graph of Future Value versus yield. All of the variation in Future Value is explained by variation in yield.

$$R^2 = \frac{\exp lained.\mathrm{var}\,iation}{total.\mathrm{var}\,iation}$$

Revisiting the NASDAQ graph we now see that R^2 is .675. The ratio of explained to unexplained variance is .675, that is, variation in time explains 67.5% of the variation in NASDAQ index. Over the long term, the best time to buy the NASDAQ index is early.

> "
> Question: When's the best time to plant a tree?
> Answer: Twenty years ago, or today.
> "
> ... anonymous

From the graph, it appears that long-term the NASDAQ index regresses to the trendline. The index moves back toward the trendline when it is far from the trendline.

The *coefficient of correlation, r,* is the square root of R^2 and varies between -1 and +1, depending on whether correlation is negative or positive. The closer r is to Ø the less the dependent variable price is determined by the independent variable time.

$$r = \pm \sqrt{\frac{\exp lained.\mathrm{var}iation}{total.\mathrm{var}iation}}$$

The standard error of estimate (SEE) is to trend what standard deviation is to mean. SEE is calculated by taking the square root of the average of the squares of the differences between trend and price.

$$SEE = \sqrt{\frac{\sum (Y - Y_{est.})^2}{N}}$$

$$SEE = \sqrt{\frac{\sum (\Pr ice - Trend)^2}{Number.of.prices}} = \sqrt{Average(\Pr ice - Trend)^2}$$

The properties of SEE are analogous to standard deviation, in that, if we draw lines parallel to the trendline at distances ±1SEE the lines will include 68% of the data points. Lines ±2SEE will include 95% of the data points and lines ±3SEE will include 99.7% of the data points.

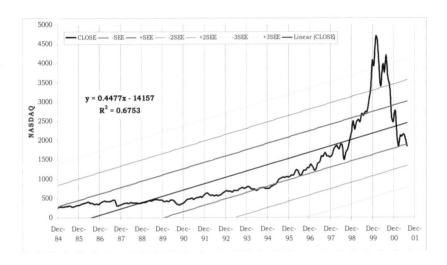

This NASDAQ graph expands on earlier ones with the addition of SEE parallel lines at ± 1, 2 and 3 SEE. Except for the year between late 1999 and late 2000, prices stayed pretty much within the ± 1 SEE lines. However, during that period the NASDAQ rose far beyond the +3 SEE line. Equity prices frequently rise or fall more than expected from analysis of trend and SEE. As Bernstein said, "Dependence on reversion to the mean for forecasting the future tends to be perilous when the mean itself is in flux."[20]

Earlier in this book, page 19, there is a graph of a normal curve representing the dispersion of data points around a mean. A trendline is like a mean but with the complication of time. A residual plot shows the distribution of data points around the trendline. R^2 in the NASDAQ graph above is .6753, not too high. Therefore, we don't expect the residual plot histogram to look exactly like a normal curve.

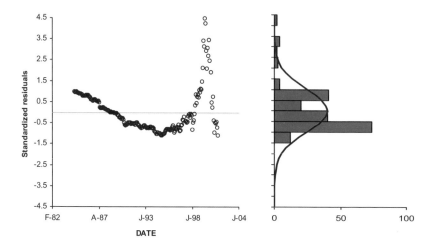

Analyse-It Software, Ltd.

The residual plot is in 2 parts: the left graph shows individual data points plotted as standard deviations away from the trendline, the right graph shows a histogram of number of data points at each SEE away from the trendline. The superimposed normal curve shows that the linear curve is not a very good fit. That is, NASDAQ Composite value is dependent on more than just time, or NASDAQ Composite value's dependence on time is non-linear. A good fitting linear curve should have a residual plot with data points scattered randomly on either side of the Ø-line, without long periods on either side. The NASDAQ Composite value spends long periods below and above its trendline.

How do you know whether the market is trending, and how do you know whether the market is trending up or down? Which trend is important to you, the short, intermediate, or long trends?

Tushar S. Chande, PhD in *BEYOND TECHNICAL ANALYSIS*[21] uses ADX, RAVI and AROON to determine trend.

The average directional index (ADX) indicator was developed by J. Welles Wilder Jr., and it is a lagging indicator sensitive to time covered. ADX is an oscillator that fluctuates between Ø and 100. Even though the scale is from Ø to 100, readings above 60 are relatively rare. Low readings, below 20, indicate a weak trend and high readings, above 40, indicate a strong trend. The indicator does not grade the trend as bullish or bearish, but merely assesses the strength of the current trend. A reading above 40 can indicate a strong downtrend as well as a strong uptrend. Usually the direction the ADX is moving is more important than the ADX value. Chande uses a rising 18-day ADX above 20 as an indication of trending. A rising ADX above 20 indicates the market is trending and any other value indicates that the market is ranging.

Chande also uses the Range Action Verification Index (RAVI) indicator, another lagging indicator sensitive to time covered. RAVI is based on the difference of 2 simple moving averages (SMA). Using a long SMA of 65 days and a short SMA of 7 days, a RAVI greater than 3 and rising indicates trending. Chande believes that RAVI responds more predictably than ADX.

$$RAVI \quad ABS \quad \frac{SMA_7 \quad SMA_{65}}{SMA_{65}} *100$$

Chande later developed the AROON indicator for detecting trends.[22] The AROON indicator consists of 2 lines, AROON(up) and AROON(down). AROON(up) for a given time-period is calculated by determining how much time (on a percentage basis) elapsed between the start of the time-period and the point at which the highest closing price during that time-period occurred. When the stock is setting new highs for the time-period, AROON(up) will be 100. If the stock has moved lower every day during the time-period, AROON(up) will be Ø. AROON(down) is calculated in just the opposite manner, looking for new lows instead of new highs.

Technically, the formula for AROON(up) is [(# of periods) - (# of periods since highest close during that time)] / (# of periods) x 100. The formula for AROON(down) is [(# of periods) - (# of periods since lowest close during that time)] / (# of periods) x 100.

For example, consider plotting a 10-period AROON(up) line on a daily chart. If the highest closing price for the past 10 days occurred 6 days ago (4 days since the start of the time-period), AROON(up) for today would be equal to ((10-6)/10) x 100 = 40. If the lowest close in that same period happened yesterday (i.e. on day 9), AROON(down) for today would be 90.

The AROON Oscillator is a single line that is defined as the difference between AROON(up) and AROON(down). All three AROON indicators take a single parameter which is the number of time-periods to use in the calculation. Since AROON(up) and AROON(down) both oscillate between Ø and +100, the AROON Oscillator ranges from -100 to +100 with Ø serving as the crossover line.

When AROON(up) and AROON(down) are moving lower in close proximity, it signals a consolidation phase is under way and no strong trend is evident. When AROON(up) dips below 50, it indicates that the current trend has lost its upwards momentum. Similarly, when AROON(down) dips below 50, the current downtrend has lost its momentum. Values above 70 indicate a strong trend in the same direction as the AROON (up or down) is under way. Values below 30 indicate that a strong trend in the opposite direction is under way.

The AROON Oscillator signals an upward trend is under way when it is above Ø and a downward trend is under way when it falls below Ø. The farther away the oscillator is from the Ø-line, the stronger the trend.

The goal of trend catching systems is to get into a position when the trend starts and to get out when the trend changes. The indicators are lagging so entries come after the trend has started or stopped. Therefore, for these indicators to produce profitable trades the markets must continue to trend after entry. Chande found trends lasting 15 to 18 days in the markets he looked at in the early '90s. Chande tested trending and anti-trend systems and concluded that for the average position trader with average commission costs and slippage, trend-following strategies are probably a better choice. The anti-trend systems he tested were not based on ADX or RAVI, but rather on stochastic oscillators and moving average crossovers.

Trend length importance is relative to whether you are an investor or a trader, a position trader or day trader. At one end of the continuum, investors are most interested in long-term trends, and at the other end day traders may be interested only in what will happen in the next few minutes. Chande chose ADX and RAVI parameters appropriate for position traders planning on holding positions from a few days to a few weeks.

Michael P. Turner is also a proponent of trend trading stating,

> "History does repeat itself, and historical patterns do rematerialize over time. The goal of technical analysis is to find a trend in progress and capitalize on it before the trend dissipates."[23]

> "Remember, the trend is your friend. Don't fight it. If the
> market is surging, go long. If it is tanking, go short.
> Don't try to pick bottoms or go against the prevailing
> trend unless a clear, substantiated reversal has material-
> ized."[24]

Another proponent of trend following is Jonathan Hoenig who started his 2/15/2001 column at <u>Smart-Money.com</u> with

> "My adult life began the day I understood persistence of
> trend. This undeniable trading truth dramatically in-
> creased my profitability and changed the way I look at the
> world."

He went on to claim that just as the seasons follow predictable trends, so do market psychology and stock prices. Stocks move in trends, and trends tend to persist. He agrees that long-term past performance may give no indication of future performance, but believes recent past performance tends to be an excellent indicator of near-term future performance, and adds that long-term performance starts out as short-term performance. He believes that when a stock begins moving in one direction, the law of inertia is often enough to continue the trend. Hoenig thinks it far more likely a strong stock will get stronger than that a weak stock will turn around. However, he goes on to state that most people would rather buy weak stocks in the hope that they'll become strong again, rather than strong stocks that most likely will get even stronger.

Reversal

Reversal systems are regression to the mean, anti-trend, reversion systems. The trader's profit is dependent on a change in the current market direction. The reversal trader loses if the present trend continues. The reversal trader believes the market overreacts, that prices go too high when people are optimistic and go too low when people are pessimistic or uncertain.

Dichotomy – Trending, Reversion

Chande, Turner and Hoenig express views on stock price movement that seem to be at the opposite end of the *regression to the mean* continuum from Bernstein and Drach. Can both views be right? More important, can following Chande and Hoenig make us money, more money than following Bernstein and Drach? I don't know Chande or Hoenig's investment/trading results. I know that Drach has a 95% win rate over 25 years. There is probably a place for strategies loyal to both views. The market is broad enough, complex enough and dynamic enough that both views can probably generate winning strategies. It is probable that the success of one view over the other is dependent on where the market is in its continuous movement between ranging and trending.

At first, it seems unlikely, nearly impossible, that both trend following and reversion trading systems work. Trend following is based on the price continuing to move in the same direction while reversal is based on the price changing direction.

One way to look at it is that reversal systems are trying to get you in before the new price trend develops, while trend following systems try to get you in after the trend is confirmed.

Another way to look at it is from the time horizon, multiple cycles viewpoint. It is possible to justify a long entry while the long-term trend is up, while justifying a short for the same security because the short term trend is down. Price action is often described by the securities' position in its short, intermediate, and long-term cycles.

Another way to look at it is from the diversity of the market. Some instruments, or groups of instruments, may trade better with trend following than with reversal systems.

Once you think about it for a while, you will be able to hold both the trend following and reversion ideas in somewhat equal regard. This is okay, however be careful how you adopt trading rules. If you are a trend follower, it may be good to adopt the rule "Buy high, sell higher." If you are a reversal trader, your rule may be "Buy low, sell high." If you are a trend follower, a good rule to adopt could be "Sell losers, ride winners," while the reversal trader responds to the same price action by "Averaging down." As you think through the rules of the trade, evaluate rules in the context of your underlying strategy.

Even when conceptually you grasp the logic of both trend following and reversion, your back-testing may push you to trust your nest egg to one strategy over the other. Most of my funded strategies are based on reversion through the *Trend Regression Portfolio Strategy*.

There is a reversal story in *THE PLUNGERS AND THE PEACOCKS* about old men and the market. The old men take wheelbarrows of money to Wall Street when pessimism is high and prices are low. Then when optimism is high and prices are high, the same old men take money, with profits, from Wall Street and add to their real estate holdings.

THE PLUNGERS AND THE PEACOCKS (150 years of Wall Street), Dana L. Thomas 1967

Part II — Trend Regression Portfolio Strategy

The objective of the *Trend Regression Portfolio Strategy* is to beat the market, to better the reward/risk return of buying and holding index unit trusts. Part II includes results from back-testing strategies that worked, and results from those that didn't. I know, I know, you are in a hurry and only want to know what works. Please bear with me.

Premise

The *Trend Regression Portfolio Model* is a reversal system and the basic premise behind it is regression to the mean, or to the trend.

Using the *Trend Regression Portfolio Model* to manage a portfolio involves a series of steps. First select a group of stocks expected to work together to create a profitable model. Then, buy undervalued stocks and sell overvalued stocks. *Undervalued stocks are those that are furthest below trend and overvalued stocks are those furthest above trend.* Then, adjust equity to cash ratio to reflect position in market cycle.

The three step process:

1. Select a group of stocks to track (master list).
2. Buy and sell from the group (entry and exit).
3. Adjust equity level (market timing).

borrows heavily from Robert F. Drach's methodology. Pretty straightforward; find some stocks you think will go up, buy those that are currently most oversold, and adjust the amount purchased to reflect current market.

3. Back-testing

Back-testing models facilitate experimenting with different investment ideas without risking capital.

Getting the stock price data into Excel has been problematic or time consuming in the past, however, now price data collection is getting easier and less expensive. The price data from any MoneyCentral chart displayed on your computer screen is exportable from the MoneyCentral web site into Excel. Excel 2002 makes it easier than in previous versions with its improved ability to link to internet data. Shareware programs are now available to either pull historical data directly into Excel or save data directly to files readable by Excel. I have tested DownloadXL[25] to bring historical daily price data directly into Excel and HQuote[26] Downloader for writing .csv files readable by Excel. Currently I use DownloadXL to bring historical data into Excel, and write the data to .csv files in my Stock Data folder. When I need current stock prices in Excel, I use MSN Stock Quote Functions for 20-minute time delayed prices, or cut and paste Scottrade.com real time prices.

There are other sources of equity price data. Some are free, some require subscription fees. The *Trend Regression Portfolio Strategy* models work with historical price data for 50 equities in one worksheet, updated weekly.

For each back-test run, the model works backwards from the most recent data calculating the trades for each week. Each week the model calculates indicators and picks 3 long entries and 3 short entries. The model assumes every position is opened and closed weekly and calculates gain or loss between Fridays' closes.

Data collection and back-testing can create numerous files. I wish I gotten better organized earlier. Now, I keep all my files grouped under one folder in subfolders that make sense to me. I have a 2 PC network, so I can keep my core folder and its backup synchronized with a few keystrokes.

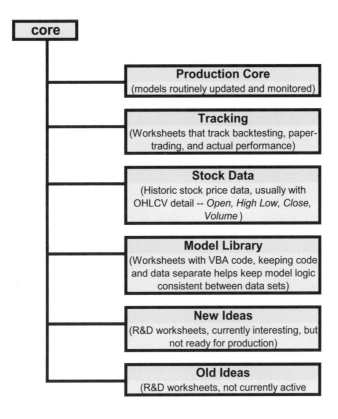

This organization of files discussion probably seems trivial and out of place in this book. However, lack of organization coupled with poor memory has been a time waster for me, and lack of organization coupled with lack of backup could be a disaster. Equipment failure can be exasperating, but most instances requiring file recoveries, from backup, result from human error. The actual organization structure used is less important than the fact that your structure makes sense to you, and is consistent with your goals. The above organization works for me, but it took several years to evolve.

Construction

Portfolio models built in Excel 2002 use closing prices 7 days apart. Each copy of the model handles one set of equities. A few early copies of the model also included PEG (Price/Earnings / Growth), in addition to closing prices.

Selecting Equities (Master List)

First step is selecting a group of equities to study.

Number of Equities

Each copy of the model handles a set of 50 equities, and is designed to recommend 3 long and/or short recommendations per time-period. The number of equities and number of buy and sell recommendations are constant in each model. The list of 50 equities is equivalent to Drach's master list, although Drach's list has more than 50 equities.

Screens

Screens (filters) are used to find 50 equities for the model. Screens are designed to find equities that work with the model. Work in the sense that trading the model produces profit. Screens were set up to find stocks with correlated price movement, had high slope to SEE ratios, or had similar fundamentals.

Correlation

One strategy for finding a portfolio of stocks is to find stocks that have moved together in the past. AIQ Trading Expert Pro[27] has a module that finds stocks with high correlation to a standard from within the AIQ database of about 3,000 equities.

Excel's Analysis ToolPak Add-in can calculate correlation after historic price data is imported. Of course, finding equities whose price moves have correlated in the past doesn't necessarily produce a list of equities that will move together in the future.

High Slope/SEE

Another strategy for finding a portfolio of stocks is to find stocks that have high, consistent stock price growth. Slope of the price trendline measures growth and SEE measures the variation around the trendline. Excel can calculate slope, SEE and the Slope/SEE ratio. Stocks with the highest Slope/SEE ratio have the highest, most consistent stock price growth.

Fundamentals

Another strategy for finding a portfolio of stocks is to identify stocks that have similar fundamentals. This is the strategy followed by Drach to build his master list. Equities that pass his fundamental tests gain a place on his list.

Several internet sites provide useful stock screening capability. These sites provide the capability to build a screen, or filter. Screens are sets of rules, or tests. Screens produce lists of equities that pass the screen's rules. Rules can involve price levels, capitalization, earnings, growth, EPS, and many of other pieces of information, depending on the internet site.

Some of the sites I have used:[28]

Microsoft	http://moneycentral.msn.com/investor/finder/predefstocks.asp
Wall Street City	http://www.wallstreetcity.com/stocks/stocks_main.html
Individual In-	http://search.individualinvestor.com/individualinvesto

vestor	r/General_Free_Search.html?
Silicon Inves-tor	http://www.siliconinvestor.com/stockscreen/advanced screen.gsp
Zacks	http://my.zacks.com/screening/custom/custom_index. php3
Equity Trader	http://www.equitytrader.com/html/top_twenty_potenti al.asp
NASDAQ	http://www.nasdaq.com/asp/guru_screener.asp

There are many other screening sites, some requiring payment. The easy availability of this screening capability is amazing, and the internet is evolving with new sites potentially providing even more functionality and utility. Over the last few years, the moneycentral.msn.com site has become the site I use most often.

Excel 2002 provided a leap forward with its ability to link website content to Excel Worksheets. An Excel 2002 model can use web site data without re-keying or cutting and pasting. Sometimes it is a little tricky if the page needed is behind a sign-on procedure, but when it works, it saves time and offers protection from keying errors. Once you build a screen, Excel 2002 can link a worksheet to the screen, and update the worksheet with new screen information automatically.

Introduction of new equities

Once a model is set up and in production (being traded), how do you introduce new equities? If a model's equity indicators are all price based it is mechanically simple, just copy new equities' price data over old equities' price data. Emotionally it is sometimes a little harder if you like the company being tossed, or if tossing the company means closing a losing position.

The need for equity replacement occurs when equities in the model no longer meet the screen requirements. If the screen is creating a lot of turnover in the tracking set, transaction costs will limit the model's ability to trade profitably.

Products and companies go through life cycles. Most companies eventually go out of business or fade from prominence. *Trend Regression Portfolio Strategy* relies on lots of data, 3 to 10 years of weekly price data. *Trend Regression Portfolio Strategy* is not trying to catch upstarts, but trying to profit from price cycles in growing, stable, established companies.

Companies go through life cycles. The Dow Industrial Index has existed for 100 years only because the component companies have changed. The most recent change in late 1999 added Intel (INTC), Microsoft (MSFT), Home Depot, Inc. (HD), and SBC Communications, Inc. (SBC) to replace Chevron Corp. (CHV), Goodyear Tire & Rubber Co. (GT), Sears, Roebuck & Co. (S), and Union Carbide Corp. (UK).[29] General Electric is the only name from the original 1896 list of Dow Industrials still in the Dow. The original list contained mostly agriculture and natural resources companies. The current list is more diverse with manufacturer, retailer, drug, technology, communication, entertainment, and fast food companies important in the current economy. The Dow Industrial Index has a longer life expectancy than any single component because it replaces companies that are aging with companies that are earlier in their life cycles.

Companies go through life cycles. The only constant is change: earnings change, customers change, growth rates change. New companies emerge. Old companies adapt, merge, or wither. The universe of company equities available for a portfolio changes over time.

For the *Trend Regression Portfolio Strategy* company life cycle leads to deterioration in suitability of any 50 stock grouping. The rate of deterioration will depend on the stocks, and on external factors.

Buy/Sell Variables (Entries & Exits)

Buy/Sell decisions for equities within the group are based on indicators calculated for individual equities. For the Portfolio Model it is the relative indicator value rather than the absolute value that is important.

Equity Indicators

The portfolio models handle 6 indicators at a time. Many indicators can serve as a basis for trading decisions. One measure of the magnitude of indicator choices available from basic price/volume histories is Ward Systems Group, Inc.'s inclusion of over 800 indicators in NeuroShell Trader.[30] Some of the indicators I have tried are discussed below.

For reversal systems like *Trend Regression Portfolio Strategy*, the indicators' job is to measure where we are in the cycle between oversold and overbought. Indicators are calculated from objective data, mostly open, high, low, close, and volume. However, the indicators function is to measure perception, the market's perception of the true value of the equity.

Price%

Price% is the current price divided by the price X weeks ago. In a reversal system the equities that are lowest relative to where they where X weeks ago are purchased. If it is a hedging strategy, the equities that are highest relative to where they where X weeks ago are shorted, in proportion to equities purchased. The models handle a range of X from 3 to 50 weeks.

Relative Price%

Relative Price% is derived from Price%. It is the current Price% divided by the Price% X weeks ago or the current Price%, relative to the Price% X weeks ago. In a reversal system, the equities that have the lowest value of Price% divided by the Price% X weeks ago are purchased. If it is a hedging strategy, the equities that are highest relative to where they where X weeks ago are shorted, in proportion to equities purchased.

Relative Price

Relative price is the current price divided by the projected price (trend price) for the current time-period. The projected price is the trend calculated with an X week least square line. In a reversal system, the equities that are farthest below their X week trend are purchased. If it is a hedging strategy, the equities that are highest relative to their trend are shorted, in proportion to equities purchased.

Obviously Price%, Relative Price%, and Relative Price are closely related. When one works, as a trading indicator, they usually all work. Often one of the three works much better than the other indicators.

PEG

The NASDAQ site (www.nasdaq.com) supplies good PEG graphical displays and defines their PEG calculation:

> "PEG ratio - which is the Price Earnings ratio divided by the growth rate. In this case we use the forecasted growth rate (based on the consensus of professional analysts) and forecasted earnings over the next 12 months. In theory, the lower the PEG ratio the better - implying that you are paying less for future earnings growth."

Intuitively PEG seems like a potentially useful statistic, but PEG history is hard to get. Back-testing is hard without the historical data. I collected weekly data, building my own history, but I collect for only 100 equities, which made it difficult to introduce new equities.

In a reversal system the equities with the lowest PEG are purchased. If it is a hedging strategy, the equities with the highest PEG are shorted, in proportion to equities purchased.

PEG seems like it should work better than it has. Results haven't justified the effort needed to maintain the history. A larger historical database and the back-testing it would permit could increase the usefulness of PEG as a *Trend Regression Portfolio Strategy* indicator.

Relative PEG

Relative PEG is the current PEG divided by the PEG X weeks ago. In a reversal system the equities that have the lowest PEG relative to where they where X weeks ago are purchased. If it is a hedging strategy, the equities with PEG highest relative to where they where X weeks ago are shorted, in proportion to equities purchased.

Slope

Slope is the slope of a regression (least squares trendline) based on X weeks of data. In a reversal system the equities with the lowest slope are purchased. For a hedging strategy, the equities with the highest slope are shorted, in proportion to equities purchased.

Slope*SEE

SEE is the Standard Error of Estimate calculated for the most current X weeks. Slope*SEE is slope multiplied by the SEE. If 2 equities have the same negative slope, the model would be more likely to buy the one with the lower SEE. In a reversal system the equities with the smallest Slope*SEE are purchased. For a hedging strategy, the equities with the largest Slope*SEE are shorted, in proportion to equities purchased.

Slope/SEE

Slope/SEE is slope divided by SEE. In a reversal system the equities that have the lowest Slope/SEE are purchased. If it is a hedging strategy, the equities that have the highest Slope/SEE are shorted, in proportion to equities purchased. If 2 equities have the same negative slope, the model would be more likely to buy the one with the higher SEE.

Having both Slope*SEE and Slope/SEE started as an experiment. I expected one to be discarded. Neither has been used in a funded portfolio, but neither has been eliminated from consideration. For some reason Slope*SEE seems to work better for timing going long and Slope/SEE seems to work better for timing going short.

Smoothing-weeks

The number of weeks used in indicator calculations, for example, the *number of weeks* back used as a base to calculate Price% and Relative PEG. Capital "X" denotes the smoothing-weeks variable in the indicator descriptions above. Smoothing-weeks is just one variable throughout the model. When it changes, it changes for all calculations. Any calculation within a simulation run that uses a week variable uses the same smoothing-weeks value. All of the equity selection indicators mentioned above and all of the market timing indicators mentioned later use the same smoothing-weeks value for each iteration of the model. Superior back-test results could be obtained by optimizing different weekly values for each place *number of weeks* is used in a calculation. It is less certain that results from trading the better-optimized model would be better.

HILO Model

This model is named as homage to Drach's book, *High Return Low Risk Investment*, not for the town on the east coast of the Big Island, Hawaii or for Woody Harrelson's movie *Hi-Lo Country*. Equity selection for this model used a fundamentals screen for the 2 rules Drach weighted highest:

Earnings Predictability

Earnings Growth

The selections were made at www.individualinvestor.com, screening with selections for EPS Consistency 5-Year, EPS Growth 5-Year, and Projected EPS Annualized 5-Year all set to High as Possible. Using this screen in late 2000 produced this group of 50 equities.

HILO MODEL EQUITIES

	Symbol	Company Name	Exchange
1	AA	Alcoa Inc.	NYSE
2	ADP	Automatic Data Processing, Inc.	NYSE
3	AFL	AFLAC Incorporated	NYSE
4	AVY	Avery Dennison Corporation	NYSE
5	BEN	Franklin Resources, Inc.	NYSE
6	C	Citigroup Inc.	NYSE
7	CBH	Commerce Bancorp, Inc.	NYSE
8	CYN	City National Corporation	NYSE
9	DG	Dollar General Corporation	NYSE
10	DOV	Dover Corporation	NYSE
11	FDO	Family Dollar Stores, Inc.	NYSE
12	FNM	Fannie Mae	NYSE
13	GDW	Golden West Financial Corporation	NYSE
14	GE	General Electric Company	NYSE
15	GPT	GreenPoint Financial Corp.	NYSE
16	HD	Home Depot, Inc.	NYSE
17	HDI	Harley-Davidson, Inc.	NYSE
18	INTC	Intel Corporation	NASDAQ
19	JKHY	Jack Henry & Associates, Inc.	NASDAQ
20	JNJ	Johnson & Johnson	NYSE
21	KRB	MBNA Corporation	NYSE
22	LLTC	Linear Technology Corporation	NASDAQ
23	LLY	Eli Lilly and Company	NYSE
24	LOW	Lowe's Companies, Inc.	NYSE
25	MDT	Medtronic, Inc.	NYSE
26	MER	Merrill Lynch & Co., Inc.	NYSE
27	MHP	McGraw-Hill Companies, Inc.	NYSE
28	MRK	Merck & Co., Inc.	NYSE
29	MWD	Morgan Stanley Dean Witter & Co.	NYSE
30	MXIM	Maxim Integrated Products, Inc.	NASDAQ

	Symbol	Company Name	Exchange
31	NTRS	Northern Trust Corporation	NASDAQ
32	NYT	New York Times Company	NYSE
33	OMC	Omnicom Group Inc.	NYSE
34	PAYX	Paychex, Inc.	NASDAQ
35	RCL	Royal Caribbean Cruises Ltd.	NYSE
36	RE	Everest Re Group Ltd.	NYSE
37	SCH	Charles Schwab Corporation	NYSE
38	SEIC	SEI Investments Company	NASDAQ
39	SGP	Schering-Plough Corporation	NYSE
40	SNV	Synovus Financial Corp.	NYSE
41	STT	State Street Corporation	NYSE
42	TCB	TCF Financial Corporation	NYSE
43	TIF	Tiffany & Co.	NYSE
44	TJX	TJX Companies, Inc.	NYSE
45	TROW	T. Rowe Price Group, Inc.	NASDAQ
46	USB	U.S. Bancorp	NYSE
47	UTX	United Technologies Corporation	NYSE
48	WAG	Walgreen Co.	NYSE
49	WFC	Wells Fargo & Company	NYSE
50	WMT	Wal-Mart Stores, Inc.	NYSE

Interestingly, even though the selection screen was patterned after Drach's, only the 18 blue equities in the HILO table above were on Drach's master list. Drach's screening is more comprehensive, and likely less mechanical.

Buy recommendations were generated by sorting on Price% and selecting the three equities that were lowest relative to X weeks ago. The model optimized on 3 smoothing-weeks, 3 weeks ago. The model optimizes by a simple exhaustive test. It tests each smoothing-week option by tracking trades triggered each week using the current iteration's value for smoothing-week. Smallest smoothing-week value, largest smoothing-week value and step size are entered for each optimization run. The lowest, smallest week value is 3, and the highest, largest week value is 50. Because the back-test recalculates all trades for all weeks, it can take a long time, hours, sometimes days. Step size reduces the number of iterations, smoothing-weeks can vary in steps of 2, 3, etc.

The HILO model stops short of the Drach's market timing step. The goal was to skip market timing and take advantage of regression to the trend for the HILO group of equities while minimizing risk by hedging. To reduce market fluctuations, impact on portfolio equity, positions are hedged instead of timed. Hedging is accomplished by shorting, by maintaining a long/short ratio of 50/50. The goal of hedging is to remove the effect of market swings and isolate the effect of the Equity Indicator. Risk can be split into 2 parts. Stock risk comes from the individual company. Market risk comes from the broad market or industry, which includes the company. Because the stock price movements of different equities do not perfectly correlated, hedging can only mitigate, not eliminate market risk.

The 50 equities of the group are sorted from lowest indicator value to highest. The lowest 3 are purchased and the highest 3 are sold. The lowest 3 are the ones most likely to go up in price based on the indicator returning to the mean. The highest 3 are the ones most likely to go down in price based on the indicator returning to the mean. If the market moves up, the longs should go up a little more than average and the shorts should go up a little less than the market. If the market moves down, the shorts should go down a little more than average and the longs should go down a little less than the market. Therefore, if the indicator works and the price action of stocks correlate, the portfolio should gain value, regardless of which way the market goes.

The model optimized to smoothing-weeks of 3 with a long Price% indicator and a short Slope/SEE indicator. That is, the model back-tested best when it purchased the three equities with lowest relative price to 3 weeks ago, and shorted the three equities with the highest Slope/SEE based on 3-week trend. Both long and short entries optimized on the same smoothing-weeks, because the model supports only one smoothing-weeks value per iteration. Results for a 150-week back-test 12/11/1998 through 11/2/2001 are:

Relative Gain	204%
R^2	0.96
%Gain	1.1%
RRR (Risk Reward Ratio)	37.5%
MAX drawdown	10.3%
TRiPS%	**0.8%**
$Gain	$ 1,066

These results seem okay. But, what do the really mean? How are they calculated?

Performance

The back-testing models exist to calculated performance measures given different inputs. After all, the reason for spending the time running back-tests is to see how different strategies would have worked in the past. What are the best measures of performance of the individual strategies or models? Good performance measures should take into account both return and risk. Return is the amount of increase or decrease in equity, or how much the system makes relative to the investment, or how much money the system makes relative to the passage of time. Risk is the amount of volatility in return, or the potential for experiencing losses in equity. A brief description of four performance measures; relative gain, NAV, R^2, and TRiPS% follows:

Relative Gain

Relative Gain measures the performance of a portfolio against a benchmark. Popular benchmarks are the indexes (Dow Jones Industrial Average, S&P 500, NASDAQ Composite, etc.) or the index funds (DIA, SPY, QQQ, etc.). The relative gain is calculated by first dividing the portfolio current value by the portfolio starting value and the index current value by the index starting value, then by dividing the portfolio result by the index result. Relative gains over 100 mean that the model portfolio has grown faster than the index.

For the *Trend Regression Portfolio Strategy* models, the index is the weekly sum of prices for the 50 equities in the group. Index performance measures performance of a buy and hold strategy that purchases equal shares of 50 equities in the group at the start of the back-test and holds them through the back-test. Equal initial investments are assumed in both the model portfolio and the buy and hold index strategy. Ending equity in the Portfolio Model equals ending equity in the buy and hold index strategy times the relative gain.

NAV

NAV (Net Asset Value) is important for keeping track of performance of portfolios or accounts where deposits and withdrawals continue after establishment of an account. Calculations parallel those for company capitalization and stock price. At the time of the initial funding, an amount of units is assumed and the NAV equals the dollars in the portfolio divided by the number of units. Each time a deposit or withdrawal is made the number of units is changed based on the amount of the change and the current NAV (dollars in portfolio divided by units).

I'm calling them units to distinguish them from shares of individual equities held in the portfolio. It is like setting up a company whose business it is to buy and sell shares of equities for profit. The shares of equities are inventory. The units of the trading company are ownership of the trading company.

R^2 of Equity Curve

The reason for trading is to make money, and the equity curve tracks portfolio value over time. Standard linear regression calculations can then measure the quality of a portfolio's equity curve.

Linear regression of equity curves produces the formula:

y = ax + b

equity = gain(loss)per period * number of periods + starting balance

The amount of money you have (equity) equals the amount of average gain or loss per period times the number of periods since the start plus your initial capital. The gain or loss is statistically the slope, and the bigger slope is, the better the equity curve. An interesting point here is that the variables are money and time. The blue line in the following graph shows the equity curve for the HILO model, with a linear regression line and formula.

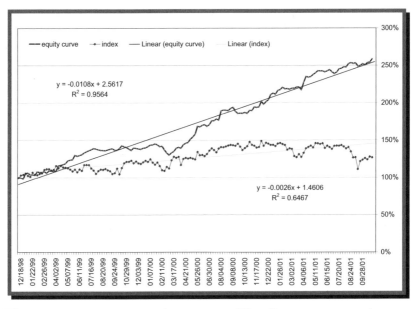

This is a percent equity curve. The linear regression shows an origin, starting balance, of 100% and a slope

of just over 1% during the 150 weeks of the back-test. The linear regression line is the straight line that best summarizes the movement of the stock (equity) over the time-period.

The magenta line is the HILO index equity curve. This is the equity curve for purchasing and holding a basket of the 50 equities in the HILO model. Notice the index equity curve has lower return (.26% versus 1.08%), and higher risk (R^2 of 0.6467 versus 0.9564 for the HILO model equity curve). This flies in the face of efficient market theory contention that return and risk are inversely correlated.

A quirk in the model reversed the signs in the calculated linear regression lines.[31] The corrected linear regression formula for the HILO portfolio equity curve is %equity = .0108 * week – 2.5617. The .0108 slope is the amount of increase in the percent equity's linear regression trendline each week. This 1.08% compares to the 1.1 % reported %Gain in the first HILO model table. The 1.1 %Gain is the average weekly change in the percent equity curve itself, not the trendline. The trendline slope maybe a better predictor of weekly gain as it is not distorted by beginning or ending outliers. In the graph above the beginning and ending points are not too far off the trendline, and they are both on the same side of the trendline. So slope and average weekly change are close.

Remember drawdown is inherent in any investment/portfolio management strategy. Equity doesn't change uniformly from period to period. Equity curves aren't usually smooth, but generally the smoother they are the better. Better, as in easier to trade, easier to stick with the plan. Smoothness is measured by the standard error of estimate (SEE). The smaller the SEE, the smoother the equity curve is. The smaller the SEE, the lower equity volatility and risk are.

A potential problem with using dollar slope and SEE to evaluate portfolio strategies is that they only provide valid comparisons for constant size portfolios. For example, a slope of $1,000 for a $100,000 portfolio is probably good, but a slope of $1,000 for a $1,000,000 portfolio is clearly not as good. Similarly, a SEE of $10,000 for a $1,000,000 portfolio is probably okay, but a SEE of $10,000 for a $100,000 portfolio is clearly not as good. Using percent equity curves avoids scale problems and makes equity curves between model runs comparable, even when initial investments are different.

R^2 is the ratio of explained variation to total variation. It measures how well an equation or trendline describes or explains the relationship between variables. For the equity curve, there are 2 variables total value and time, with value the dependent and time the independent variable. The closer R^2 is to 1 the more variation in equity is explained by progress of time. High R^2 is good, especially if accompanied by high positive slope. If account equity is used to buy a fixed rate certificate of deposit R^2 is 1, but the slope may be much less than can be achieved purchasing equities.

TRiPS%

The TRiPS% statistic brings together return and risk into a single performance measure. The best way to eliminate scale as a problem, while maintaining the flexibility to model different size portfolios, is to calculate performance statistics as ratios or percentages: In the following, %Gain and %Median are substitutes for slope and %SEE substitutes for SEE.

- %Gain = average weekly gain / equity risked
- %Median = Median weekly gain / equity risked
- RRR = %Gain / %SEE (%SEE is weekly SEE / equity risked)
- Win% = Winning trades divided by total trades

- Max% Drawdown = 1 - Minimum of current equity divided by maximum equity
- TRiPS% = (%Gain + %Median) * RRR * (Win%/.5) * (1-Max% Drawdown)

TRiPS% is a risk adjusted per period percent equity increase expectation. %Gain and %Median measure weekly returns. RRR[32] measures dispersion of weekly returns. Win% measures the ratio of winning trades to losing trades. Max % Drawdown tracks how far equity fell from back-test high. TRiPS% seems a good generalized measure of the potential of different strategies as it incorporates both return and risk. TRiPS% is a risk adjusted %Gain, an approximation of expected future model performance.

Return is measured with %Gain and %Median. Including both penalizes models that have high mean returns because of a few large winning trades. Models with %Gain and %Median about the same are less volatile.

RRR (Risk Reward Ratio) is calculated by dividing the average weekly %Gain by SEE as a percent of equity risked. RRR measures dispersion or volatility relative to return and is a proxy for risk. Some investor/analysts[33] use the reciprocal of RRR, coefficient of variation (CV) is %SEE divided by %Gain.[34]

Win% is a measure of how tradable the model is. Models with high win ratios are easier to trade than models with low win ratios. Wins are calculated weekly. If an individual equity is held for 3 weeks and it gains every week the model counts that as 3 wins. If an equity is held for 3 weeks and it gains 2 weeks and loses 1 week, that counts as 2 wins and 1 loss; even if the loss is greater than the 2 wins.

Max% Drawdown is a another measure of how tradable the model is. Models with little drawdown are easier to trade than models with large drawdowns. Max% Drawdown is also a measure of risk. In some ways, it is a better measure of risk than RRR because it focuses on pain (loss), rather than on volatility. Big gains increase volatility without increasing trader pain.

All of the four methods of measuring performance discussed above are valid and important. However, *Trend Regression Portfolio Strategy* back-testing models concentrated on TRiPS%. TRiPS% is the output the models optimize for. The optimal values for variables are those that produce the highest TRiPS% for the back-test. Relative Gain, Gain (slope), and R^2 are calculated and recorded for each test. NAV isn't calculated because neither additional investments nor withdrawals occur during the back-test.

Getting back to the HILO model performance results:

Relative Gain	204%
R^2	0.9593
gain%	1.1%
RRR (Risk Reward Ratio)	37.5%
MAX drawdown	10.3%
TRiPS%	**0.8%**
$Gain	$ 1,066

The relative gain 204% is:

$$\operatorname{Re} lativeGain = \frac{(EndEquity/StartEquity)}{(EndIndex/StartIndex)}$$

$$\operatorname{Re} lativeGain = \frac{(259/100)}{(127/100)} = 204$$

The index is the sum of share prices of the 50 equities in the model group. In 150 weeks, the model equity climbed from 100 to 259 and the index climbed from 100 to 127. So, at the end of the 150 weeks of the back-test the model portfolio's equity is 204% of the buy and hold index ending equity.

R^2 of 0.9593 for the equity curve compares to R^2 of 0.6467 for the index curve. Thus, following the model strategy with this group of equities is less risky than buying and holding a portfolio of equal shares of the 50 equities in the group.

Gain% is the average weekly gain(loss) divided by the average weekly capital risked. In this case $1,066/$96,474 equals 1.1%.

Risk Reward Ratio is Gain% divided by SEE. In this case 1.1 / 2.9 equals 37.5%. SEE is much bigger than Gain%, so RRR is small. The variation around the Gain% is greater than the Gain% itself, so expect weeks with loses. With Gain% of 1.1 and SEE of 2.9 there is 95% probability of a weekly gain (or loss) being between (4.8%) and 7.0%, a pretty big range. There is 67% probability of a weekly gain (or loss) being between (1.9%) and 4.1%.

There is a 50% probability of having a weekly gain of 1.1% or greater, a 16% chance of having a weekly gain of 4.1% or greater, and a 2% chance of having a weekly gain greater than 7.0%. There is a 50% probability of having a weekly gain(loss) less than 1.1% gain, a 16% chance of having a weekly loss greater than 1.9%, and a 2% chance of having a weekly loss greater than 4.8%

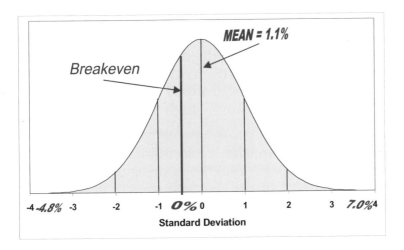

We can use the normal curve to estimate what proportion of the weeks we should expect to have gains.
Knowing that the Ø standard deviation point is 1.1%
and the standard deviation is 2.9%, we estimate that
0% (breakeven) is 1.1/2.9 = .38 standard deviations left
of the curve's midpoint. Drawing a vertical line at .38
standard deviations left of the midpoint allows us to estimate that 60% of the data points fall to the right of 0%
return. Therefore, in 60% of the weeks we expect to do
better than breakeven, and in 40% of the weeks we expect to take a loss. This estimate compares to actual
back-test results of 56.5% win ratio for trades and 63%
win rate for weeks. Weekly win rate is based on dollar
gain or loss for week, not on whether there were more or
fewer winning trades.

We estimated the 60% weekly win rate from the
above graph. It is also possible to calculate the win rate
or look it up in statistical tables. Looking up .38 in a
normal curve area table yields .148. Adding .148 to .5
sums to .648 or 65% expected win rate. Sixty-five percent of the normal curve is to the right of breakeven.

MAX drawdown is maximum reduction in equity from historic high during the back-test. Reduction in equity is (equity high up to and including the current week minus current equity) divided by historic high, for each week of the back-test. In this case, in the week 3/3/00 to 3/10/00 equity dropped to $130,465, a drop of 10.3% from the historic high (to that point) of $145,416 reached in the week of 1/21/00 to 1/28/00.

TRiPS% is a composite performance measure that adjusts Gain% for risk. TRiPS% is designed to be a reasonable estimate of future average weekly percent gain in portfolio equity. The TRiPS% calculation (% Gain + % Median) * RRR * (Win%/.5) * (1-Max % Drawdown) was discussed earlier. In this case (0.011+0.009) *.565/.5*(1-0.103) = 0.008 = 0.8%

$Gain is the average dollar gain in equity each week. This number becomes meaningful if you know the initial investment, or if the initial investment is held constant across all back-tests. If you are using different model iterations to compare strategies it is good to use a constant initial investment, say $100,000 or $1,000,000. However, when you start trading a model it is often better to use the real portfolio value, as the model calculates the number of shares to buy and sell.

Construction 2

I mentioned earlier Drach's three steps, we covered the "master list" and "entries and exits" but we skipped over Drach's second step, "market timing."

Equity Level (Market Timing)

The goal of market timing is to be in the market (long) when prices are going up and out of the market (or more extreme, short) when prices are falling.

Drach's 'market timing' step varies the portion of the portfolio in equities. Drach is always long, never short, but he varies equity/cash ratio depending on market conditions. Many investment advisors warn against trying to time the market, preaching adherence to buy and hold strategies. However, Drach has successfully timed the market for a quarter century.

Buy and holders use 2 variations of the same logic to argue against timing. First, they claim that the risk of being out of the market when it advances is too great. They believe market advances occur in short bursts, and the probability of "market timers" being out of the market when it advances are high. Second, they state back-testing of market timing strategies show they don't work.

Market Timing Indicators

Market timing indicators signal equity level targets to the model. Equity level is the percent of the portfolio's equity invested, or at risk. The following indicators seem to have some potential as market timing indicators.

%Down

%Down is the percentage of equities in the model that are below their price of X weeks ago. This is a Drach indicator. He actually recommends using P/E, rather than price, but thinks price is an okay second choice. He uses the percentage of equities that have fallen from 4 weeks ago as threshold levels for buy and sell signals. He believes that for equities with stable earnings and earnings growth, changes in P/E measure changes in sentiment or emotion. %Down is an advance/decline momentum oscillator ranging from 0%, if all 50 equities are up, to 100%, if all 50 equities are down.

The advantage of Price over P/E is that historical data are easier to obtain for back-testing.

%Long

Another advance/decline momentum oscillator, taking many different forms but often based on the previously mentioned %Down. Usually the more equities below where they were X weeks ago, the higher the %Long. One form is %Long equals 1 minus (current % of equities below X weeks ago minus minimum % of equities below X weeks ago) divided by range of % of equities below X weeks ago. Range and minimum are for the last 150 periods.

$$\%Long = 1 - \frac{current\%Down - \min imum\%Down}{\max imum\%Down - \min imum\%Down}$$

Mod %Long

Based on %Long, and modified to adjust for current market position versus market trend.   Mod %Long equals %Long times current % Long times trend market sum of 50 equities divided by current sum of 50 equities.   That is, Mod %Long equals %Long times the ratio of trend of model index to current model index.   Mod% Long is larger than %Long when the market is above trend and smaller when the market is below trend.

Both %Long and Mod %Long attempt to improve model performance over performance with %Down. %Long adjusts %Down to make it oscillate through a complete Ø to 100 by adjusting for the range %Down has oscillated through. This increases the variation in equity invested, as a percent of account value.   Mod %Long increases the amplitude of %Long in the direction current price is moving from the trend.   This increases equity invested if %Long is high while current prices are lower than calculated trend.

SMA

The Simple Moving Average (SMA) is the moving average of the 50 equities sum, for the last X weeks.

Market SEE

The Market Standard Error of Estimate is the SEE of 50 equities sum, for the last X weeks.   The smaller Market SEE the more the market is trending, as SEE measures how widely values (closing prices) are dispersed from the trend.   Dispersion is the difference between the actual value (closing price) and the trend value.   The larger the difference between the closing prices and the trend price, the higher SEE will be and the higher the volatility. The closer the closing prices are to the trend, the lower SEE and the lower the volatility.

RAVI

The Range Action Verification Index (from page 43) is calculated using the 50 equities sum, for the last X weeks. A RAVI greater than 3, and rising, indicates trending.

AROON

A Tushar S. Chande indicator, the AROON oscillator is calculated using the 50 equities sum, for the last 7 weeks. The AROON Oscillator signals an upward trend is under way when it is above Ø and a downward trend is under way when it falls below Ø. The farther away the oscillator is from the Ø-line, the stronger the trend.

KST System

The KST System, invented by Martin Pring[35] is a weighted average Rate of Change (ROC) indicator. The concept behind KST is that equity prices are in more than one cycle at a time. All the time, anytime, equities have positions on waves of short, intermediate, and long-term cycles. For instance, an equity's price might be climbing in its short term cycle, while falling in its intermediate cycle and climbing in its long term cycle. Pring's KST System combines 3 KST indicators short, intermediate and long into a Market-Cycle Model. Each KST indicator is a weighted average of moving averages of 4 different duration ROC indicators. For instance:

$$Short\ .term\ .KST\ =$$
$$(ROC\ 10\,)MA\,10\,*.1 + (ROC\ 15\,)MA\,10\,*.2$$
$$+ (ROC\ 20\,)MA\,10\,*.3 + (ROC\ 30\,)MA\,15\,*.4$$

Short-term KST equals the weighted average of 10 period moving average of 10 period ROC, 10 period moving average of 15 period ROC, 10 period moving average of 20 period ROC, and 15 period moving average of 30 period ROC.

HILO Model, Part 2

Getting back to the HILO model.

Taking the HILO model discussed earlier and adding a market timing adjustment, changes model performance. The model inputs were changed to eliminate short positions and to vary the percentage of portfolio value invested in equities to %Down. If at the end of the current week 44% of the equities in the group are lower in price than they were X weeks ago then 44% of the portfolio value is invested in equities.

	Timed	Hedged	m001 T b(w) H¹
Relative Gain	195%	204%	-9%
R²	0.99	0.96	0.03
gain %	2.3%	1.1%	1.2%
RRR (Risk Reward Ratio)	29.9%	37.5%	7.7%
MAX drawdown	6.4%	10.3%	3.8%
TRiPS%	**1.1%**	**0.8%**	**0.4%**
$Gain	$ 981	$ 1,066	$ (86)
% long	43 %	50 %	
% short	-	50 %	

Interesting results; R², Gain%. Max Drawdown, and *TRiPS%* all improved, but Relative Gain, RRR and $Gain moved in the opposite direction. The model optimized at 7 weeks, composite indicator. The model can optimize for smoothing-weeks and for indicator (one of six individual indicators, or a three indicator composite indicator). The model's composite indicator uses sorted indicator input and averages indicator rank for three indicators. In this case the three indicators are Relative Price, Slope*SEE and Slope/SEE. First, the 50 equities of the group are sorted in ascending order for each indicator and assigned a rank from 1 to 50. Then the ranks are summed for each equity, and sorted on the summed rank. The composite idea is another borrowed from Drach. In Drach's experience the composite doesn't necessarily outperform other indicators. Drach uses three indicators, earnings, yield and price. The *Trend Regression Portfolio Strategy* models provide for 6 indicators plus the composite. Each optimization picks the optimal of the 7 possibilities. The composite is of three indicators, and isn't optimizing. In current versions of the model, the 3 component indicators of the composite have to be selected before the optimization.

The reason Relative Gain and $Gain are worse, in the previous table, is that less of the portfolio's equity is used. Notice at the bottom of the Hedged column the % long and % short total 100%. All of the equity available is used. At the bottom of the Timed column, the 43% indicates that over the back-test period average portfolio equity used was 43%. The timed strategy risked less of the available equity and got a better return on what it risked. The R^2 and drawdown improved because the average amount of capital at risk was less. Gain% climbed and RRR fell as actual trades made were more risky. It is not really the individual trades that were more risky, but the weekly combination of trades. Remember in the Hedged strategy, the portfolio has some protection from overall market moves with long positions balanced by short positions. The goal of the Hedged Strategy is to gain from relative moves of equities within the group, rather than from market moves.

So, what's the best strategy, hedging or timing? To preserve my status as an amateur economist, I have to say "on one hand ... but then on the other hand." It really depends on you. If you need a strategy for an IRA account, timing is the only choice as IRA accounts can't allow shorting. In a regular account, the investor has to balance off ending equity (Relative Gain) versus sleeping at night (MAX drawdown).

Both the Timed and Hedged strategies pursue the goal of balancing risk and return. What if, return is your sole goal, will increasing risk by eliminating hedging and market timing increase return?

	HILO 100% Long	HILO Timed	L b(w) T
Relative Gain	312%	195%	117%
R²	0.96	0.99	-3%
Gain%	2.0%	2.3%	-0.3%
RRR (Risk Reward Ratio)	33.9%	29.9%	4.0%
MAX drawdown	10.9%	6.4%	-4.5%
TRiPS%	**1.1%**	**1.1%**	**0.0%**
$Gain	$1,961	$981	$980
% long	100%	43%	

100% of available portfolio equity is used to purchase the three equities with the lowest composite ranking each week. In this case the composite components are Slope, Slope*SEE, and Slope/SEE.

The increases in Relative Gain, and $Gain are dramatic, but the surprising result is that TRiPS% doesn't change. R2 and MAX Drawdown do reflect the assumption of more risk, but RRR improves, indicating less risk relative to reward. The investor who followed this model over the 150 months ending 11/2/01 would have risked more then twice as much equity per week, and ended with twice as much gain. An investor starting with $100,000 would have ended with $312,000 versus $195,000 for the timed strategy (assuming index is flat). However, the %100 Long investor would see more volatility and drawdown of portfolio equity.

HILO Model Scenario Summary

	Index B&H	Hedged	Timed	100% Long
Relative Gain	100%	204%	195%	312%
R^2	0.65	0.96	0.99	0.96
Gain%	0.4%	1.1%	2.3%	2.0%
RRR (Risk Reward Ratio)	4.8%	37.5%	29.9%	33.9%
MAX drawdown	25.3%	10.3%	6.4%	10.9%
TRiPS%	**0.03%**	**0.8%**	**1.1%**	**1.1%**
$Gain	$190	$1,066	$981	$1,961

All of the HILO model regression to mean strategies outperformed buy and hold the index. The impressive thing is not the amount $Gain or Gain% improved, but that the increase in return was accompanied by a reduction in risk over the index buy and hold strategy.

These performance statistics might make it seem easy to beat the HILO index, but as the table shows, the HILO index itself out

Cumulative %Gain 12/11/98 – 11/02/01	
Index	Gain(loss)
HILO..............	27%
S&P 500.........	(7)%
Dow..............	6%
NASDAQ........	(14)%

performed the major indexes. During the 150-weeks of the back-test the HILO index gained 27% compared to a 7% loss for the S&P 500. The Gain(Loss) values in the table are for the 150-weeks 12/11/1998 through 11/02/2001.

Of course, all of these performance measures are after the fact, historical, which means they may not be repeated. Past performance is not a guarantee of future performance. Because the HILO equities were selected in late 2000 based on earnings consistency and growth, it is not too surprising that they beat the indexes during the back-test.

For the period 1/1/2001 through 11/21/2001 the HILO index performance only beat the NASDAQ. During that period the

| Cumulative %Gain 1/1/01 through 11/21/01 ||
Index	Gain(loss)
HILO………...	(12)%
S&P 500……….	(11)%
Dow…………...	(8)%
NASDAQ……....	(28)%
HILO Hedged..	22%

HILO Hedged Model gained 22%. Better than any index, and about the same as my Drach account's 19% gain. If you take the HILO Hedged 0.8% TRiPS% times the 44 weeks of this test and add that 35% to the HILO loss of 12%, the sum 23 is pretty close to the HILO Hedged performance of 22%. Don't you love it when a plan comes together? Well don't get too excited as the HILO Hedged 0.8% *TRiPS%* back-test result comes from models with price data through 11/21/01, thus including the tables time-period 1/1/01 through 11/21/01. The model optimization and confirmation test time-periods overlap.

The basic premise of hedging is that it is possible to isolate equity indicator accuracy by reducing the impact of market cycles. If the group is homogeneous, individual equities should be pushed in the same direction by market cycles. If the equity indicator works the relatively oversold equities should increase more than the relatively overbought equities when the market advances. In addition, the relatively overbought equities should decrease more than the relatively oversold equities when the market declines. The basic justification for hedging is that the market cannot be timed, and this calls for a 50/50 long/short ratio. However, the HILO model showed that with the right combination of equities and market indicators there can be gains from market timing.

To maximize return an investor would always be 100% short when the market is going down and 100%

long when the market is going up. In the HILO Timed model holdings ranged from 5% to 98% long. A later run used the same indicator, %Down, for market timing but increased timing adjustments by targeting a range from 100% short to 100% long. There was no hedging the portfolio was either long or short. Which direction (long or short) and the dollar amount (long or short) depended on the %Down value.

	Short & Long Timed	Long Timed	S&L b(w) L
Relative Gain	160%	195%	35%
R^2	0.97	0.99	0.02
gain %	1.8%	2.3%	0.5%
RRR (Risk Reward Ratio)	23.6%	29.9%	6.2%
MAX drawdown	8.5%	6.4%	2.1%
TRiPS%	**0.6%**	**1.1%**	**0.6%**
$Gain	$ 668	$ 981	$ (312)
% long	0.38	0.38	
% short	0.40	-	

The *Short & Long Timed* model lost to the long only timed model in every performance measure recorded. The *Short & Long Timed* model reduced gain and increased risk over the Long Timed model, but still performed better than buy and hold. The portfolio was short 58% of the time during a time (150-week backtest) when the HILO index advanced 27%. The average short equity was $40,432 and the average long equity was $38,518. Because the portfolio was never long and short at the same time the average equity risked was less than 40%. This model optimized on 6 Smoothing-weeks and Composite indicator for long selection and Slope indicator for short selection.

Earlier I stated, "To maximize return an investor would always be 100% short when the market is going down and 100% long when the market is going up." The Short and Long Timed model didn't really do that. When optimizing instead of moving from 100% long to

100% short then back to 100% long, it moved along the continuum between 100% long and 100% short.

The next table compares the previous Short & Long Timed model to a new Short & Long Switched model. The switched model is either 100 % long or 100% short.

	Switched	Short & Long Timed	S b(w) T
Relative Gain	239%	160%	79%
R^2	0.97	0.97	0.00
gain %	1.4%	1.8%	0.4%
RRR (Risk Reward Ratio)	26.4%	23.6%	2.8%
MAX drawdown	10.3%	8.5%	1.8%
TRiPS%	**0.7%**	**0.6%**	**0.1%**
$Gain	$ 1,333	$ 668	$ 665
% long	0.97	0.38	
% short	0.97	0.40	

The improvement in Relative Gain and $Gain was expected as the amount of equity at risk more than doubled climbing from less than 40% to almost 100%. The improvements in TRiPS% and RRR are small and unexpected. I had also expected R2 to decline. Maybe sometimes what feels more risky, isn't. On the other hand R^2 and RRR measure volatility around the center, whereas MAX drawdown measures only loss, and in this case increases to over 10%.

Previously, we looked at timing the market to take advantage of the effects of market cycles, and at hedging to reduce or eliminate the effect of market cycles. Another possibility is varying the hedging ratio from 50/50 depending on Market Indicator values. This is taking the Long Timed model and adding a short position to use the remaining equity. So if the %Down indicator calls for a 60% long level an offsetting 40% short position is established.

	Timed Hedge	50/50 Hedged	T b(w) 50/50
Relative Gain	242%	204%	38%
R^2	0.98	0.96	0.03
gain %	1.4%	1.1%	0.3%
RRR (Risk Reward Ratio)	37.1%	37.5%	0.4%
MAX drawdown	6.0%	10.3%	4.3%
TRiPS%	**1.0%**	**0.8%**	**0.2%**
$Gain	$ 1,358	$ 1,066	$ 292
% long	0.76	0.50	
% short	0.24	0.50	

The Timed Hedge model is an improvement over the 50/50 Hedged model. Every performance measure except RRR improves, and it is close. However, neither the Timed Hedge nor the 50/50 hedged model performs as good as the 100% Long model.

Test Time-period

Back-test results depend on time-period covered. Most of my model runs covered 150-weeks, about 3 years, backwards from the date of the model run. Nothing magic about 3 years, I wanted a long period, but not so long that it eliminated too many stock candidates for lack of history.

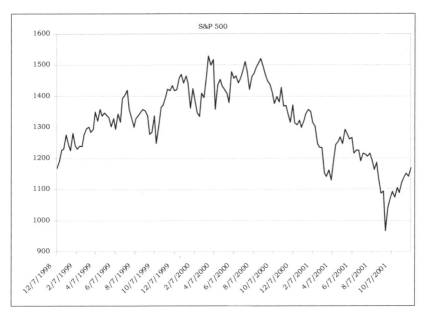

The time-period chosen for back-tests is important to optimization. You want to optimize over a time-period with price movement similar to what you expect in the future. Generally, the longer the back-test, the more variety in price movement captured. The S&P 500 graph shows why I was using 150-weeks, lots of volatility but no net change from beginning to end. This is what I was expecting for the future, volatility without a clear trend. Actually, I was expecting some growth, but still expecting volatility to be the dominant theme of the market.

I tried 520-weeks, 10 years, for HILO 100% Long model. *TRiPS%* was a little less at 0.7% versus 1.1%.

	10 year	3 year	
	100% Long	100% Long	10 b(w) 3
Relative Gain	110%	312%	(202)%
R^2	0.98	0.96	.02
Gain%	1.2%	2.0%	(0.8)%
RRR (Risk Reward Ratio)	28.1%	33.9%	5.8%
MAX drawdown	4.1%	10.9%	6.8%
TRiPS%	**0.7%**	**1.1%**	(0.4)%
$Gain	$1,250	$1,961	$(711)

To keep the 10 year test as comparable as possible to the 3 year test, I forced optimization on Composite. Smoothing-weeks and Proportion Timed then optimize to 3 weeks, 0% timed. The model was always long, but the equity/cash ratio was adjusted based on number of equities that were lower in price than 3 weeks ago, number out of 50 in the HILO equity selection. That the HILO model optimized at 3 weeks, 0% timed on both the 3-year and 10-year test is a positive indication of the stability and robustness of the HILO model.

The improvement in R^2, RRR and Max drawdown are a direct result of the longer time-period of the test, and the upward slope of the trend. Weekly movements relative to the prior week's accumulated base, become smaller as time advances. Time becomes more of a determining factor in what the new week's accumulated base will be. This could mean the longer you trade a model, or strategy, the less risk there is. Look at the relationship between the HILO 100% Long index and equity curves in the chart below.

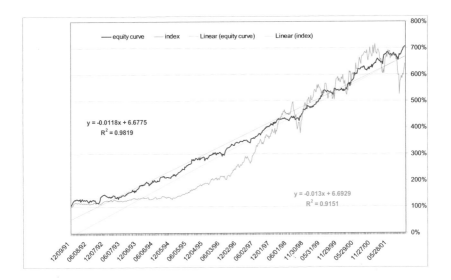

There have been periods when the index has outperformed the HILO 100% Long model. However, at the
end the index and equity curves are not that far apart
and it looks like their trendlines have converged. The
Trend Regression Portfolio Strategy model equity curve is
much smoother than the index curve. The equity curve
has less variability, is less risky.

I tried a 1 year, 52 week, test, without optimization.

	1 year	10 year	3 year	
	100% Long	100% Long	100% Long	1 b(w) 3
Relative Gain	227%	110%	312%	(85)%
R²	0.92	0.98	0.96	(.04)
Gain%	2.5%	1.2%	2.0%	0.5%
RRR (Risk Reward Ratio)	38.9%	28.1%	33.9%	5.0%
MAX drawdown	14.5%	4.1%	10.9%	(3.6)%
TRiPS%	**1.9%**	**0.7%**	**1.1%**	**0.8%**
$Gain	$2,430	$1,250	$1,961	$469

TRiPS% climbed compared to longer back-tests. Reasonable *TRiPS%* in the three different time-periods
confirm the value of the HILO selection. Relative Gain

should be a function of time. Relative Gain should increase as time span increases given HILO model growing faster than HILO index. The 312% to 227% Relative Gain for 3 year and 1 year is as expected. The 110% for 10 year is lower than expected, because of the time from early 1995 to early 2000 where the index was growing faster than the model. R^2 is expected to increase with time span for curves with positive slope as time explains more and more of the change in equity from the origin. Gain% and $Gain both get better as time span decreases, because of better match between model and market conditions during those times rather than just the smaller time span. RRR and Max Drawdown move in opposite directions. As time span increases percent drawdown decreases, improves. This is because as the difference between the current value and the origin increases equal dollar drawdowns are smaller percent drawdowns. As time span decreases RRR increases, improves, because of a better match between model and market conditions during those times rather than just the smaller time span.

I decide to revise the *Trend Regression Portfolio Strategy* model to allow changing the end date of the test. Up to now all tests ended with the most recent date in the price database. After updating the model, I planned to make 5 runs, of 50-weeks within the last 150-weeks of data. I used a random number generator to pick end dates, but kept hitting Excel's recalc [F9] until I got five covering most of the available time span.

Set Duration, Random Time-period *Back-tests*

	1 50-week	2 50-week	3 50-week	4 50-week	5 50-week	ave
Relative Gain	226%	218%	229%	200%	194%	213%
R^2	0.92	0.96	0.93	0.95	0.93	0.94
Gain%	2.5%	2.4%	3.2%	2.9%	2.8%	2.8%
RRR	38.8%	39.7%	45.4%	43.8%	41.7%	41.9%
Drawdown	14.7%	12.0%	7.2%	16.7%	15.5%	13.2%
TRiPS%	**2.1%**	**2.2%**	**3.1%**	**2.5%**	**2.3%**	**2.4%**
$Gain	$2,420	$2,326	$3,125	$2,824	$2,698	$2,678
end date	12/07/01	08/25/01	04/30/01	01/20/01	12/22/00	
Index Gain	95%	98%	111%	118%	121%	

I was surprised by both the level and consistency of performance. I checked out the model and ran 5 more tests.

Set Duration, Random Time-period *Back-tests*

	ave 1-5	6 50-week	7 50-week	8 50-week	9 50-week	10 50-week	Ave.
Relative Gain	213%	243%	244%	213%	200%	212%	218%
R2	0.94	0.93	0.93	0.95	0.95	0.95	0.94
Gain%	2.8%	3.0%	1.8%	2.7%	2.9%	2.7%	2.7%
RRR	41.9%	44.2%	27.5%	44.4%	43.8%	42.3%	41.2%
Drawdown	13.2%	8.8%	12.4%	8.4%	16.7%	9.3%	12.2%
TRiPS%	**2.4%**	**2.9%**	**1.2%**	**2.7%**	**2.5%**	**2.5%**	**2.4%**
$Gain	$2,678	$2,866	$1,779	$2,651	$2,824	$2,561	$2,607
end date	12/22/00	03/23/01	09/23/01	05/22/01	01/16/01	06/23/01	
Index Gain	121%	100%	79%	112%	118%	105%	

Other than the one outlier low *TRiPS%* for the 7th test ending 9/23/01, the second set of five is not too different from the first. With this set of 10 tests, an interesting relationship between Relative Gain and Index Gain caught my eye.

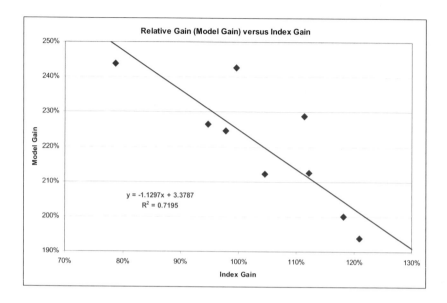

Relative Gain and Index Gain are inversely correlated, as Index Gain decreases Relative Gain increases. Relatively speaking, the model works best in a bear market. The *Trend Regression Portfolio Strategy* HILO model reduces the risk of drawdown over buy and hold.

I'm still concerned about the high *TRiPS%*, so I try 10, 5-week tests, with random end dates. Average *TRiPS%* climbs to 9.2%. I try 10, 10-week tests, with random end dates; average *TRiPS%* is 2.4%. I try 10 20-week tests; *TRiPS%* is 1.8%. As expected, Relative Gain, R^2, and MAX drawdown all climb as the duration of the test increases. Gain%, and $Gain seem unrelated to duration of test. RRR seems independent of duration of test. *TRiPS%* seems higher with short duration tests, but most of that may be caused by the reduced drawdown of short tests. *TRiPS%* may not be that a good comparison statistic, between tests of different length. Of the 40 tests done (4 durations times 10 tests each), only 2 suffered a loss for the test period. The 2 losers were 5-week tests.

Set Duration, Random Time-period *Back-tests*

	ave 5-week	ave 10-week	ave 20-week	ave 50-week
Relative Gain	112%	121%	150%	218%
R^2	0.49	0.48	0.72	0.94
Gain%	3.2%	2.3%	2.3%	2.7%
RRR	58.0%	36.7%	35.3%	41.2%
MAX drawdown	4.9%	9.5%	13.5%	12.2%
TRiPS%	**9.2%**	**2.4%**	**1.8%**	**2.4%**
$Gain	$ 3,115	$ 2,190	$ 2,257	$ 2,607
Index Gain	101%	99%	98%	106%

I mentioned that 2 of the 5-week tests had negative gain, here are results of all 10 of the 5-week tests.

Set Duration, Random Time-period *Back-tests*

	1 5 Wk	2 5 Wk	3 5 Wk	4 5 Wk	5 5 Wk	6 5 Wk	7 5 Wk	8 5 Wk	9 5 Wk	10 5 Wk	Ave 5 Wk
Relative Gain	126%	114%	130%	106%	120%	98%	100%	118%	100%	106%	112%
R2	0.91	0.12	0.84	0.02	0.28	0.65	0.14	0.91	0.04	0.98	0.49
Gain%	7.6%	2.2%	6.0%	1.6%	1.8%	0.7%	1.4%	8.4%	0.2%	4.0%	3.2%
RRR	135%	22.8%	59.7%	38.1%	21.1%	20.0%	19.6%	115%	3.8%	193%	58.0%
MAX drawdown	0.0%	9.1%	0.0%	5.5%	11.3%	6.9%	10.7%	0.0%	6.0%	0.0%	4.9%
TRiPS%	33%	1.0%	8.6%	1.8%	0.5%	0.1%	0.5%	27%	0.0%	19%	9.2%
$Gain	$7,398	$2,166	$5,760	$1,592	$1,758	$(682)	$1,353	$8,053	$(177)	$3,931	$3,115
end date	11/02	04/13	05/09	06/21	10/07	07/04	02/28	05/18	07/16	12/07	
Index Gain	104%	96%	110%	98%	92%	95%	96%	110%	98%	109%	101%

Not only are there losers in the 5-week tests, there is a lot of variability in performance results. For instance, the average RRR is 58%, which is good indicating that Gain% is large relative to the standard deviation of Gain%. However, between tests the standard deviation for RRR is 68% for 5-week, 15% for 10-week, 8% for 20-week, and 5% for 50-week. Therefore, although Gain% variation between weeks of the 5-week test is much smaller than between weeks of the longer tests, the variation of Gain% between tests is much greater for 5-week tests than for longer tests.

The same is true for TRiPS%. Variation between the weeks of each 5-week test is much smaller than between weeks of the longer tests, however, the variation of TRiPS% between 5-week tests is much greater than for longer tests.

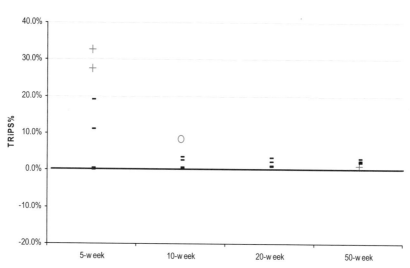

The graph show TRiPS% for each of the 40 tests in this series. Distributions are much tighter for longer duration tests.

The increased variability of short duration tests implies increased risk in adopting a *Trend Regression Portfolio Strategy* for a 5-week period in comparison to a longer period. *Trend Regression Portfolio Strategy* is not a short-term proposition. Another telling point, in favor of a longer-term commitment, comes from a revisit to the Relative Gain versus Index Gain relationship.

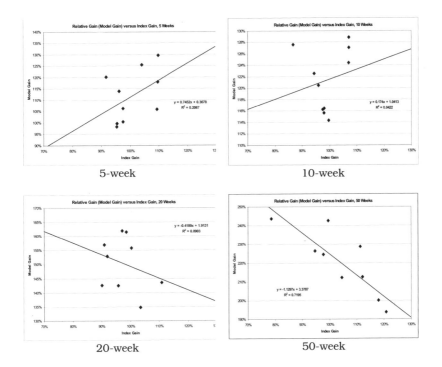

5-week

10-week

20-week

50-week

Notice the slope of Relative Gain versus Index Gain. In the shorter tests Relative Gain and Index Gain are positively correlated. The more the index group goes up the more the model portfolio goes up and vice versa. Using *Trend Regression Portfolio Strategy* short term, increases market risk. The model portfolio moves in the same direction as the model, but more.

Once the test period gets to 20-weeks, the relationship between Relative Gain and Index Gain has switched to inversely correlated. Using *Trend Regression Portfolio Strategy* long term decreases market risk.

Of course, the 3 smoothing-weeks, 0%-timed optimization was done on a relatively long period, 150-weeks. Optimizing on a different duration (length of back-test) or on a different time-period (different calendar dates of back-test), produces different results. You should optimize on price data that you feel is representative of future price moves.

Short duration back-tests are especially problematic as demonstrated in the following table.

	150-week optimized	5-week optimized	5 B(W) 150
Relative Gain	226%	160%	(66)%
R²	0.92	0.73	(0.19)
Gain%	2.5%	2.1%	(0.4)%
RRR (Risk Reward Ratio)	38.8%	26.3%	(12.4)%
MAX drawdown	14.7%	17.9%	(3.3)%
TRiPS%	**2.1%**	**0.7%**	(1.4)%
$Gain	$ 2,420	$ 1,042	$ (1,378)
% long	0.97	0.50	
end date	12/7/2001	12/7/2001	
Smoothing-weeks	**3**	**25**	
Index Gain	95%	95%	

The table compares performance of different Smoothing-week, Proportion Timed combinations for the 50-week period ending 12/7/2001. The 3 Smoothing-weeks, 0% Proportion Timed combination was achieved by optimizing on the 150-weeks ending 12/7/2001. The 25 Smoothing-weeks, 100% Proportion Timed combination was achieved by optimizing on the 5-weeks ending 7/4/2001. Usually the fewer data points used in calculating an indicator the more volatile it is; the faster it reacts to current price changes. There is no shorting in these tests, so the larger the portion timed, the lower average risked capital. I speculated that the combination of longer Smoothing-weeks and less average capital risked would reduce return and reduce risk. However, the 5-week optimization missed on every performance measurement, reducing return and increasing risk across the board.

This is not to say that short time duration test optimizations will always produce less performance than longer duration test optimizations. This is just a warning that test duration and time-period selected for optimization can have a significant impact on optimization solutions and subsequent trading results.

I confess, I cheated a little by deliberately picking a time-period that performed poorly using the 3 Smoothing-week, 0% Proportion Timed combination as inputs. I expected that a time-period, that didn't do well with the 3,0 combination, would optimize on a combination, that wouldn't produce good results where the 3,0 combination had. Column 6 of the *Set Duration, Random Time-period* Back-tests table on page 91, is the source of my short time-period selection. Later, I optimized on the 5-week test that produced the best results with the 3,0 combination and that 5-week period ending 11/4/2001 optimized to 3 Smoothing-weeks, and 0% Proportion Timed, same as 150-week optimization.

Returning now to the comparison between different length tests using the HILO 100% Long model, I'll focus on the central limit theorem. The central limit theorem gives a better perspective on the test duration impact on optimization solutions and subsequent trading results. The HILO 100% Long model 150-week test optimization results column has been added to the previous table.

Set Duration, Random Time-period *Back-tests*

	ave 5-week	ave 10-week	ave 20-week	ave 50-week	HILO 150-week
Relative Gain	112%	121%	150%	218%	312%
R^2	0.49	0.48	0.72	0.94	0.96
Gain%	3.2%	2.3%	2.3%	2.7%	2.0%
RRR (Risk Reward Ratio)	58.0%	36.7%	35.3%	41.2%	33.9%
MAX drawdown	4.9%	9.5%	13.5%	12.2%	10.9%
TRiPS%	**9.2%**	**2.4%**	**1.8%**	**2.4%**	**1.1%**
$Gain	$ 3,115	$ 2,190	$ 2,257	$ 2,607	$1,961
Index Gain	101%	99%	98%	106%	106%

The central limit theorem states that the mean of means of samples taken from a population will converge on the mean of the population[36]. The weekly $Gain for the 150-weeks ending 12/7/2001 is the population. The weekly $Gain is calculated by the HILO model each week based on the 3 Smoothing-week, 0% Proportion Timed inputs. Regardless of the number of weeks covered by the test, the $Gain for individual calendar weeks will be the same. All of the other performance statistics are derived from the weekly $Gain. If enough 5-week, 10-week, 20-week, or 50-week tests are done using the same data that generated the 150-week $1,961 average gain the mean of those tests will converge on $1,961.

The 150-week optimization finds the best answer for the 150-week period, which is not necessarily the best for any smaller time-period within the 150-weeks. Any optimization for a subset of the 150-week, tested on all of the 150-week data will have a performance equal to or less than the longer optimization. However, the performance will only be equal if the shorter optimization Smoothing-weeks and Proportion Timed is identical to the 150-week optimization.

This does not mean a long optimization will always produce a superior guide to future trading. It will depend how the future unfolds. Is the future price action more like the long test period, or more like the short test period? It is probable that the Smoothing-week, Proportion Timed combination that was optimum is not going stay optimum. We hope the future optimum will be close to the back-test optimum.

Proportion Timed

Proportion timed is the amount of equity that is not hedged, the amount that is traded subject to market indicator values.

We looked at timing the market to take advantage of the effects of market cycles, at hedging to reduce or eliminate the effect of market cycles, and at varying the hedging ratio from 50/50 depending on Market Indicator values. What if part of the portfolio is hedged 50/50 and part is a timed hedge? What portion of the portfolio equity should be timed?

The %Timed Hedge model optimizes in 2 directions Smoothing-weeks and Proportion Timed. The best *TRiPS%* is highest when Smoothing-weeks is 8 and Proportion Timed is 10. Ninety percent of the portfolio equity is hedged 50/50 and 10 percent is hedged with long at %Down and short at 100% minus %Down. This results in limiting the long percent of equity to the range 45% to 55%. Short percent of equity is also limited to the range 45% to 55% as short percent equals 100% minus long percent of equity.

	%Timed Hedge	Hedged	%TH b(w) H
Relative Gain	222%	204%	18%
R^2	0.98	0.96	0.02
gain %	1.3%	1.1%	0.1%
RRR (Risk Reward Ratio)	42.6%	37.5%	5.1%
MAX drawdown	6.6%	10.3%	3.7%
TRiPS%	1.0%	0.8%	0.3%
$Gain	$ 1,211	$ 1,066	$ 145
% long	49%	0.50	
% short	51%	0.50	

The preceding %Timed Hedge model started from an un-timed position of 50/50 hedging. The next model, %Timed Long starts from an un-timed position of 100% long. Seventy percent of the portfolio equity is long and 30 percent is hedged with long at %Down and short at 1 minus %Down. This results in limiting the long percent of equity to the range 70% to 100%. Short percent of equity is then limited to the range 0% to 30% as short percent equals 100% minus long percent of equity.

	%Timed Long	%Timed Hedge	T Long B(W) T&H
Relative Gain	287%	222%	64%
R^2	0.99	0.98	0.01
gain %	1.8%	1.3%	0.5%
RRR (Risk Reward Ratio)	38.6%	42.6%	4.0%
MAX drawdown	5.7%	6.6%	0.9%
TRiPS%	1.5%	1.0%	0.5%
$Gain	$ 1,777	$ 1,211	$ 566
% long	0.84	49%	
% short	0.16	51%	

The %Timed Long strategy outperforms the %Timed Hedged strategy on every performance measure except RRR. The decrease in RRR is probably related to the fact that hedging ratios changed from near 50/50 to 84% long.

Because *Trend Regression Portfolio Strategy* Excel models are built with non-smooth functions (if and lookup), locally optimum solutions can exist that are not the optimal solution. For instance in the diagram below (for the % Timed Long model), a local optimal exists at 35 Smoothing-weeks and 0% proportion timed. But the global optimum, within the constraints of Smoothing-weeks between 3 and 50, and proportion between Ø and 100, is 8 smoothing-weeks and 30% Proportion Timed.

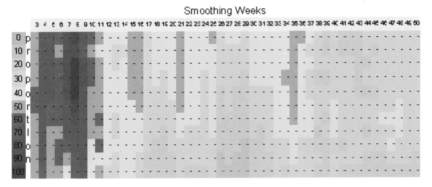

In the diagram above (R-map, Robustness Map), Smoothing-weeks from 3 to 50 is the x-axis along the top, and Proportion Timed is the y-axis along the left margin. Colors range from dark green optimal solution to dark orange least-optimal solution. The R-map makes it easy to see that for this model there is more than one locally optimal solution, but only one globally optimal solution. Determination of optimal solution is based on *TRiPS%* for each combination of Smoothing-weeks—Proportion Timed.

These models determine optimal solution by exhaustive testing. They cycle through every possible solution leaving a trail of portfolio performance statistics. The advantages of exhaustive testing are that it finds the globally optimal solution, it produces the above diagram, and it is easy to understand. The disadvantage is that each run takes hours.

The diagram helps to form judgments about how robust the optimal solution is. The more green cells around the optimal solution, the more likely it is that the optimal solution is robust. Robust means likely to work in the future. The future optimal solution is likely to be different from the back-test optimal solution. However, if many solutions around the back-test optimal are also good, maybe the future optimal will land close enough to create future gains in portfolio equity. The diagram shows how sensitive the model is to having the exact optimal Smoothing-week, Proportion Timed combination.

A close-up of the area around the optimal solution shows the *TRiPS%* values the colorization is based on.

Smoothing Weeks

		3	4	5	6	7	8	9	10	11	12	13
0	p	0.80%	1.08%	1.07%	0.86%	1.25%	1.35%	1.02%	0.83%	0.70%	0.60%	0.55%
10	r	0.80%	1.08%	1.04%	0.81%	1.19%	1.27%	0.95%	0.73%	0.66%	0.61%	0.47%
20	o	0.71%	1.06%	0.99%	0.87%	1.18%	1.43%	1.12%	0.89%	0.78%	0.61%	0.48%
30	p	0.79%	1.07%	1.03%	0.90%	1.20%	1.49%	1.15%	0.85%	0.78%	0.59%	0.61%
40	o	0.82%	1.04%	1.10%	0.91%	1.16%	1.47%	1.07%	0.72%	0.72%	0.54%	0.56%
50	r	0.82%	0.99%	0.86%	0.88%	1.02%	1.30%	0.99%	0.71%	0.78%	0.59%	0.61%
60	t	0.79%	1.01%	0.90%	0.86%	1.02%	1.20%	1.07%	0.78%	0.84%	0.57%	0.49%
70	l	0.78%	0.99%	0.75%	0.79%	1.00%	1.04%	1.11%	0.76%	0.81%	0.56%	0.47%
80	o	0.72%	0.99%	0.78%	0.92%	0.85%	1.03%	0.97%	0.62%	0.88%	0.56%	0.52%
90	n	0.75%	0.98%	0.71%	0.91%	0.71%	0.90%	0.98%	0.61%	0.57%	0.53%	0.45%
100		0.69%	0.95%	0.71%	0.76%	0.59%	0.85%	0.97%	0.59%	0.67%	0.49%	0.44%

Both Smoothing-weeks and Proportion Timed have an impact on *TRiPS%*. TRiPS% declines no matter what direction you move away from the optimal 8 Smoothing-weeks and 30% Timed. Every combination one step away stays above 1% *TRiPS%*. However, 2 steps in either direction away from the Smoothing-weeks optimal reduces score below 1% *TRiPS%*.

Picking the optimal Smoothing-week—Proportion Timed combination can be important. For the %Timed Long model *TRiPS%* ranges from a low of .1% at 28 weeks–100% timed to the optimal 1.5% at 8 weeks–30% timed.

A big advantage of exhaustive models that calculate every combination, over linear programming or neural networks, is the R-map.

Earlier I mentioned the length of back tests and optimization. Remember from page 50, short optimizations can give higher TRiPS% than long optimizations, but short optimizations can not give optimal values that will perform better in a longer back-test, which contains the short optimization period, than optimal values obtained from an optimization done on the longer period.

Here is an R-map for a 1-year optimization.

TRiPS%

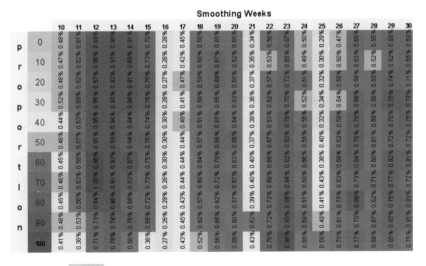

The minimum TRiPS% is 0.26% and the maximum is 1.00%, a range of 0.74%. Next is an R-map for the same group of equities, but optimized over 10 years, instead of 1 year.

TRiPS%

Smoothing Weeks

proportion	10	11	12	13	14	15	16	17	18	19	20	21	22	23	24	25	26	27	28	29	30
0	0.61%	0.65%	0.70%	0.65%	0.78%	0.74%	0.72%	0.70%	0.66%	0.73%	0.73%	0.73%	0.75%	0.79%	0.52%	0.72%	0.50%	0.77%	0.76%	0.75%	0.76%
10	0.62%	0.66%	0.70%	0.64%	0.78%	0.75%	0.72%	0.69%	0.69%	0.74%	0.74%	0.74%	0.76%	0.80%	0.53%	0.73%	0.72%	0.78%	0.77%	0.76%	0.76%
20	0.63%	0.68%	0.74%	0.68%	0.82%	0.79%	0.74%	0.71%	0.71%	0.76%	0.77%	0.76%	0.77%	0.83%	0.53%	0.74%	0.73%	0.79%	0.79%	0.80%	0.80%
30	0.65%	0.68%	0.72%	0.89%	0.83%	0.80%	0.76%	0.75%	0.72%	0.78%	0.77%	0.78%	0.82%	0.83%	0.56%	0.74%	0.76%	0.80%	0.79%	0.81%	0.90%
40	0.64%	0.71%	0.76%	0.89%	0.83%	0.81%	0.77%	0.75%	0.72%	0.78%	0.79%	0.78%	0.80%	0.84%	0.57%	0.76%	0.56%	0.81%	0.80%	0.81%	0.80%
50	0.66%	0.69%	0.74%	0.89%	0.82%	0.79%	0.76%	0.74%	0.72%	0.79%	0.79%	0.79%	0.80%	0.84%	0.57%	0.76%	0.56%	0.80%	0.78%	0.79%	0.80%
60	0.66%	0.69%	0.74%	0.88%	0.82%	0.80%	0.77%	0.76%	0.75%	0.80%	0.81%	0.81%	0.85%	0.61%	0.78%	0.77%	0.81%	0.80%	0.81%	0.79%	
70	0.64%	0.69%	0.75%	0.83%	0.81%	0.80%	0.77%	0.75%	0.73%	0.80%	0.81%	0.80%	0.85%	0.62%	0.78%	0.75%	0.81%	0.79%	0.79%	0.90%	
80	0.64%	0.57%	0.75%	0.85%	0.81%	0.80%	0.75%	0.75%	0.73%	0.80%	0.81%	0.80%	0.84%	0.61%	0.77%	0.61%	0.78%	0.77%	0.79%	0.76%	
90	0.61%	0.64%	0.70%	0.82%	0.77%	0.75%	0.72%	0.71%	0.70%	0.76%	0.77%	0.76%	0.77%	0.79%	0.63%	0.73%	0.61%	0.76%	0.75%	0.63%	0.74%
100	0.57%	0.58%	0.65%	0.74%	0.70%	0.68%	0.66%	0.67%	0.64%	0.69%	0.72%	0.72%	0.72%	0.74%	0.68%	0.68%	0.59%	0.69%	0.70%	0.69%	0.69%

min	0.50%
max	0.89%

There is a lot less variation in color for the 10-year back-test. Minimum TRiPS% is 0.50% and the maximum is .89%, a range of 0.49%. TRiPS% for the longer optimization has a narrower range of optimized values. One implication of these 2 R-maps is that there was less cost of being wrong (not trading with the optimal input variables) over the 10-year term than over the one-year period. If you followed the 17 smoothing-weeks, 90% timed strategy for the one year of the back-test your TRiPS% was only .26%. However, the worst combination for the 10-year back-test, 26 smoothing-weeks, Ø percent timed, had a TRiPS of .50%. The worst 10-year strategy is twice as good as the worst 1-year strategy.

Another implication of the R-maps is that TRiPS% scores for Smoothing-weeks—Proportion Timed combinations revert to their mean over time. The worst combinations will probably have better scores in the future and the optimal combinations will probably have worse scores in the future. That doesn't necessarily mean that the worst combinations last year will produce the best results this year. The standard deviation of TRiPS% scores was 0.18% for the 1-year back-test and 0.07% for the 10-year back-test.

Below is an updated summary of HILO model runs, sorted from worst to best *TRiPS%*.

HILO Model Runs

	Index	Short & Long Timed	Switched	Hedged	% Timed Hedge	Timed Hedge	Long Timed	100% Long	% Timed Long
Relative Gain	100%	160%	239%	204%	222%	242%	195%	312%	287%
R²	0.65	0.97	0.97	0.96	0.98	0.98	0.99	0.96	0.99
Gain%	0.4%	1.8%	1.4%	1.1%	1.3%	1.4%	2.3%	2.0%	1.8%
RRR %	4.8%	23.6	26.4%	37.5%	42.6	37.1	29.9	33.9	38.6%
Drawdown	25%	8.5%	10.3%	10.3%	6.6%	6.0%	6.4%	11%	5.7%
TRiPS%	0.0%	0.6%	0.7%	0.8%	1.0%	1.0%	1.1%	1.1%	1.5%
$Gain	$190	$668	$1,333	1,066	1,211	1,358	$981	1,961	$1,777
% long	100%	38%	97%	50%	49%	76%	43%	100%	84%
% short	-	40%	97%	50%	51%	24%	-	-	16%

All eight variations on the HILO theme produced better results for the back-test period than the buy and hold index strategy. The eight *Trend Regression Portfolio Strategy* models not only increased return but also lowered risk relative to the buy and hold the index strategy. The table is sorted by *TRiPS%*, as the models are built to optimize on *TRiPS%*. Remember *TRiPS%* has risk and return components combined in one measure. I like *TRiPS%*, and of the models above, the one I would trade is %Timed Long. If you are less risk adverse you might trade 100% Long as it produced higher Relative Gain and $Gain. However with its high RRR and small

MAX Drawdown none of the other models is less risky than % Timed Long. Actually, I like the HILO model enough that I have traded the 100% Long model in an IRA account.

Carefully picking the 50 equities for the group is important, but the 8 model comparison above shows tuning the long/short assumptions also has an impact on results. *TRiPS%* increases nearly 3 fold between Short & Long Timed and %Timed Long.

You might be thinking "WOW eight is a lot of model runs for the HILO group of equities." More to come, there are a few wrinkles we haven't explored yet.

Reversal/Trending Switch

The basic model assumes regression to the mean, but sometimes trends continue, instead of reversing. The model allows changing sort order depending on market indicators. The model normally sorts indicators so most overbought are sold but can be changed so most overbought are bought. At the same time, the model normally buys most oversold but can be changed to sell most oversold. Most overbought is the equity that has the largest positive equity indicator reading. For instance, the equity with the largest % Price increase for X weeks or highest Slope for X week trend is overbought relative to other equities in the group of 50.

A market indicator trigger is set as a switch% at the point in the market indicator's range where we want to change sort direction. For instance, if the market indicator is SEE as a percent of ending equity, the range is .6% to 6.4%, and the switch% is input as 25% the threshold will be 2.04%. If SEE% falls below 2.04%, the equity indicator sort order is switched to descending. The descending order sort causes most overbought equities to be bought.

The %Timed Long model was rerun to reverse sort order when %SEE drops below 25$^{%}$ of range.

	Trend Switch 25%	%Timed Long	S B(W) T
Relative Gain	213%	287%	(74)%
R2	0.96	0.99	(0.03)
gain %	1.2%	1.8%	(0.6)%
RRR (Risk Reward Ratio)	25.9%	38.6%	(12.7)%
MAX drawdown	12.0%	5.7%	6.3%
TRiPS%	**0.5%**	**1.5%**	**(1.0)%**
$Gain	$ 1,149	$ 1,777	$ (628)
% long	0.84	0.84	
% short	0.16	0.16	

The results are not good with Trend Switch 25% losing to %Timed Long for every performance measure. However 25% is only one of 100 possible values. Results with Trend Switch at 10% improves *TRiPS%* to 1.6%. Optimal Smoothing-weeks–Proportion Timed stays at 8 weeks–30% timed. All performance measures except R^2 improved.

	Trend Switch 10%	%Timed Long	TS10 b(w) %TL
Relative Gain	296%	287%	9%
R^2	0.98	0.99	(0.01)
gain %	1.9%	1.8%	0.1%
RRR (Risk Reward Ratio)	40.6%	38.6%	2.0%
MAX drawdown	5.6%	5.7%	0.1%
TRiPS%	**1.6%**	**1.5%**	**0.1%**
$Gain	$ 1,848	$1,777	$ 71
% long	0.84	0.84	
% short	0.16	0.16	

With the Trend Switch set at 10% the sort order was switched only 11 times during the 150-week back-test.

The back-tests in this Chapter lead to the following generalizations about *Trend Regression Portfolio Strategy*:

a. *Trend Regression Portfolio Strategy* seems to work, in all but 2 of the back-tests discussed so far, following an optimized *Trend Regression Portfolio Strategy* gained more than a buy and hold strategy for the model's 50 equities.

b. Hedging and Timing impact performance, but don't necessarily improve the performance over staying 100% Long.

c. Some optimizations seem quite robust as shown by the Smoothing-weeks, Proportion Timed colored grid and by the 3-year and 10-year tests for HILO equities optimizing at same Smoothing-weeks, Proportion Timed combination.

d. *Trend Regression Portfolio Strategy* works better for longer time-periods, i.e. the longer it is used.

e. For longer tests, Relative Gain and Index Gain are inversely correlated, as Index Gain decreases Relative Gain increases. Therefore, *Trend Regression Portfolio Strategy* reduces drawdown as relatively speaking; the model works best in a bear market.

f. Short duration optimizations may produce high future returns. However, historic short duration optimizations cannot yield better returns than historic longer period optimizations for the longer historic period, if the shorter period is contained in the longer period.

g. Not only is model performance, *TRiPS%*, sensitive to indicator sort order, it seems performance is generally better for reversal (ascending sorts), than for trend following (descending sorts).

h. There are times when trend following will produce better performance than reversal.

We haven't exhausted all the HILO group models there are many more equity and market indicators possible. However let's think about stock picking for awhile.

4. Stock Picking

Earlier we introduced the topic of selecting stocks for the Trend Regression Portfolio Theory model. Why bother, why not just take 50 stocks at random? Isn't regression to the mean a universal rule and shouldn't it work regardless of which stocks are in the model?

Random

On my first try at randomness, I picked 50 random stocks by searching on analyst rating of hold, limiting the result to 100, and starting alphabetically throwing out equities that didn't have 200 weeks of data. The resulting group of 50 equities includes: ACO,ACTM, ADC,CDA,CEBC,CIB,CICI,CLYS,CM,COA,CRC,CRGO, CTI,CYLK,DA,DLW,DRF,ELIX,EPR,EX,FBBC,FELE, FLA,FLAG,FRDM,GEL,GL,GNL,GXP,HDNG,HSKA,INDB, IPS,ISEC,ISKO,JNC,JQH,KLM,KUB,LANC,LVEL,MAA, MABA,MCRS,MEAD,MTLG,MYS,NATR,NSPR,ONCO.

The idea for searching on analyst rating came from some earlier work I had done trying to make money on analyst ratings. To my chagrin, I found no correlation between analyst buy or strong buy ratings and subsequent price increases. Now I am surprised at how good the results for the Random Hold group were.

	Random Hold	HILO 100% Long	R b(w) H
Relative Gain	562%	312%	250%
R^2	0.96	0.96	0.00
gain %	2.6%	2.0%	0.6%
RRR (Risk Reward Ratio)	24.6%	33.9%	9.3%
MAX drawdown	16.9%	10.9%	6.0%
TRiPS%	**0.9%**	**1.1%**	**0.2%**
$Gain	$ 2,517	$ 1,961	$ 556
% long	100%	100%	

The random stock pick produced better return, with more risk than the HILO pick. The Relative Gain is inflated by decline in the Random index, but the Gain% improvement and $Gain improvement are impressive.

This strong return and reasonable *TRiPS%* was not what I expected. I surmised that maybe my random selection wasn't really random. Therefore, I tried again taking the 500 equities of S&P 500, listed them alphabetically, assigned them a number, and then picked 50 numbers at random, eliminating duplicates. The resulting group of 50 equities includes: ABC,AGN,AVY,AZO,BLL,CAT,CI,CMCSK,CMVT,D,DE,DLX,DVN,EDS,F,FDX,FRE,GPC,GPS,HCA,HIG,HRC,IFF,JNJ,KEY,LIZ,LXK,MSFT,MXIM,MYG,NSI,ONE,PG,PMCS,PNW,RAL,RHI,SWK,SYK,TGT,TMK,TROW,TRW,TXN,UCL,UVN,WEN,WHR,WIN.

The results for Random 500 are not as good, as for Random Hold.

	Random 500	HILO 100% Long	T b(w) H
Relative Gain	211%	312%	(101)%
R^2	0.96	0.96	0.00
gain %	0.9%	2.0%	1.1%
RRR (Risk Reward Ratio)	23.4%	33.9%	(10.5)%
MAX drawdown	11.9%	10.9%	(1.0)%
TRiPS%	**0.4%**	1.1%	(0.7)%
average/wk	$ 897	$1,961	$ (1,064)
% long	56%	100%	
% short	44%	0%	

The results are better than buy and hold of a Random 500 index. This may mean regardless of how bad your stock picks are you can improve your return and reduce risk by using *Trend Regression Portfolio Strategy*. The random stock pick results still bother me because it is better than expected. So, I look at a random selection from the stocks in the NASDAQ 100. WOW!

	Random QQQ	HILO 100% Long	RQ b(w) H
Relative Gain	602%	312%	290%
R^2	0.97	0.96	0.01
gain %	3.4%	2.00%	1.4%
RRR (Risk Reward Ratio)	23.1%	33.90%	10.8%
MAX drawdown	16.9%	10.90%	6.0%
TRiPS%	**1.1%**	**1.1%**	**0.0%**
$Gain	$ 3,246	$1,961	$ 1,285

The TRiPS% matches the HILO 100% Long at 1.1%. Remember, the HILO screen was for companies with consistent earnings and growth. The Random QQQ was a random selection from the largest 150 NASDAQ companies. The QQQ models are named after the NASDAQ 100 Trust, Series 1, which has the ticker symbol QQQ. However, the QQQ models are not limited to the 100 companies in the NASDAQ 100 Trust, Series 1. The Random QQQ performance is amazingly good, with *TRiPS%* 1.1, however there is more risk with RRR lower and Max Drawdown greater. R^2 is actually better because the slope of the Random QQQ equity curve is 0.0285, much greater than 0.0208 for the HILO 100% Long equity curve. Because the slope is larger, time explains more of the variance in equity.

The equity curve is interesting showing close correlation between the Random QQQ index and the Random QQQ—*Trend Regression Portfolio Strategy* equity curve through early 2000.

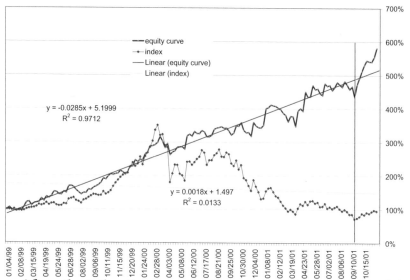

After that the 2 curves pull apart with the index falling and the *Trend Regression Portfolio Strategy* rising. The model's equity curve rises when the index is rising and rises when the index is falling. Pretty amazing, but unexpected, so I 'time out' to audit the model and contemplate more stock selection schemes.

I audited the model to confirm that the weeks with the biggest gains in Random QQQ *Trend Regression Portfolio Strategy* equity checks out. I verify that in the week 1/1/01 – 1/8/01 the model produced a $49,975 profit. The trading week 1/1/01 is Monday 1/1/01 through Friday 1/5/01. Trading weeks are labeled with Monday's date and the weekly closing price is Friday's close. The model buys BIGT, PCLN, and NETA at

Symbol	Company	Shares	Week 1/1/01 Close	Week 1/8/01 Close	per Share Gain	Total Gain
BIGT	Pinnacle Holdings, Inc.	3,800	$8.5625	$9.9375	$1.375	$5,225
PCLN	Priceline.com Inc.	18,800	$1.7188	$2.9688	$1.250	$23,500
NETA	Network As-sociates	6,800	$4.7500	$7.8750	$3.125	$21,250
						$49,975

Friday's close $8.5625, $1.7188, and 4.75 and sells at the following Friday's close $9.9375, $2.9688, and $7.875. These three round trips create gains of $5,225 for BIGT, $23,500 for PCLN, and $21,250 for NETA. The weeks closes are confirmed and the $49,975 profit is confirmed. Other weeks are audited and check out okay. The Random QQQ *Trend Regression Portfolio Strategy* model is 100% long and optimized 27 weeks and 0% timed. That is, the model was 100% long every week, with no adjustments for market cycles. Although the model was optimized for smoothing-weeks and proportion timed, no effort was made to look for a hedging or sort-order switching strategy. So, better back-test results may be possible.

The good result for Random QQQ still bothered me. I was sure I had investigated regression to the mean strategies with NASDAQ stocks in the past, and given them up as dead ends. Maybe the performance of the back-test on this random QQQ selection was just blind luck. I decided to invest some time in selection of NASDAQ stocks.

The table below compares the first random QQQ with five more QQQ models.

	Random QQQ	Random QQQ 2	Random QQQ 3	Random QQQ 4	Random QQQ 5	Random QQQ 6
Relative Gain	593%	465%	438%	472%	698%	559%
R2	0.97	0.88	0.94	0.93	0.92	0.94
Gain%	3.36%	3.06%	3.23%	3.33%	3.81%	3.5%
RRR	23.09%	23.55%	25.13%	27.91%	29.76%	24.5%
Drawdown	16.86%	16.72%	21.33%	13.32%	15.52%	21.5%
TRiPS%	**1.1%**	**1.3%**	**1.3%**	**1.7%**	**2.1%**	**1.4%**
$Gain	$3,246	$2,966	$3,117	$3,225	$3,678	$ 3,348
% long	100%	100%	100%	100%	100%	100%
Weeks	27	20	17	3	3	3
Index Gain	97%	111%	122%	119%	111%	100%

The *TRiPS%* for every test is good. Remember, I was surprised by how good the first test Random QQQ was, but now that test turns out to have the lowest *TRiPS%* of the lot. MAX drawdown in all tests is a little high and RRR is a little low, but the returns are high enough to bring *TRiPS%* up. Random QQQ 5's *TRiPS%* is unusually high. The Index gain of all 150 equities 98%. That is after 150-weeks the sum of 150 equities prices is 98% of starting sum of 150 equities. As the number of Random QQQ models run increases, for the same 150-weeks, the mean index Gain should approach 98%. Based on these six random models, I expect that as the number of Random QQQ models increases the mean *TRiPS%* would approach 1.3 or 1.4%.

The grouping of optimum smoothing-weeks at 3, and to a lesser extent around 20, is surprising. I expected a more random distribution. This may imply that there is some magic, some universality, to 3 smoothing-weeks.

The spread of *TRiPS%* from 1.1% to 2.1% indicates that stock selection has a bearing on how TRiPS models perform.

Some Non Random Selections

In order to improve TRiPS% I tested 2 non random selections.

First I selected from the NASDAQ 150 biggest companies the companies with the most consistent price growth by screening for price trendline slope divided by price trendline SEE. The result was Stable Grow QQQ including the 50 equities: CYTC, IDPH, GENZ,CEFT,BBBY,ERTS,AMGN,CHIR,NVDA,GILD, BMET,ADVP,SBUX,ESTS,LLTC,NVLS,FLEX,MCHP, MXIM,USAI,HGSI,CMCSK,MEDI,PDLI,CHKP,ADBE, PTEN,SYMC,MLNM,TMPW,DISH,KLAC,IDTI,PLCM, XLNX,ALTR,QCOM,AHAA,TQNT,SANM,BEAS,LRCX, SEBL,INTU,MERQ,BGEN,EMLX,ORCL,ATML,BRCD.

I had convinced myself that prices of companies that have prices growing consistently should regress to the trend. I was still using my Drach inspired belief that solid fundamentals would isolate price changes due emotion. I was assuming consistently growing prices were a reflection of consistently growing earnings and solid fundamentals. However, the Stable Growth QQQ model didn't work well.

	Random Average	Stable Growth QQQ	SG B(W) R
Relative Gain	537%	187%	350%
R2	0.93	0.91	0.02
Gain%	3.4%	2.5%	0.8%
RRR (Risk Reward Ratio)	25.7%	27.6%	1.9%
MAX drawdown	17.5%	13.8%	3.7%
TRiPS%	**1.5%**	**1.3%**	**0.2%**
$Gain	$3,264	$2,466	($798)
% long	100%	100%	
Smoothing-weeks	12.5	5	
Index Gain	110%	247%	

The carefully selected group of 50 didn't better the average of the random picks. *TRiPS%* was less, Gain% and $Gain were less, but RRR improved and MAX Drawdown was reduced. Relative Gain was a lot less because the group was selected based on its growth and the index itself grew by 147%. *TRiPS%* at 1.3% was better than that of the lowest random selection with 1.1%, and quite a bit lower than the best random selection with *TRiPS%* of 2.1%.

The next selection was based on correlation with QQQ (the NASDAQ 100 Trust, Series 1). The result was Corr QQQ including the 50 equities: QQQ,ERICY,NXTL, JDSU,CSCO,XOXO,RBAK,INKT,MFNX,BVSN,ARBA, CMRC,MCLD,VIGN,BRCM,BIGT,VRSN,PMCS,SUNW, VTSS,INTC,INSP,TERN,AAPL,ITWO,OPWV,GSPH,ASML, YHOO,ADCT,CNXT,ISSX,AFFX,NTAP,VLNK,LVLT,IMNX, GMST,VRTS,TXCC,ORCL,AMAT,FDRY,QLGC,SCMR, ATML,RMBS,RIMM,XLNX,RFMD

The correlation with QQQ model beats the average of the random tests on every measure. *TRiPS%* at 2.2% is higher than the highest random selection back-test score of 2.1%.

	Random Average	Corr QQQ	C B(W) R
Relative Gain	537%	936%	399%
R^2	0.93	0.96	0.03
Gain%	3.4%	4.6%	1.3%
RRR (Risk Reward Ratio)	25.7%	30.4%	4.7%
MAX drawdown	17.5%	14.0%	3.6%
TRiPS%	**1.5%**	**2.2%**	**0.8%**
$Gain	$3,264	$ 4,483	$1,219
% long	100%	100%	
% short	0%	0%	
Smoothing-weeks	12.5	4	
Index Gain	110%	82%	

There is only a 30% overlap between the **QQQ** 6 model selection and the Correlated **QQQ** model. Fifteen of fifty stocks show up in both groups (ARBA, ATML, CNXT, FDRY, GSPN, IMNX, INTC, ITWO, JDSU, NTAP, NXTL, RBAK, RIMM, TXCC, VLNK). The absence of significant overlap between the selections for the 2 best performing models could mean there is a significantly better group of 50 equities hidden in the 150 largest NASDAQ companies. Maybe correlation is not the best selection screen. Maybe **QQQ** (the NASDAQ 100 Trust, Series 1) is not the best correlation base; correlation with the NASDAQ Composite or with a particular equity could produce a better selection.

Below is a summary of the **QQQ** runs:

	worst Random QQQ	Best Random QQQ 5	Random Average	Stable Growth QQQ	Corr QQQ
Relative Gain	593%	698%	537%	187%	936%
R2	0.97	0.92	0.93	0.91	0.96
Gain%	3.36%	3.81%	3.37%	2.5%	4.6%
RRR	23.09%	29.76%	25.66%	27.6%	30.4%
Drawdown	16.9%	15.5%	17.5%	13.8%	14.0%
TRiPS%	**1.1%**	**2.1%**	**1.5%**	**1.3%**	**2.2%**
$Gain	$3,246	$3,678	$3,264	$ 2,466	$ 4,483
% long	100%	100%	100%	100%	100%
Smoothing-wks	27	3	12.5	5	4
Index Gain	97%	111%	110%	247%	82%

The Correlated **QQQ** model is only .1% better than the best Random **QQQ** mode, as for *TRiPS%*. However, the Correlated **QQQ** model is better than the best Random **QQQ** model in every performance measure recorded. For now at least, the Correlated **QQQ** model seems pretty good. Remember the search is for robust models we can believe in enough to fund, not just for absolute best back-test *TRiPS%*.

I am surprised that all these QQQ models have *TRiPS%* over 1.0%. I find it interesting that the Correlated QQQ model was able to stay 100% long and deliver impressive gains, while the Correlated QQQ 50 index decreased in value to 82% of start value.

The equity curve for Correlated QQQ is impressive, climbing with the Correlated QQQ 50 index through early 2000, then continuing to climb while the Correlated QQQ 50 index tanked through the last 9 months of 2000 and first 9 months of 2001.

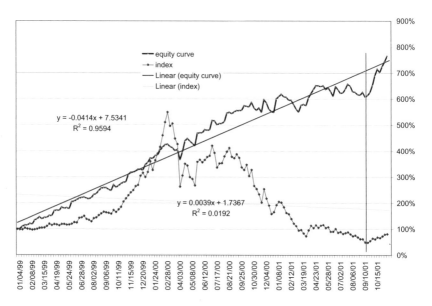

R^2 for the Correlated QQQ *Trend Regression Portfolio Strategy* at .96 is much, much better than the R^2 for the Correlated QQQ index at .02.

The histogram from the residual plot for the Correlated QQQ *Trend Regression Portfolio Strategy* is far from a normal distribution in spite of the high R^2. It looks like there are trends or cycles in the residuals.

Residual Plot for Correlated QQQ Trend Regression Portfolio Strategy

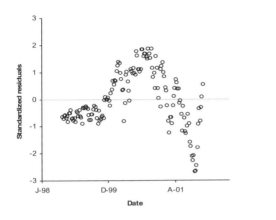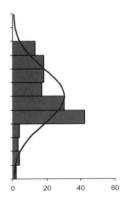

Analyse-It Software, Ltd.

The histogram from the residual plot for the Correlated QQQ Index doesn't come close to a normal distribution. There are trends or cycles in the residuals, with the residual plot looking very much like the index curve itself. The SEE for the index is 1.2339% versus 0.3737% for the Correlated QQQ Trend Regression Portfolio Strategy model.

Residual Plot for Correlated QQQ Index

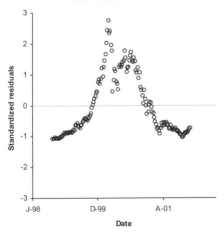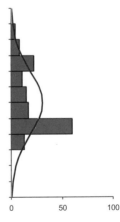

The preceding charts plot deviation from the equity trendlines for Correlated QQQ *Trend Regression Portfolio Strategy* and Correlated QQQ Index. The following graph plots residuals from the trendline of weekly $Gain.

Residual Plot for weekly $Gain for Correlated QQQ Trend Regression Portfolio Strategy

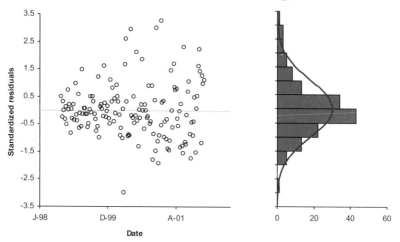

Analyse-It Software, Ltd.

This plot shows a much more normal distribution of residuals, and there doesn't appear to be any pattern in the standardized residuals. The big difference between the $Gain data and the earlier data is that $Gain is non-cumulative. The cumulative nature of the equity curve data affects the residual because the part carried over from the previous week is larger than the weekly change.

$Gain for Correlated QQQ Trend Regression Portfolio Strategy

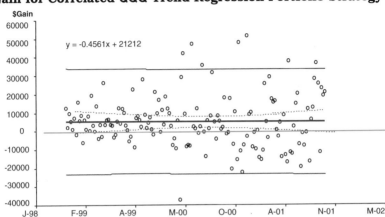

Analyse-It Software, Ltd

The trend of $Gain over the 150-weeks is virtually flat with average $4,483 losing $0.4561 per week. The trendline in the $Gain graph above is the thick blue line. The dashed blue lines define the Confidence interval band, the range around the fitted regression line likely to contain the population regression line with 95 % probability. The black lines farther out are the Prediction interval band, the range around the fitted regression line likely to contain future observations with 95% probability. A wide interval would indicate that the regression line is not a good fit, and that the trend formula will not accurately, or usefully, predict future values.

I like the Correlated QQQ *Trend Regression Portfolio Strategy* $Gain graph; almost the entire *confidence interval band* is above Ø, and 93 of the 150 weekly data points are above Ø.

In our quest to determine if careful selection of our 50 equities is important, we looked at 9 random selections with *TRiPS%* from 0.4% to 2.1%, and 3 careful selections with *TRiPS%* from 1.1% to 2.2%. This is hardly a resounding endorsement of careful selection, but a clear vote for the *Trend Regression Portfolio Strategy* itself. Actually, the large range of these back-test *TRiPS%* results obtained by trying different groups of 50 equities shows that equity selection is important. However, most carefully selected equity groups haven't performed better than the random selections. Let's try a few more careful selections.

Pre-selected

First, let's try letting someone else select for us. We'll look for published groupings of 50 companies. Two that come to mind immediately are the Business Week Fifty and the Motley Fool 50.

Business Week selects the 50 companies of the S&P 500 index it determines are best performers by dint of growth, management effectiveness, and returns to shareholders. The *TRiPS%* at 0.6% is less than the HILO model's 1.1%. The Business Week Fifty loses to HILO on all performance measures.

	Business Week Fifty	HILO 100% Long	BW b(w) H
Relative Gain	256%	312%	(56)%
R²	0.92	0.96	(0.04)
Gain%	1.7%	2.0%	(0.3)%
RRR (Risk Reward Ratio)	23.8%	33.9%	(10.1)%
MAX drawdown	14.4%	10.9%	(3.5)%
TRiPS%	**0.6%**	**1.1%**	**(0.5)%**
$Gain	$ 1,635	$1,961	$ (326)
% long	100%	100%	
% short	0%	0%	
Smoothing-weeks	3	3	
Index Gain	136%	128%	

The *Trend Regression Portfolio Strategy* does outperform buy and hold Business Week Fifty index. The

Business Week Fifty index outperformed the HILO index.

The Motley Fool's Fool 50 is a selection of 50 best companies based on a voting and review process. The Motley Fool promotes the Fool 50 as an index for measuring the state of the economy rather than as a portfolio of stocks one should own. I made 2 substitutions. I took Berkshire Hathaway (BRK.A) out, because I was sure my models couldn't handle the $70,000 stock price. I added in Tyco International Ltd. (TYC), simply because it was first in the Business Week Fifty. I also switched Enron (ENE) out and Family Dollar Stores (FDO) in. I wrongly thought ENE's fall to $.26 was causing an error in my model. FDO just happened to fit alphabetically in the hole ENE left. Including TYC, 10 companies appear on both the Business Week Fifty and Fool 50 (AMAT, AOL, C, EMC, MRK, ORCL, SUNW, TXN, TYC, and XOM).

The Fool 50 does worse than the Business Week Fifty as a base for a *Trend Regression Portfolio Strategy.* Tom and David, what's up?[37] I shouldn't pick on the brothers as they weren't trying to select companies for the *Trend Regression Portfolio Strategy.*

	Motley Fool 50	HILO 100% Long	BW b(w) H
Relative Gain	323%	312%	(11)%
R^2	0.74	0.96	(0.22)
Gain%	1.4%	2.0%	(0.6)%
RRR (Risk Reward Ratio)	18.3%	33.9%	(15.6)%
MAX drawdown	26.9%	10.9%	(16.0)%
TRiPS%	**0.4%**	**1.1%**	**(0.7)%**
$Gain	$ 1,384	$1,961	$ (577)
% long	100%	100%	
% short	0%	0%	
Smoothing-weeks	23	3	
Index Gain	97%	128%	

The Fool 50 *Trend Regression Portfolio Strategy* model has a *TRiPS%* of only 0.4%. The Fool 50 *Trend Regression Portfolio Strategy* model managed to grow at over $1,000 per week while the Fool 50 index declined 3%. The Fool 50 *Trend Regression Portfolio Strategy* model didn't beat any random QQQ model, but it beat buy and hold Fool 50 index.

The big spread between the Business Week Fifty, Fool 50 *Trend Regression Portfolio Strategy* models' performances around .5% *TRiPS%* and the best QQQ selections around 2.0% *TRiPS%*, once again points out the importance of equity selection. However, it doesn't really solve the problem of how to pick equities for the model. Neither the Business Week Fifty nor Fool 50 companies were selected based on their suitability for the *Trend Regression Portfolio Strategy*. Maybe, as for *Trend Regression Portfolio Strategy* models, these selections should be considered random.

Well anyway, if somebody else's 50-company selection made the model better, it would make it too easy.

More Non-Random Selections

This model, LEAP 50, is named for Long-Term Equity AnticiPation Securities® (LEAPS®). LEAPS are options that have expirations more than 9 months out. There are thousands of companies whose shares trade daily, but only about 400 that have LEAPS. Companies that have LEAPS are bigger, more active than average. LEAPS companies were ranked from largest capitalization and lowest P/E. The 100 companies with best combined capitalization, P/E rank and 200 weeks of price data were correlated with SPY. SPY plus the 49 equities most closely correlated with SPY were placed in the LEAP 50 model. There is an overlap of 13 equities between HILO and LEAP 50 (ADP, C, GE, HD, INTC, JNJ, KRB, MER, MRK, MWD, UTX, WFC, WMT)

The results are not so good.

	LEAP 50	HILO 100% Long	L b(w) H
Relative Gain	187%	312%	(125)%
R²	0.92	0.96	(0.04)
Gain%	1.7%	2.0%	(0.3)%
RRR (Risk Reward Ratio)	22.1%	33.9%	(11.8)%
MAX drawdown	11.3%	10.9%	(0.4)%
TRiPS%	0.6%	1.1%	(0.5)%
$Gain	$ 755	$1,961	$ (1,206)
% long	10%	100%	
% short	0%	0%	
Smoothing-weeks	11	3	
Index Gain	114%	128%	

LEAP 50 loses to HILO on every measure. Perform-ance is about the same as the Business Week Fifty model, and a little better than the Fool 50 model. The dollar gain is small because of timing, as the average proportion long is 46%. I wanted a LEAPS strategy to work, so I tried a new screen from the 100 equity pre-screen. This time I wanted to maximize volatility. My volatility indicator was (high-low)/high times SEE/trend, that is % range * % SEE. The larger this number the more volatile the equity's pricing.

LEAP 50v performance was only marginally better than LEAP 50, with a TRiPS% of 0.7%. I still wanted a LEAP 50 model to work, as I was thinking about possi-ble option plays.

I go back to the QQQ dataset. Even the worst ran-dom QQQ model is as good as or better than any careful selection. The 50-company selection for the best QQQ model is based on correlation to QQQ. I had also tried consistent stock price growth as a selector, now I decide to try volatility.

The Volatile QQQ model doesn't measure up to the Correlation QQQ model. In spite of a 28 company overlap (ADCT, ARBA, BIGT, BRCM, BVSN, CMRC, CNXT, FDRY, GSPN, INKT, INSP, ITWO, JDSU, LVLT, MCLD, MRNX, NTAP, OPWV, PMCS, RBAK, RMBS, SCMR, TERN, VIGN, VLNK, VRSN, XOXO, YHOO) the Volatile QQQ model has .7% lower *TRiPS%*, and is lower on all measures except Relative Gain.

	Volatile QQQ	Corr QQQ	V b(w) C
Relative Gain	2167%	961%	1207%
R^2	0.87	0.96	(0.09)
Gain%	3.9%	4.6%	(0.7)%
RRR (Risk Reward Ratio)	25.8%	30.4%	(4.5)%
MAX Drawdown	16.8%	14.0%	(2.8)%
TRiPS%	**1.6%**	**2.2%**	**(0.7)%**
$Gain	$ 3,779	$4,483	$ (704)
% long	100%	100%	
Smoothing-weeks	3	4	
Index Gain	31%	82%	

The big Relative Gain is interesting. The Volatile QQQ index fell to 31% of its starting value. *Trend Regression Portfolio Strategy* reduces risk. The *Trend Regression Portfolio Strategy* model suffered a Max Drawdown of 17% while the index had a Max Drawdown of 80% and ended at 69% drawdown.

I've mentioned the overlap between the company selections of the various models tested. Overlap gives a feel for how different the 50-company groups are. When different models are used for simultaneous trading for different portfolios, they should have no overlap. Overlap compromises risk management. The price action that causes the equity to be picked as a buy or sell candidate is likely to cause the equity to be picked in other models. Multiple buys or sells of the same equity would put too much of the trader's total equity into one security.   A systematic investor/trader would never put more than 10% of his/her equity in any single stock

Overlap between equities of different models is probably okay if the models are used serially for the same portfolio or account. One of the difficulties with switching between models is premature exit from a position. The more overlap between models, the less likely a premature exit.

The back-tests in this Stock Picking chapter lead to the following generalizations about Equity Selection:

i. Stock picking, selection of 50 equities to track in a model, has a big impact on the Trend Regression Strategy Portfolio model's performance.

j. There is more than one way to select groups that yield tradable performance, TRiPS% over 1.0%.

k. Groupings that seem intuitively to have potential don't necessarily produce good back-test results.

5. Entries & Exits

The *Trend Regression Portfolio Strategy* models discussed so far looked for entries and exits based on Price%, Relative Price, Slope, Slope*SEE, and Slope/SEE. Of 261 model runs, 83 optimized on Rel Price, 63 on Comp, 57 on Price%, 25 on Slope*SEE, and 6 on Slope (more detail in Appendix). As I mentioned earlier, there are hundreds of indicators available to trigger entry and exit decisions. Indicators range from simple to complicated, from moving averages to Moving Average Convergence Divergence (MACD), from range to volatility.

MACD

First MACD. The MACD signal is the exponential moving average of the difference between a short (fast) exponential price close moving average and a long (slow) exponential price close average. The most popular periods are 26 for the long, 12 for the short and 9 for the signal. I let the model vary the number of weeks, but kept the 26, 12, 9 ratio. I tried 3 variations *MACD signal*, *MACD signal %* (MACD signal/long exponential average), *MACD signal % up* (MACD signal % when up; that is, for a buy MACD signal % must be lowest, but higher than last week. The theory behind *MACD signal % up* is MACD is a leading indicator, so you should wait until MACD signal has changed direction, started up, before placing a trade.

MACD turns out to be a better indicator for the LEAP 50 model. *TRiPS%* climbs to 1.1% and all measures improve except R^2.

	LEAP 50 MACD	LEAP 50	M B(W) L
Relative Gain	289%	255%	34%
R^2	0.87	0.96	(.09)
Gain%	1.6%	1.3%	0.3%
RRR (Risk Reward Ratio)	31.6%	23.9%	7.7%
MAX drawdown	10.4%	13.6%	3.2%
TRiPS%	1.1%	0.6%	0.5%
$Gain	$ 1,561	$ 1247	$ 314
% long	100%	97%	
opt weeks	43	29	
Index Gain	114%	114%	

When price indicators (Price%, Rel Price, and Rel Price%) were replaced with MACD indicators LEAP 50 optimized on MACD signal.

MACD doesn't improve Correlated QQQ. When Price%, Relative Price%, and Relative Price, were replaced with MACD signal, MACD signal %, and MACD signal % up, Correlated QQQ optimized on SEE*slope. Forcing the Correlated QQQ to optimize on MACD reduced TRiPS% to 0.5%, all performance measures were worse than for the model which optimized on SEE*slope. The original Correlated QQQ model had optimized on Price% with TRiPS% of 2.2%. When forced to optimize on only MACD indicators, Correlated QQQ optimized on MACD signal. MACD signal% was close, but MACD signal % up had a Gain% of only 1.2%, half the gain for MACD signal, and MACD signal %.

	CORR QQQ MACD FORCED	CORR QQQ MACD	F B(W) M
Relative Gain	524%	886%	(401)%
R²	0.57	0.95	(0.36)
Gain%	2.2%	4.6%	(2.4)%
RRR (Risk Reward Ratio)	16.4%	26.2%	(9.8)%
MAX drawdown	31.9%	18.4%	(13.5)%
TRiPS%	**0.5%**	**1.5%**	**(1.0)%**
$Gain	$ 2,079	$ 4,296	$ (2,217)
% long	100%	100%	
Smoothing-weeks	17	3	
Index Gain	78%	84%	

Okay, the jury is out on MACD; one win, one loss. Let's try a different equity group, HILO.

	HILO MACD f	HILO 100% Long	F B(W) L
Relative Gain	169%	312%	143%
R²	0.91	0.96	(0.05)
Gain%	0.9%	2.0%	(1.1)%
RRR (Risk Reward Ratio)	14.6%	33.9%	(19.3)%
MAX drawdown	18.1%	10.9%	(7.2)%
TRiPS%	**0.2%**	**1.1%**	**(0.9)%**
$Gain	$ 822	$1,961	$ (1,139)
% long	97%	100%	
Smoothing-weeks	27	3	
Index Gain	137%	128%	
opt indicator	**MACD**	**comp**	

None of the MACDs (MACD, MACDsig%, or MACDsig%up) improves HILO 100% Long over the composite ranking of Slope*SEE, Slope, Slope*SEE.

So MACD brings up performance of the LEAP 50 model, but does nothing for Correlated QQQ or HILO models, one win, 2 losses.

RSI

On to RSI, Relative Strength Index developed by Welles Wilder in 1978. RSI oscillates between Ø and 100. High RSI, above 70, indicates equity is over-bought, and low RSI, below 30, indicates equity is oversold. RSI can be a leading indicator, reversing direction before the equity price trend itself changes. RSI is calculated by dividing x period average of upward price changes by x period average of downward price changes adding 1, then dividing that intermediate by -100 and adding 100.

$$RSI = \left(\frac{-100}{\left(\dfrac{average.x.period.upward.price.change}{average.x.period.downward.price.change} \right) + 1} \right) + 100$$

I tried RSI on the LEAP 50, HILO, and Correlated QQQ equity selections. LEAP 50 performed better using RSI.

	LEAP 50 RSI*Trend%	LEAP 50	RSI B(W) org LEAP
Relative Gain	337%	255%	82%
R^2	0.98	0.96	0.02
Gain%	1.9%	1.3%	0.6%
RRR (Risk Reward Ratio)	35.7%	23.9%	12.8%
MAX drawdown	6.8%	13.6%	6.8%
TRiPS%	**1.4%**	**0.5%**	**0.9%**
$Gain	$ 1,889	$ 1247	$ 642
% long	100%	97%	
% short	-		
Opt Smoothing Weeks	31	29	
Index Gain	114%	114%	

The LEAP 50 RSI bettered the original LEAP 50 model on all return and risk measurements. *TRiPS%* almost tripled from 0.5% to 1.4%. R^2 is an impressive 0.98 and MAX drawdown is only 6.8%.

The Correlated QQQ model didn't benefit from a switch from price to RSI indicators. All performance measures suffered from the switch.

	CORR QQQ RSI*%T	Corr QQQ	RSI B(W) Q
Relative Gain	829%	963%	(133)%
R^2	0.91	0.96	(0.05)
Gain%	3.8%	4.4%	(0.7)%
RRR (Risk Reward Ratio)	25.2%	28.7%	(3.5)%
MAX drawdown	17.8%	14.5%	(3.3)%
TRiPS%	**1.3%**	**1.8%**	**(0.5)%**
$Gain	$ 3,637	$ 4,308	$ (672)
% long	100%	100%	
% short	-	-	
Opt Smoothing-weeks	9	4	
Index Gain	78%	78%	
Optimized Indicator	**RSI*%T**	**Price%**	

The HILO 100% Long model didn't benefit from a switch from composite slope indicators to RSI indicators. All performance measures suffered from the switch. The composite slope indicator ranked equities by each of Slope, Slope*SEE, and Slope/SEE; added the ranks; then re-ranked by the sum of the ranks.

	HILO RSI	HILO 100% Long	RSI B(W) L
Relative Gain	228%	312%	(84)%
R²	0.95	0.96	(0.01)
Gain%	1.4%	2.0%	(0.6)%
RRR (Risk Reward Ratio)	24.9%	33.9%	(9.0)%
MAX drawdown	12.9%	10.9%	(2.0)%
TRiPS%	**0.6%**	**1.1%**	**(0.5)%**
$Gain	$ 1,353	$ 1,961	$ (608)
% long	100%	100%	
% short	-		
Opt Smoothing-weeks	5	3	
Index Gain	127%	128%	
Optimized Indicator	**RSI**	**comp**	

So RSI brings up performance of the LEAP 50 model, but does nothing for Correlated **QQQ** or HILO models, one win, 2 losses.

Williams %R

On to Williams' %R. This Larry Williams developed momentum indicator measures oversold/overbought levels. Most financial technicians think Williams' %R to be a leading indicator, changing direction ahead of equity price. Williams's %R is calculated dividing the difference between recent high minus today's close by recent high minus recent low and then multiplying by -100. This produces a range of values between Ø and -100. Low readings, lower than -80, mark oversold conditions and high readings, higher than -20 denote overbought conditions.

$$W\% = \left(\frac{highest.high.x.weeks - today.close}{highest.high.x.weeks - lowest.low.x.weeks} \right) * -100$$

To keep things comparable I stick with the 3 equity sets used for the MACD and RSI tests (LEAP 50, Correlated QQQ, and HILO).

The LEAP 50 model benefited slightly from a switch from composite slope indicators to Williams' %R indicators. *TRiPS%* increased 0.1%, percent return declined, but risk was reduced.

	LEAP 50 W%R	LEAP 50	W%R B(W) L
Relative Gain	242%	255%	(13)%
R²	0.96	0.96	0.00
Gain%	1.1%	1.3%	(0.2)%
RRR (Risk Reward Ratio)	25.6%	23.9%	1.7%
MAX drawdown	9.3%	13.6%	4.3%
TRiPS%	**0.6%**	**0.5%**	**0.1%**
$Gain	$ 1,105	$ 1,247	$ (142)
% long	100%	97%	
% short	-	-	
Opt Smoothing-weeks	3	29	
Index Gain	109%	113%	
Optimized Indicator	**W%R**	**rel price**	

The HILO 100% Long model didn't benefit from the switch from composite slope indicators to Williams' %R indicators.

	HILO W%R	HILO 100% Long	H%R B(W) L
Relative Gain	220%	312%	(92)%
R^2	0.97	0.96	(0.01)
Gain%	1.2%	2.0%	(0.8)%
RRR (Risk Reward Ratio)	26.4%	33.9%	(7.5)%
MAX drawdown	10.8%	10.9%	0.1%
TRiPS%	**0.6%**	**1.1%**	**(0.5)%**
$Gain	$ 1,206	$ 1,961	$ (755)
% long	100%	100%	
% short	-		
Opt Smoothing-weeks	13	3	
Index Gain	127%	128%	
Optimized Indicator	**W%R**	**Comp**	

The Correlated **QQQ** model didn't benefit from a switch from price to Williams' %R indicators. All performance measures suffered from the switch.

	QQQ W%R*%T	CORR QQQ Long	W%R*%T B(W) L
Relative Gain	598%	963%	(365)%
R^2	0.69	0.96	(0.27)
Gain%	2.5%	4.4%	(1.9)%
RRR (Risk Reward Ratio)	16.3%	28.7%	(12.4)%
MAX drawdown	32.1%	14.5%	(17.6)%
TRiPS%	**0.4%**	**1.8%**	**(1.4)%**
$Gain	$ 2,414	$ 4,308	$ (1,894)
% long	100%	100%	
% short	-		
Opt Smoothing-weeks	7	4	
Index Gain	76%	78%	
Optimized Indicator	**W%R*%T**	**% price**	

So Williams' %R holds up performance of the LEAP 50 model, but it does nothing for Correlated QQQ or HILO models, one tie, 2 losses. After trying MACD, RSI, and Williams' %R it appears that suitability of different indicators for *Trend Regression Portfolio Strategy* is highly dependent on the equities in the model. The

LEAP 50 equities responded best to these three new indicators. LEAP 50 model performance held even or gained with all indicators. Correlated QQQ and HILO models performed better without the new indicators.

Comparison MACD, RSI, Williams %R

	LEAP 50 MACD	LEAP 50 RSI *Trend%	LEAP 50 W%R	LEAP 50	RSI *Trend% B(W) L
Relative Gain	293%	337%	242%	255%	82%
R^2	0.86	0.98	0.96	0.96	0.02
Gain%	1.6%	1.9%	1.1%	1.3%	0.6%
RRR	30.8%	35.7%	25.6%	23.9%	11.8%
Drawdown	11.2%	6.8%	9.3%	13.6%	6.8%
TRiPS%	**1.0%**	**1.4%**	**0.6%**	**0.5%**	**0.9%**
$Gain	$1,520	$1,889	$1,105	$1,247	$642
% long	100%	100%	100%	97%	
% short			-	-	
Weeks	43	31	3	29	
Index Gain	110%	114%	109%	113%	
Optimized Indicator	**MACD**	**RSI*T**	**W%R**	**rel price**	

The biggest improvement for new indicators came in the LEAP 50 equities with the use of the RSI*Trend indicator. *TRiPS%* climbed to 1.4%. R^2 is an impressive 0.98 and MAX drawdown is only 6.8%. Remember I wanted LEAP 50 to work, so I could investigate some option strategies.

That the MACD, RSI, and Williams' %R didn't perform better than the previously mentioned indicators should not be too surprising. Their originators and proponents haven't suggested using them as inputs into *Trend Regression Portfolio Strategy* models. *Trend Regression Portfolio Strategy* uses these indicators by comparing them between equities, while other traders use them for trading an individual equity. Other traders look not only at indicator value but also at direction indicator is moving, indicator movement versus other indicators, and indicator movement versus price moves.

It is possible that MACD, RSI, and Williams' %R in combination can deliver better performance. It is also possible that MACD, RSI, or Williams' %R in combination with an earlier indicator can deliver better performance. Indicators discussed fall into three groups, the relative price group, the slope group, and the new group. In the price group Price% has been the most successful indicator. In the slope group, Slope * SEE has been most successful. In the new group, RSI has been the most successful. A LEAP 50 model with these three indicators and their combination all available optimized on RSI*Trend. Forcing the model to optimize on the composite indicator resulted in a lower *TRiPS%*

The back-tests in this Entries and Exits chapter lead to the following generalizations about Entries and Exits:

l. Choice, of which indicators to use for generating buy and sell signals, has a big impact on model performance.

m. The same indicator is not likely to be best for all models.

n. More than one indicator has yielded tradable performance, that is, TRiPS% over 1.0%.

o. Sometimes the right indicator can save a group from extinction.

p. The best indicator in back-tests is not necessarily the best indicator for the future.

6. Market Timing

The *Trend Regression Portfolio Strategy* models discussed so far, looked to adjust equity to cash ratio entries based on the number of equities that were lower priced than X weeks ago. The more equities that had fallen in price the higher the equity portion of the portfolio. As mentioned earlier, there are hundreds of indicators available with potential for triggering market-timing decisions.

Another variable for market timing is the range of investment position. In an ideal situation, your Portfolio would be 100% long when the market is going up, and 100% short when the market is falling. This is the maximum position range, 100% long to 100% short. Depending on the indicator, it may be useful to limit the range.

Other considerations for the range are hedging and stepping. Is the midpoint of the continuum from 100% long to 100% short 0% equities, all cash? Or, is the midpoint of the continuum 50% long and 50% short, balanced hedge? Should the model vary equity levels continuously or jump in steps of 10%, 25%, 100%, or X%? The optimum midpoint is all cash if the market-timing indicator is superior to the equity entry/exit indicator. The optimum midpoint is 50/50 hedge if the market-timing indicator is inferior to the equity entry/exit indicator. Superior, in this instance, means has more impact on the profitability of the strategy.

There are more indicators available for markets than for individual equities, because of the number of equities. There are all the same indicators as for equities based on open, high, low, close and volume, plus indicators based on the distribution of equities into categories. For instance, the Advance/Decline Line (A/D Line) is the relationship between the number of advancing equities and the number of declining equities. A/D Line is calculated by adding the number of equities increasing in price today minus the number of equities decreasing in price today to yesterday's cumulative total.

Most of the market timing done in models discussed so far comes from the Drach derived indicator, %Down. %Down is the percent of equities that have a lower price than they had X weeks ago. The models have all used a contrarian's approach increasing investment in longs as the %Down increased. A few models increased investment in shorts as the %Down decreased.

%Long

The AG1 model is one of the few that didn't optimize 100% long. Optimizations on %Down and %Long are compared in the table below.

	AG1 %Long	AG1 %Down	B(W) %Down
Relative Gain	236%	185%	51%
R²	0.98	0.99	(0.01)
Gain%	2.3%	1.6%	0.7%
RRR (Risk Reward Ratio)	35.7%	42.9%	7.2%
MAX drawdown	7.8%	4.9%	(2.9)%
TRiPS%	**1.8%**	**1.3%**	**0.5%**
$Gain	$ 2,978	$ 2,111	$ 867
% long	85%	43%	
% short	15%	57%	
Index Gain	181%	181%	

Using %Long as a market timing indicator, instead of %Down increases return and risk. All measures of return, Relative Gain, Gain% and $Gain are better while all measures of risk, R², RRR, and MAX drawdown are worse. Replacing %Long with Mod%Long didn't change the results. The AG1 model optimized using the Price% indicator to sort equities for long entries. The %Long AG1 and Mod%Long AG1 models optimized using the S*SEE indicator to sort equities for long entries. All three models used the S/SEE indicator to sort equities for short entries.

KST Indicator

Martin Pring didn't develop KST for *Trend Regression Portfolio Strategy.* He is more of a momentum person,

> "...knowledge of the maturity and direction of the main
> trend can be of the utmost importance since most mistakes
> are made moving against the direction of the main trend."

Mr. Pring uses his KST System to generate entry and exit signals considering short-term, intermediate, and long-term cycles.

Trend Regression Portfolio Strategy is not specifically short-term, intermediate, or long-term as far as trades are concerned, as it optimizes indicators over a 3 to 50 week range of smoothing-weeks. In the first KST test the DMT model was modified to incorporate a KST Indicator that varied with smoothing-weeks, but keeping the same relative durations and weights as the Long-term line in Pring's Table 7.1 on page 159 of *Martin Pring on Market Momentum.* Pring's Long-term KST Indicator equals the weighted average of 6-week moving average of 9-week ROC, 6-week moving average of 12-week ROC, 6-week moving average of 18-week ROC, and 9-week moving average of 24-week ROC. The results were good, but not as good as the 100% long DMT model.

	DMT KST	DMT 100%	KST B(W) 100%
Relative Gain	143%	236%	(93)%
R^2	0.95	0.95	(0.01)
Gain%	2.5%	2.6%	(0.1)%
RRR (Risk Reward Ratio)	29.1%	30.4%	(1.3)%
MAX drawdown	9.8%	14.7%	4.9%
TRiPS%	**1.2%**	**1.5%**	**(0.3)%**
$Gain	$ 3,423	$ 6,817	$ (3,394)
% long	49.6%	100%	
Smoothing-weeks	4	29	
Index Gain	202%	202%	

Drawdown is reduced but all other performance measures are worse. The average amount of capital risked is just less than 50%. Risking less capital is only a good thing when the market is going against you. Even though the KST Indicator timed model did not do as well as the 100% long model, it did beat the %Down timed model.

	DMT KST	DMT %Down	KST B(W) %Down
Relative Gain	143%	104%	39%
R^2	0.95	0.95	0.00
Gain%	2.5%	2.5%	0.0%
RRR (Risk Reward Ratio)	29.1%	25.7%	3.4%
MAX drawdown	9.8%	10.4%	0.6%
TRiPS%	**1.2%**	**1.1%**	**0.1%**
$Gain	$ 3,423	$ 2,003	$ 1,420
% long	49.6%	29.4%	
Smoothing-weeks	4	29	
Index Gain	202%	202%	

Hedging in the KST Indicator DMT model should help improve utilization of capital.

	DMT KST 50/50 Hedge	DMT 100%	KST B(W) 100%
Relative Gain	150%	236%	-86%
R^2	0.97	0.95	0.02
Gain%	1.4%	2.6%	1.1%
RRR (Risk Reward Ratio)	44.1%	30.4%	13.6%
MAX drawdown	4.1%	14.7%	10.5%
TRiPS%	**1.0%**	**1.5%**	**-0.5%**
$Gain	$ 3,755	$ 6,817	$ (3,062)
% long	49%	100%	
% short	48%	-	
Smoothing-weeks	7	29	
Index Gain	202%	202%	

Hedging does employ more capital and increases $Gain over the long only DMT with equity varied by KST Indicator. However, the KST hedge model optimizes on a 50/50 hedge rather than on a hedge varied by KST value. Forcing KST Indicator timing decreases TRiPS%, but $Gain increases a little.

	DMT KST Timed Hedge	DMT 100%	KST B(W) 100%
Relative Gain	152%	236%	-84%
R^2	0.97	0.95	0.02
Gain%	1.4%	2.6%	1.1%
RRR (Risk Reward Ratio)	32.1%	30.4%	1.7%
MAX drawdown	8.5%	14.7%	6.1%
TRiPS%	**0.7%**	**1.5%**	**-0.8%**
$Gain	$ 3,850	$ 6,817	$ (2,967)
% long	47%	100%	
% short	50%	-	
Smoothing-weeks	7	29	
Index Gain	202%	202%	

The KST Indicator has some potential, beating Down% as a market timing indicator for the DMT stock group. In the DMT KST tests to this point the DMT Indicator anticipated reversals, buying more equities when KST is the lowest. Another way to use the KST Indicator is to use KST Indicator slope to anticipate reversals or jump on trends.

	DMT KST Hedge on Slope switched	DMT KST Hedge on - Slope	DMT KST Hedge on Slope	DMT KST TIMED LONG	DMT KST LONG on - Slope	DMT 100%	KST B(W) 100%
Relative Gain	115%	162%	150%	143%	142%	236%	-94%
R^2	0.82	0.97	0.97	0.95	0.96	0.95	0.01
Gain%	0.8%	1.6%	1.4%	2.5%	2.5%	2.6%	0.1%
RRR	18.5%	34.6%	44.1%	29.1%	30.2%	30.4%	0.2%
Drawdown	11.0%	9.0%	4.1%	9.8%	13.6%	14.7%	1.1%
TRiPS%	**0.3%**	**0.8%**	**1.0%**	**1.2%**	**1.4%**	**1.5%**	-0.2%
$Gain	$2,258	$4,220	$3,755	$3,423	$3,399	$6,817	$(3,418)
% long	48%	51%	49%	50%	50%	100%	
% short	49%	46%	48%	0%	0%	-	
Weeks	18	7	7	4	29	29	
Index Gain	202%	202%	202%	202%	202%	202%	

None of the KST Indicator slope timed models matched the TRiPS% or $Gain of the 100% Long DMT model. DMT 100% Long always has all money in portfolio in long positions. KST slope timed models should appeal to risk adverse, as all of the DMT KST Indicator slope timed models had a lower drawdown than the 100% Long DMT model.

The DMT KST Long on –Slope model (long on minus slope model) reduces money in long positions on a reversal basis. The lower the KST Indicator slope, the more money invested in long positions. The DMT KST Long on –Slope model has the highest TRiPS% of any KST model. The DMT KST Timed Long model reduces money in long positions on a reversal basis. The lower the KST Indicator, the more money invested in long positions. The DMT KST Hedge on Slope model increases money in long positions and decreases the money in short positions on a trend-catching basis. The higher the KST Indicator slope, the more money invested in long positions. The lower the KST Indicator slope, the more money invested in short positions. The DMT KST Hedge on –Slope model reduces money in long positions and increase the money in short positions on a reversal basis. The lower the KST Indicator slope, the more money invested in long positions. The higher the KST Indicator slope, the more money invested in short positions. The DMT KST Hedge on Slope switched model reduces money in long positions and increases the money in short positions on a trend-catching basis. The higher the KST Indicator slope, the more money invested in long positions. The lower the KST Indicator slope, the more money invested in short positions. The DMT KST Hedge on Slope switched model changes individual stock picks from reversal to trend catching strategy if KST Indicator slope is in top half of its range.

Maybe it's just the DMT model, maybe KST will work for another group of equities.

	AG1 KST	AG1 %Down	B(W) %Down
Relative Gain	193%	185%	8%
R^2	0.96	0.99	(0.03)
Gain%	1.7%	1.6%	0.1%
RRR (Risk Reward Ratio)	37.0%	42.9%	(5.9)%
MAX drawdown	8.1%	4.9%	(3.2)%
TRiPS%	**1.1%**	**1.3%**	**(0.2)%**
$Gain	$ 4,522	$ 4,300	$ 222
% long	48%	43%	
% short	52%	57%	
Smoothing-weeks	3	12	
Index Gain	181%	181%	

Maybe not, KST doesn't improve TRiPS% for the AG1 model, either. Although return improves, it is not enough to overcome the increase in risk. Remember AG1 improved from 1.3% to 1.8% by using the %Long indicator instead of the %Down indicator.

AROON

AROON was developed by Tushar S. Chande to measure direction and magnitude of trend. Chande calculated positive and negative indicators plus an oscillator, which at extremes was -100 for strong negative trend and +100 for strong positive trend. For *Trend Regression Portfolio Strategy* the oscillator was modified, by proportioning the range to fit between Ø and 100, so it could be used directly as % long. Testing was done on the HILO model equity group. Rather than sticking with Chande's 10 period AROON, calculations were varied with Smoothing-weeks

	HILO AROON	HILO 100%	100% B(W) AROON
Relative Gain	218%	319%	(101)%
R²	0.97	0.97	0.00
Gain%	2.4%	2.1%	0.3%
RRR (Risk Reward Ratio)	35.1%	35.7%	0.6%
MAX drawdown	**5.2%**	**10.8%**	**5.6%**
TRiPS%	**1.4%**	**1.5%**	**(0.1)%**
$Gain	$ 3,187	$ 5,508	$ (2,321)
% long	51%	100%	
% short	0%	0%	
Index Gain	126%	126%	

TRiPS% for the AROON timed HILO model is a little lower than for the 100% long model. Gain% on trades and drawdown are better, but because less equity is risked $Gain and Relative Gain are substantially less. The AROON timed HILO model optimized on 3 smoothing-weeks. TRiPS% drops to 0.3% at 4 smoothing-weeks and never gets above 0.7% with the 0.7% recorded at 50 smoothing-weeks. Although 1.4% TRiPS is close to the 1.5% of the 100% model, the AROON model will likely be less robust.

Because AROON is designed as a trend confirmation indicator, as opposed to a impending reversal indicator, a second optimization was undertaken with equity selection sort order reversed when AROON values climbed above 50.

	HILO AROON switched	HILO 100%	HILO B(W) A S
Relative Gain	157%	319%	(161)%
R^2	0.91	0.97	(0.06)
Gain%	1.3%	2.1%	(0.7)%
RRR (Risk Reward Ratio)	19.4%	35.7%	(16.3)%
MAX drawdown	8.6%	10.8%	2.2%
TRiPS%	**0.5%**	**1.5%**	**(1.1)%**
$Gain	$ 1,818	$ 5,508	$ (3,690)
% long	51%	100%	
% short	0%	0%	
Index Gain	126%	126%	

The change didn't alter the amount of equity risked each week, but performance deteriorated, with every measure, except drawdown, worse than for the HILO 100% model. Although performance is poor, this model is probably more robust than the non-switched AROON as optimized smoothing-weeks is 43, smoothing-weeks from 42 through 46 are 0.4% or better, and smoothing-weeks from 38 to 50 are 0.3% or better.

Maybe it's just the HILO model, maybe AROON will work for another group of equities.

	AG1 AROON hedged	AG1 AROON long	AG1 AROON ma long	AG1 %Down	AROON B(W) %Down
Relative Gain	248%	173%	191%	185%	6%
R2	0.97	0.97	0.96	0.99	(0.03)
Gain%	2.4%	2.7%	2.9%	1.6%	1.3%
RRR (Risk Reward Ratio)	41.0%	36.2%	40.4%	42.9%	(2.5)%
MAX drawdown	13.0%	9.4%	6.9%	4.9%	(2.0)%
TRiPS%	**1.6%**	**2.1%**	**2.3%**	**1.3%**	**1.1%**
$Gain	$6,377	$ 3,948	$4,592	$4,300	$292
% long	72%	56%	59%	43%	
% short	28%	0%	0%	57%	
Index Gain	181%	181%	181%	181%	
Smoothing-weeks	39	3	4	12	

AROON does work as a market-timing indicator for the AG1 group of equities. TRiPS% is better for three AROON tests made than for the base %Down market timed model. The best TRiPS% came from the *AG1*

AROON *ma long* model, which averaged AROON over 3 weeks (ma = moving average). The *AG1* AROON *ma long* model has higher return and higher risk than the AG1 %Down model.

The back-tests in this Market Timing Chapter lead to the following generalizations about Market Timing:

q. Market Timing can influence Trend Regression Strategy Portfolio model performance.
r. Choice of indicator has an impact on success of market timing.
s. Match-up of *Trend Regression Portfolio Strategy* group and indicator is important to the success of market timing. It doesn't appear that there is one indicator that will work regardless of the group.
t. Many models optimize at 100% long all the time.

The Appendix has a listing of model runs done while researching *Trend Regression Portfolio Strategy*. The listing includes date of run, input variables, and output performance statistics.

The preceding seemingly endless parade of model back-tests has probably convinced you that I am a big fan of back-testing. It is true now. Market experience is expensive. I now believe that it is important not to be in too big of a rush to become rich. It is time well spent experimenting with investment ideas using historic data, before risking your life savings. I wish I'd known then what I know now. The market doesn't know or care how smart you are or how much you need the money.

The market is like snow.

" When dealing with objective hazards, the subjective thinking our society values—How do I feel? What do I want?—can kill, because Nature doesn't care about the answers. Our assumptions, schedules, goals, and abilities make no difference to an unstable slope or a stormy ocean. ...

> Avalanches happen in certain places, at certain times, for particular reasons. The clues we need are almost always apparent if we know how to look for them and are willing to listen to the message. Too often, the victims themselves recognized the clues but ignored them."[38]

Concentrate on objective back-tests rather than wishful thinking. Back-testing shows you how your system has worked in the past, giving you an idea of what you might expect in the future. Back-testing allows you to experiment with ideas and see what those ideas would have produced in past markets.

Back-testing is not the only tool in the portfolio manager's toolkit.

7. Paper-trading

Like Back-testing, paper-trading allows practicing the steps of the system without risking capital. Paper-trading can discover flaws in the system that are not uncovered by back-testing. The flaws can be due to changes in the market or faulty construction of the model. Depending on how carefully paper-trading is tracked, it can be used to refine your understanding of how commission and slippage cost will impact portfolio performance. The back-testing models described so far have consistently ignored commissions and slippage.

Paper-trading also can allow testing of ideas not testable in back-testing. Usually the only reliable historical data available to individual DIY investors are price (open, high, low, and close) and volume. Other historical data, when available, is often too expensive for an individual to access.

The biggest disadvantage of paper-trading is that it uses up time. To build a back-testing model using years of data takes some time and energy. However, to paper-trade a strategy for 3 years would take a great deal of commitment, in addition to a lot of time and energy. A second disadvantage is that paper-trading doesn't really test the emotional demands of the system. It may take just as many keystrokes to paper-trade as it does to trade, but it doesn't take the same emotional energy. Watching your nest egg (your future financial well-being) suffer drawdown takes energy.

Paper-trading provides the time needed to learn how the system trades, and to build up your confidence in the system. No matter how good the system is, the portfolio manager won't make money with it unless he/she believes in the system. First, you need a system that works, then you need to believe the system will work. Back-testing and paper-trading help find systems that work and give the portfolio manager time to build his/her confidence in the system. When confidence is lacking, the courage required to stick with a system in drawdown can't conquer the feared risk of ruin.

Marketocracy

Marketocracy has an excellent site for testing portfolio strategy. In the summer of 2001, I started building Marketocracy portfolios for paper-trading.

Marketocracy allows you to compare your performance against other Marketocracy users and gives each user $1,000,000 to start each portfolio. Transaction costs add realism. You have to follow SEC and IRS fund manager diversification rules. At least 50% of your portfolio equity must be in equities that each comprises less than 5% of portfolio equity. No equity can account for more than 25% of your portfolio equity. No more than 5% of your portfolio equity can be in an Exchange Traded Fund (EFT), including exchange traded indices such as SPY. No short positions or margin borrowing are allowed. No more than 35% of your portfolio equity can be in cash.

At first I was put off by all the rules, and some aspects of Marketocracy seem primitive compared to FOLIO*fn*. Marketocracy doesn't have target weights and rebalancing. At FOLIO*fn* in both real and watch portfolios you can set a new list of equities with target weights within a portfolio and rebalance with a single trade. At Marketocracy you need to calculate how many shares of each equity you need to buy, then enter sells and buys for each equity. Transactions don't queue so you often have to wait for sells to clear before buys can be entered. This becomes tedious if you are placing trades after hours, as it takes 2 passes and often results in periods of rule violation.

Using Marketocracy gave me insight into *Trend Regression Portfolio Strategy*. Remember the basic *Trend Regression Portfolio Strategy* model started with 3 long and 3 short positions, but when models optimized 100% long they had only 3 long recommendations. To implement Marketocracy portfolios the same *Trend Regression Portfolio Strategy* 3 long optimizations were used. The Marketocracy portfolios bought 14.5% of each of the first 3 positions and 4.5% of the next 12 positions. Six portfolios were started between the July and the end of September 2001, and 5 survived past September. The following graph shows NAV plotted with normalized start date of 9/21/2001 for each of the 5 *Trend Regression Portfolio Strategy* based portfolios and for the S&P 500 ETF (SPY).

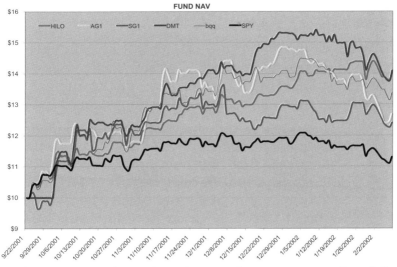

After 4 months, the 5 *Trend Regression Portfolio Strategy* Marketocracy portfolios are all ahead of SPY, and all of them are down from their peak NAV. Marketocracy has a timing report that showed that many of the stocks being sold were increasing in value as fast as or faster than the ones being held. This puts into question the decision to have only 3 long positions in the *Trend Regression Portfolio Strategy* models.

Marketocracy demonstrated what a tradable *Trend Regression Portfolio Strategy* model would look like in production. Marketocracy has a Stratification Report that lists the equities held in a portfolio listed in descending order of return. In an ideal circumstance, each week the portfolio equities with the most gain are replaced with new equities having the most potential for gain. The portfolio equities with lesser gains are held for more appreciation. New equities enter at the bottom of the report, accumulate gains, move up in the report, then move off the top of the report. In practice, the number of equities traded each week has not stabilized varying between models and between weeks. With 20 equities held, number of equities sold each week has varied between 2 and·15.

What would Drach do? Drach's goal is to have 95% of trades close at a profit. Drach might look at the *Trend Regression Portfolio Strategy* model and the Marketocracy report, and then decide on the following rules:

- Buy equities into the portfolio based on model recommendations.
- Sell equities that have met profit targets.
- Hold equities that haven't met profit targets.
- Sell equities that fall out of master list.
- Set profit target to—must be profit, must be in top 1/3 of Stratification Report.

This idea is interesting enough that a new Marketocracy portfolio, dmtprofit, is created in late June of 2002. The equity pool and *Trend Regression Portfolio Strategy* model is the same as for dmthilo. The new portfolio uses the rules above.

More on Marketocracy later.[39]

8. Trading History

Actual trading of these *"regression to the mean strategies"* started in early 2001, with increased tracking starting in June. However, models were evolving and, for me at least, trading evolving models is not a great idea.

Mistakes, often treated as problems in school and job situations, are thought by the enlightened a necessary part of learning. Mistakes in investing/trading can be expensive, and the self-directed investor/trader needs to turn mistakes into education, to get the learning he is paying for. It's like learning to play a musical instrument; you have to work you way through some sour notes to get to the sweet notes. Ultimately, hands-on experience makes a musician or an investor/trader, not book learning education.

"Failures paved my road to success," quipped Eric Bergoust when he was still in first place in 2002 Olympic Freestyle Skiing Aerials, in response to a "how did he get here" question. Unlike Olympic Freestyle skiers, trader/investors can use back-testing and paper-trading to mitigate the damage from some failures. However, back-testing and paper-trading can't eliminate all damage to your portfolio.

Real portfolios don't always live up to the back-tests they are based on. "Survivorship bias," is the overstating of return by only including survivors in the sample.[40] When we take a sample of existing companies to include in our index or in our back-test it includes only companies that exist now, not the ones that have disappeared. A gap between back-test and actual develops when purchased equities become worthless before we cash out. Another source of gap between back-test and real portfolio is transaction cost, slippage and commissions.

Slippage & Commissions

In real life, slippage and commissions count. For the trading week ending Friday, November 30, 2001, a real dollar IRA account showed nearly $1,000 loss (for the week); while the model showed I should have gained $5,000. This $6,000 swing got my attention. It turned out the difference was slippage between the model's 11/23/2001 signal price and the 11/26/2001 fill price. Most of the slippage was in 2 buys. FNM signaled at $80.55 and filled at $81.39, for a slip of $.84. LLTC signaled at $38.85 and filled at $40.85, a slip of $2.00. I had monitored slippage earlier and determined that it was not a problem, but now I wondered.

My thinking was that as my models were looking for relatively long term gains, week to week versus minute to minute, then slippage would be random with a mean of Ø. I thought most of the slippage would be from market cycles, rather than relative moves by individual equities. Because I was making approximately equal buy and sell trades in any window, I thought positive slippage would offset negative slippage. I knew that slippage could be large in this particular FOLIO*fn* Investments, Inc. account, because I was using FOLIO*fn* window trades. My model signals use Friday close, and FOLIO*fn* window trades do not execute until approximately 10:15 am Monday. I audited 163 transactions filled between 7/1/2001 and 11/30/2001. The table lists some of the transactions and a summary.

FOLIO*fn* Slippage

	Ticker	Trigger Date	Trigger	Trans-action	Fill Date	Filled Price	Buy Slip	Sell Slip	Slip
1	JNJ	6/29	$49.80	Buy	7/2	$51.36	$(1.56)		$(1.56)
2	LLTC	6/29	$44.13	Buy	7/2	$46.01	$(1.88)		$(1.88)
3	MXIM	6/29	$44.21	Sell	7/2	$45.84		$ 1.63	$ 1.63
4	SCH	6/29	$15.74	Sell	7/2	$15.60		$ (0.14)	$(0.14)
5	SGP	6/29	$36.09	Buy	7/2	$37.13	$(1.04)		$(1.04)
6	JNJ	7/6	$50.24	Sell	7/9	$51.07		$ 0.83	$ 0.83
156	MDT	11/16	$41.00	Buy	11/20	$41.39	$(0.39)		$(0.39)
157	RE	11/16	$68.16	Buy	11/20	$68.05	$ 0.11		$ 0.11

	Ticker	Trigger Date	Trigger	Trans-action	Fill Date	Filled Price	Buy Slip	Sell Slip	Slip
158	SGP	11/16	$35.45	Buy	11/20	$35.71	$(0.26)		$(0.26)
159	FNM	11/23	$80.55	Buy	11/26	$81.39	$(0.84)		$(0.84)
160	LLTC	11/23	$38.85	Buy	11/26	$40.84	$(1.99)		$(1.99)
161	MDT	11/23	$44.12	Sell	11/26	$43.71		$ (0.41)	$(0.41)
162	RE	11/23	$69.50	Buy	11/26	$68.82	$ 0.68		$ 0.68
163	SGP	11/23	$36.30	Sell	11/26	$36.31		$ 0.01	$ 0.01
	Average		$36.54			$36.26	$ 0.22	$ (0.34)	$(0.04)
	Std Dev		$15.01			$15.07	$ 2.33	$ 1.38	$ 1.95
	without 9/11								
	Average		$36.93			$37.09	$ (0.20)	$ 0.11	$(0.06)
	Std Dev		$15.51			$5.59	$ 0.80	$ 0.70	$ 0.77
	%Average						-0.6%	0.3%	-0.2%
	%Std Dev						2.2%	1.9%	2.1%

The net slippage for 163 transactions was only $.04 per share traded, but the standard deviation is high at $1.95. That means that expected slippage at 95% confidence level is from a $3.94 loss to a $3.86 gain. Backing out transactions affected by the events of 9/11 the 95%, confidence range shrinks to $1.61 loss to a $1.48 gain. The range does not seem so bad when you believe the mean will be close to Ø. The range seems intolerable when you think of 1,000 share positions and slippage of $1,000 or more. Even the mean of $.04 to $.06 per share is $40 to $60 per trade, $100 a round-trip, more than commissions.

I was placing weekly trade orders sometime over the weekend. I could eliminate some FOLIO*fn* slippage by running models after the open on Monday and placing trades before the 10:15 am window opens. However, on Maui, in the summer, that means getting up for a 3:30 am market open. I have problems with early morning executions. I usually wake at 5:00 am, but I don't think my brain gets into second gear before 6:00. I've reduced execution errors (such as wrong equity bought, wrong equity sold, wrong quantity bought or sold) by avoiding entering orders before 6:00 am HST.

I also use Scottrade for trading *Trend Regression Portfolio Strategy* models. At Scottrade, I have had some success trading after-hours, Friday afternoon, to reduce slippage. The after-hours trading is not a total solution as not all the trades I want to make are available after hours at Scottrade.

Scottrade *Slippage*

	Ticker	Trigger Date	Trig-ger	Trans-action	Fill Date	Filled Price	Buy Slip	Sell Slip	Slip
1	CPRT	8/24/01	24.58	BUY	8/27/01	24.58	(0.58)		(0.58)
2	CPRT	8/24/01	24.58	BUY	8/27/01	24.58	(0.51)		(0.51)
3	ACF	8/24/01	47.91	BUY	8/27/01	47.91	(0.41)		(0.41)
4	CHP	8/24/01	21.64	BUY	8/27/01	21.64	0.04		0.04
106	ACF	11/16/01	18.40	SELL	11/20/01	18.40		(6.05)	(6.05)
107	CMVT	11/16/01	23.67	SELL	11/20/01	23.67		0.02	0.02
108	KSS	11/16/01	66.73	SELL	11/20/01	66.73		0.72	0.72
109	APH	11/16/01	47.77	SELL	11/20/01	47.77		0.76	0.76
110	CPN	11/23/01	24.15	BUY	11/26/01	24.15	0.20		0.20
111	AIG	11/23/01	80.90	SELL	11/26/01	80.90		(0.60)	(0.60)
112	MTG	11/23/01	59.47	SELL	11/26/01	59.47		(0.43)	(0.43)
113	KSS	11/23/01	67.73	SELL	11/26/01	67.73		(0.22)	(0.22)
114	ACF	11/23/01	24.08	SELL	11/26/01	24.08		(0.17)	(0.17)
115	SCOR	11/23/01	28.63	SELL	11/26/01	28.63		(0.13)	(0.13)
	Average	$30.33				$30.33	$(0.20)	$ 0.04	(0.08)
	Std Dev	$15.63				$15.63	$ 1.27	$ 1.00	$1.15
	without 9/11								
	Average	$30.27				$30.27	$(0.03)	$ 0.00	(0.01)
	Std Dev	$15.83				$15.83	$ 0.88	$ 0.99	$0.93
	%Average						-0.1%	0.0%	0.0%
	%Std Dev						2.9%	3.3%	3.1%

Scottrade slippage gets closer to a mean of Ø than FOLIO*fn*, but the standard deviation is still high. One of the detail lines, selling ACF on 11/20/2001, shows a slippage of over $6.00, on my 300 order a loss of $1,800. I'm not unhappy with the progress of slippage's reversion to the mean, but meanwhile the standard deviation is causing pain and stress.

I decide to stop waiting for Fridays' closing prices and run models in time to catch FOLIO*fn*'s 2:45 pm Friday window and to place Scottrade orders to execute before 4:00 pm. I believe the slippage between model trigger prices and actual trade prices is due to elapsed time between trigger and execution, rather than to broker inefficiencies.

Slippage is bad; it increases risk, risk in the sense of variability of returns. However, slippage could also be a good thing if the indicators used to make entry and exit decisions are leading. It could be with a leading indicator, signals come too early, and the passage of time between signal and execution improves entry or exit relative to the trigger price.

Regardless of the indicator the whole *Trend Regression Portfolio Strategy* system is leading. Trend following systems try to catch trends after they start and ride them through conclusion. *Trend Regression Portfolio Strategy* systems try to catch the early part of a trend and jump to a more promising equity regardless of the performance of the current holdings. *Trend Regression Portfolio Strategy* is a bottom fishing strategy for longs and top skimming strategy for shorts. If a *Trend Regression Portfolio Strategy* model issues a buy signal and the equity declines in value, the model will issue a new buy for the same equity the following week. With falling prices, slippage should help get a lower buy price. However, my slippage statistics to-date don't corroborate this.

> "If you're worried about the commission, there is something wrong with your strategy."[41]

Some brokers justify high commissions by claiming better execution (less slippage[42]). I don't know. I have tried a few brokers, and haven't noticed a correlation between commission charged and execution. The broker I have had the most problem with is the one I started with 8 or 9 years ago when I first abandoned my traditional broker to go online. Their basic commission has stayed the same $14.95 + fees or $19.95 + fees depending on exchange. By today's standard this is middle priced, not low price. Some of the new non-browser trading platforms allow a lot of execution options and control. The features of these trading platforms are more important for day traders but could be advantageous for portfolio managers to improve entry and exit execution. However, for most of us it is probably best to enter market orders as quickly as possible after receipt of trigger to minimize time-caused slippage.

Most of my trades now are at FOLIO*fn* Investments, Inc. and Scottrade. FOLIO*fn* charges an annual fee of $295 for a large number of trades,[43] more trades than I need to make. Scottrade charges $7 + fees for market orders and $12 for after-hours, stop and limit orders. I like both of these brokers and have slowed down my look for something better.

FOLIO*fn* is especially good for *Trend Regression Portfolio Strategy* because it leads you to think more like a portfolio manager. It has some interesting and useful portfolio management features. You can enter orders in dollar amounts, you can change you equity to cash ratio for an entire portfolio by entering one trade, and you can easily rebalance a portfolio to maintain component equities at a set percent of the total. FOLIO*fn* makes it easy to do things with a portfolio that would require a lot of calculation, compromise, and order entry at other brokerages. For portfolio managers FOLIO*fn* provides better tools and a reasonable price.

I approached slippage as the difference between model trigger prices and actual entry price, keeping commissions and fees in a separate category. My testing shows that the time delay between model trigger and entry is the most important, controllable factor for slippage. Other authors have focused on other contributors to transaction cost. Richard C. Grinold and Ronald N. Kahn identify commissions, bid/ask spread, market impact, and opportunity cost as components of transaction cost.[44] They claim transaction costs increase with trade size and with your need for a quick trade. They mention one of the surest ways of reducing transaction cost is to reduce the number of transactions. Their testing indicates that 75% of the value added by a strategy can be obtained with half the number of trades, half the transaction cost.

To test the effect of reducing transactions, a new Marketocracy portfolio is created to track the dmthilo dataset. The following constraints should reduce the number of trades, and increase the win ratio.

- Sales limited to top third of list, in descending order of trade P&L.
- Sales limited to trades with profit.
- Sales limited to equities that drop out of the *Trend Regression Portfolio Strategy* top 20 buys.
- Buys taken starting at top of *Trend Regression Portfolio Strategy* buy list excluding equities already held.

After 4 weeks the new portfolio was averaging 5 trades per week (25% turnover), compared with 13 trades per week (65% turnover) for the unconstrained dmthilo strategy. After 4 weeks, the new portfolio was down 5 % and the unconstrained portfolio was down 3%. Marketocracy tracking includes transaction costs of $0.05 per share traded.

Leap of Faith

Earlier I mentioned that if you are a true believer in trend regression, you should switch out of models that are above trend into models that are below trend. On 12/1/01, the HILO model's equity curve was .67 SEE above its trendline, while the DMT model's equity curve was 2.01 SEE below its trendline. Both the HILO and DMT equity selections are based on earnings consistency and growth. The HILO screen was from late 2000 or early 2001, and the DMT screen was done around 10/1/2001. Even though both HILO and DMT screened for the same things, there is an overlap of only 8 companies (FDO, HDI, JKHY, KRB, LOW, PAYX, SEIC,

WAG). Six DMT equities are on Drach's master list (FAST, KRB, LOW, PAYX, TSS, and WAG). I considered switching to QQQ Correlated, but it was .21 SEE above its trendline.

It was an easy switch; both models are 100% long, HILO was recommending selling the three open positions, and 2 of the positions were winners. I sold FNM, LLTC, and RE and bought DV, DORL, BJ.

This is the same account that caused me to reinvestigate slippage. However, the large slippage was not what caused me to switch models. The first week, post

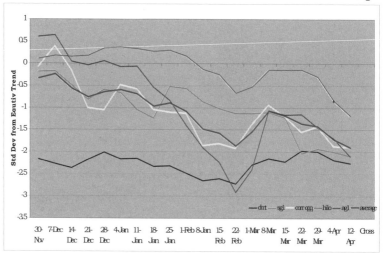

switch, was hard. DMT fell 2.9%, HILO was up 1.2%, *QQQ Correlated* climbed an amazing 26.5%, and the S&P500 advanced 2.1%. Ouch! The second week, DMT fell 0.4%, HILO was up 0.2%, QQQ Correlated fell 2.9%, and the S&P500 dropped 3.3%. Well, the switch is not vindicated yet. Ouch! The third week DMT fell 0.2%, HILO was up 0.2%, QQQ Correlated fell 2.9%, and the S&P500 climbed 1.7%. Hmmm, ouch! The graph above shows trend of SEEs deviation from equity trend continued to decline through mid April 2002.

The graph shows how (equity value – equity trend)/standard error of estimate, number of SEEs from trend moved from the switch between models on 12/3/01. I switched into DMT on 12/3/01, because model equity was low relative to its trend. It is probably a good idea to have more tradable models than you are actively trading. It seems like a good idea to switch from models that have current equity above equity trendline, although the empirical evidence to support switch timing is not too convincing.

The graph below shows *SEEs from trend* for the dmthilo model, a 10-year model with equities from the DMT and HILO models that have 10 years of price history. Notice that the *SEEs from trend* line spends long periods on either side of the trend.

dmthilo model GAIN & SEE

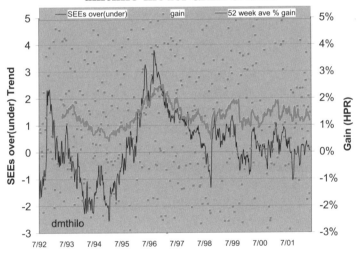

Notice also the gain (HPR, Holding Period Return) in relationship to number of SEEs. The 52-week moving average HPR doesn't appear to be inversely correlated with *SEEs from trend*. It looks like when the model is working it continues to work for a while and when it's not working it continues not working for a while.

The graph below plots correlation between HPR and *SEEs from trend*, with different offsets. Offset of 1 compares week 2 to week 1, week 3 to week 2, week 4 to week 3 .... Offset of 2 compares week 3 HPR with week 1 *SEEs from trend*, week 4 to week 2 .... Offset of 3 compares week 4 HPR with week 1 *SEEs from trend* week 5 to week 2 .... Etc.

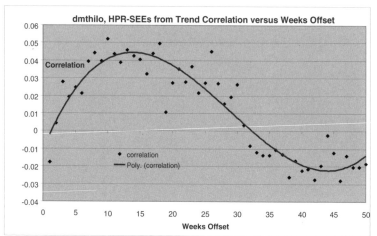

There isn't much correlation, all correlations are very close to Ø. Other than the 1 and 2 week offsets, it appears that positive HPR is associated with positive deviation from trend, through 30 week offset. The implication is that if you expect to be in the trade from 3 to 30 weeks you should put most faith, and money, in your model when its equity curve current value is above the trend of its equity curve. Because the correlations are so small, you shouldn't put too much faith in this strategy.

My 12/3/01 switch from HILO to DMT was based on reversion of current equity value to equity value trend. The switch seemed logical at the time, but I should have done more homework. It doesn't appear that you can assume there is a negative correlation between current equity values relationship to the trend (measured as *SEEs from trend*) and subsequent HPR.

A synonym for "leap of faith" might be "gambling on gut instinct." Back-testing, paper-trading, and other homework is work. Sometimes we get lazy or just impatient for the profits from a breakthrough idea. Too often, the results are surprising in an unprofitable way.

Funded Accounts versus Models

The graphs below show funded accounts against their models.

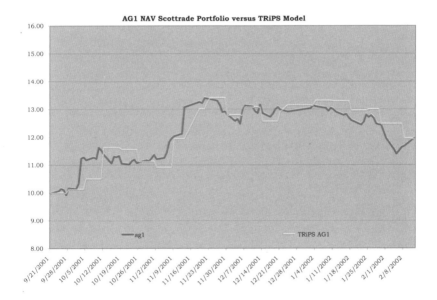

The AG1 FOLIO*fn* portfolio, red line, and TRiPS model, pink line, are tracking closely. Tracking is close, in spite of complications getting as short as the model calls for. This portfolio is at Scottrade and they don't always have the equities available to borrow so shorts can be placed.

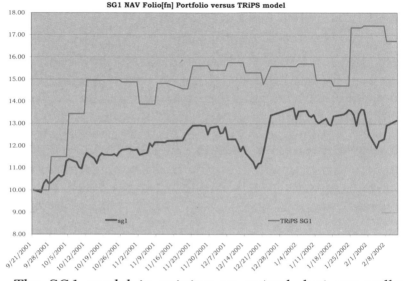

The SG1 model is gaining on actual, but generally actual and model seem to be moving in the same direction.

Now it gets ugly.

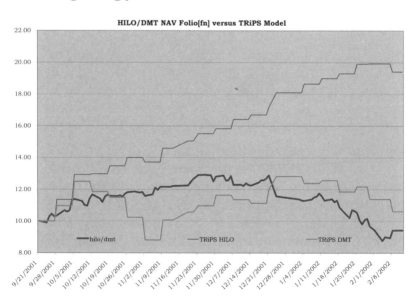

The HILO FOLIO*fn* Portfolio was losing to its TRiPS model then I switched models and made a bad situation worse. I mentioned earlier that the switch was made because DMT model equity was further below its trend-line than HILO model equity. This provided another painful reason that ideas that seem good should be tested before money is committed.

Funded portfolios don't track models exactly because re-optimizing changes historical trades, because Friday afternoon trading doesn't use weekly close data, because bad data can trigger real trades that don't appear in later corrected data models, and because models don't include trading cost. In addition, sometimes, human error screws up implementation and sometimes human emotion compromises ability to persevere following the model further into losing trades.

Marketocracy Again

The Marketocracy portfolios stretch the TRiPS models, buying 15 positions instead of 3. Earlier we saw 5 Marketocracy portfolios built on the TRiPS models performed better than SPY. They performed as well as or better than funded portfolios implemented using the buy 3 rules.

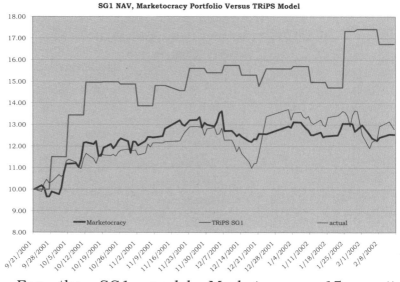

For the SG1 model Marketocracy 15 equity implementation and actual 3 equity implementation are running neck and neck. Marketocracy portfolio performance looks a little less volatile.

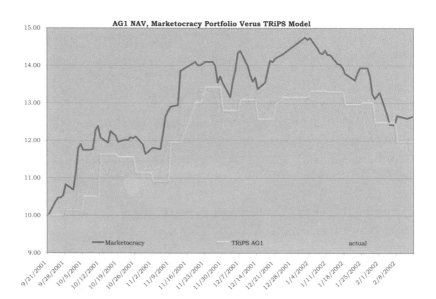

For AG1, Marketocracy portfolio, actual portfolio and the TRiPS model are tracking closely.

The close tracking of the 15-equity portfolios with the 3-equity portfolios, implies that returns may not be diminished by selecting 30% (15/50) of the groups' equities instead of 6% (3/50). Selecting more equities reduces risk.

Based on the Marketocracy results I changed actual portfolio buys to 10, to reduce risk. I also changed Marketocracy buys to 20 equities, each 4.5% of portfolio equity, to improve compliance with Marketocracy rules. It wasn't just the above graphs that forced me to increase diversification, it was more the preponderance of evidence:

1. Marketocracy portfolios performed as well as, or better than, the same model funded portfolios that had fewer equities. It seems there was no return penalty for holding more equities.

2. Marketocracy timing reports showed that sold equities were gaining price after sale. It seemed logical that increasing the number of equities held would increase the holding time of each equity held.

3. Enron[45] fallout caused three of my holdings to tank (Hanover Compressor Company, Calpine Corporation, and Tyco International Ltd.). Remember the Wall Street wisdom: "Bulls climb the stairs, bears jump out the window." Concentrating equity holdings was exposing my portfolio to more risk than I could endure.

Probably the price declines driven by the Enron effect were the emotionally trigger that increased my diversification within portfolios. Most likely, I would not have changed, when I did, without that impetuous. My reluctance to increase diversification was knowing that diversification would dilute the effect of single equity price jumps while it was diluting the effect of single equity price drops.

9. Tuning

Optimal Diversification

After decreasing risk as described above, I did some simulations to get a better feel for the risk/return trade-offs I was making. I did these simulations using statistical distribution functions from Insight.xla. The chart below indicates that best return is putting all portfolio equity into just 1 security. Best RRR (Risk Return Ratio) occurs when portfolio equity is spread among 19 equities, but improvement after 13 equities is minor.

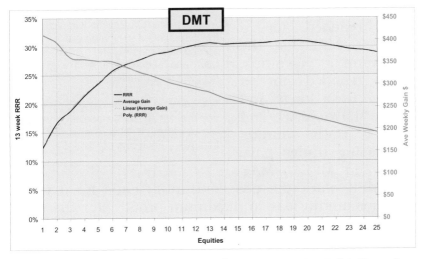

Average gain should be close to a straight line because gain was allocated from average (index in TRiPS model, $317.33 gain/trade) to average of top 3 (picked in TRiPS model, $668.67 gain/trade). This allocation makes the simplifying assumption that the advantage of following the *Trend Regression Portfolio Strategy* rather than purchasing a basket of all 50 equities is distributed evenly from top to bottom. Average weekly gain (magenta line) is gain over buying a portfolio of all 50 equities in the DMT TRiPS group. This line would reach

Ø at 50 equities. I was surprised that RRR peaked so late.

Maximum Adverse Excursion

Maximum Adverse Excursion (MAE), and the opposite direction Maximum Favorable Excursion (MFE) were popularized by John Sweeney.[46] MAE is the maximum unfavorable price reached for a trade. MFE is the maximum favorable price reached for a trade. Both longs and shorts have MAE and MFE. Both winning and losing trades have MAE and MFE. MAE

Insight.xla is a book and Excel add-in produced by Sam L. Savage, Ph.D., a pioneer in moving analytical modeling into spreadsheets. For a very reasonable price, Insight.xla provides a very readable book that combined with the add-ins and sample files provides a hands-on education on analytical modeling. The add-ins can then be used to build models useful to many trader/investors. Insight.xla covers: Monte Carlo simulation, queuing networks, Markov chains, forecasting, decision trees, and linear regression. Along the way Dr. Savage warns about the care needed to create reliable spreadsheet models, and explains uncertainty and random variables in way that is useful to trader/investors.

I recommend anybody using Excel for any business/finance modeling, invest in a copy of Insight.xla or at least visit http://www.analycorp.com/.

and MFE mark the p&l continuum ends for a trade, from maximum loss to maximum profit. For the time-period of a long position, MAE is the buy price and MFE is the sell price for maximum profit. And vice versa, MFE is the buy price and MAE is the sell price for maximum loss. Without having read the book, I understand Mr. Sweeney used MAE analysis to set stop losses, to determine the point beyond which a trade was unlikely to recover and show a profit.

I modified the transaction record for the dmthilo model to determine MAE and MFE for each transaction. Treating each week as a separate roundtrip, even when a particular security is held for multiple weeks, totals to 1,563 transactions. Of these, 904 closed at a profit and

659 at a loss. The maximum MAE was 26.5% while the maximum loss was 20.4%. The maximum MFE was 45.4% while the maximum gain was 31.8%. The 904 transactions that closed with a profit had an average MAE of 2.5%, and the 659 transactions that showed a loss had an average MAE of 5.8%. Trades that went further into a loss on average ended up closing at a loss. Putting a stop loss at -5% might have capped losses of 407 transactions, at 5%, but those transactions went on to close with an average loss of 2.7%. That is, trades that were down at least 5% ended up closing down only 2.7%. There doesn't seem to be any persistence of trend. Just because a position has moved adversely doesn't mean it will continue to move against you. Putting a stop loss at 10% reduced the number of transactions that would be stopped out to 107. Those 107 transactions went on to close with an average loss of 6.1%. That is, trades that were down at least 10% ended up closing down only 6.1%. Losing trades tended to recover some of their loss before closing.

Wondering about the effect of treating each week as a separate roundtrip, I merged multi-week trades into a single record. One hundred fifty seven transactions were eliminated; and of 1406 transactions remaining, 810 closed at a profit and 596 at a loss. The maximum MAE was 26.6% while the maximum loss was 19.1%. The maximum MFE was still 45.4% and the maximum gain was still 31.8%. The 810 transactions that closed with a profit held to an average MAE of 2.5%, but for the 596 transactions that showed a loss, average MAE climbed to 6.4%. Trades that went further into a loss on average ended up closing at a loss. Putting a stop loss at -5% would have capped losses of 389 transactions. Those transactions went on to close with an average loss of 2.6%. That is, trades that were down at least 5% ended up closing down only 2.6%. Putting a stop loss at 10% reduced the number of transactions that would be stopped out to 118 (compared to 107 transactions for weekly transaction records). Those 118 transactions went on to close with an average loss of 5.7%. That is, trades that were down at least 10% ended up closing down only 5.7%. Losing trades still tended to recover some of their loss before closing, merging multi-week trades didn't change nature of results.

Keeping with our regression to the mean theme leads to the question; "What if positions are added each time positions move 5% against us?" From the above it seems this should have a positive impact on the portfolio, although it is clearly counter to trend following traders' axiom "Don't add to losing positions." The *Trend Regression Portfolio Strategy* is "buy low, sell high." If the *Trend Regression Portfolio Strategy* model is saying an equity is relatively oversold, and then the equity declines another 5%, it becomes even more oversold.

Putting buy triggers at -5% intervals added 590 trades. These trades had an average gain of 3.9% within a range of 14.9% loss to 30.6% profit. In the table below, I've labeled this the Adverse Move Strategy. Each time a trade moves adversely 5%, another trade of the same dollar amount is added.

	Original Model Trades	With Addition of Adverse Move Trades	Adverse Move Trades	Adverse Move B(W) Original
count	1,406	1,996	590	
max	31.8%	31.8%	30.6%	-1.2%
min	-19.1%	-19.1%	-14.9%	4.2%
high	12.6%	14.2%	17.1%	4.5%
low	-9.7%	-9.8%	-9.3%	0.3%
std dev	5.6%	6.0%	6.6%	-1.1%
mean	1.5%	2.2%	3.9%	2.4%

In the table above, count is the number of trades, max is the maximum % profit in the back-test, min is the minimum % profit(loss), high and low mark the upper and lower 95% confidence levels, std dev is the standard deviation of % profit, and mean is the average % profit. Assuming equal dollar trades, the adverse move trades out perform the original trades. The mean profit is more than twice as much. Standard deviation (range, risk) does increase, but the low of the adverse move 95% confidence range is above the low of the original range. Seventy four percent of the adverse move trades are profitable, compared with 56% of the original dmthilo model trades.

This supports the following logic (rationalization). If the *Trend Regression Portfolio Strategy* model indicates an equity is undervalued relative to the rest of the equities in the model, that equity will be more of a bargain if it falls 5% in price.

I think Drach is aware of this phenomenon, because of the way he scales into positions. He never goes from 0% long to 100% long; he goes from 0% to 20%, then 20% to 40%, etc. He refers to this as time diversification. The closest I come to this is rebalancing in my FOLIO*fn* portfolios. With 10 equity positions in a portfolio, I rebalance each week so each position is 10% of the portfolio. This increases the share count of equities that have declined in price and reduces the share count of equities that have increased in price. This adds to losers and takes some of the profit from winners.

After seeing the above table, I started looking for a way to profit from the good performance of adverse move trades. Because the performance is so much better for adverse move trades, the most obvious thing to do is limit the portfolio to adverse move trades. If each trade is limited to 10% of portfolio value utilization of portfolio equity becomes a constraint. Back-testing showed average investment level would only be 4.6%. Maximum drawdown is only 1.7%, and after 10 years, ending equity is 330% of starting equity. Relaxing the 10% money management rule to 20% increases average investment level to 9.1%. Maximum drawdown climbs to 2.5%, and after 10 years, ending equity is 561% of starting equity. However peak investment would climb to 120% of portfolio value (20% margin).

	dmthilo Index	Original dmthilo Model	Adverse Move Trades	Adverse Move Trades	Adverse Move Trades	Aggressive Adverse Move Trades
% Portfolio per trade	2.0%	33.0%	10.0%	16.0%	20.0%	33.0%
Ave. Portfolio Utilization	100.0%	100.0%	11.3%	18.3%	21.9%	31.4%
Max Portfolio Utilization	100.0%	100.0%	100.0%	100.0%	120.0%	99.0%
Ending/Beginning Value	708.0%	824.0%	330.0%	482.0%	500.0%	605.0%
% Winning Trades	??	57.8%	73.6	73.0%	71.8%	70.5%
Maximum Drawdown	65.0%	32.4%	1.7%	2.4%	2.7%	3.9%
TRiPS%	??	0.642%	0.393%	0.490%	0.563%	0.622%

The table above shows adverse move strategies against the original dmthilo *Trend Regression Portfolio Strategy* model and the dmthilo index. No aggressive column has a better ending value divided by beginning value than the index, which falls short of the *Trend Regression Portfolio Strategy* model performance. The problem is utilization of the available funds. As each version of the adverse move strategy uses more of the available funds the return (ending/beginning value) goes up and drawdown goes up. Maximum drawdown on all adverse move strategies is much less than for basic dmthilo model.

What appears to be the best trading strategy, the adverse move strategy, isn't necessarily the best strategy for a portfolio. While the trade average of the underlying model doesn't have the performance of the trade average of the adverse move strategy, the portfolio return is better.

If an independent, highly uncorrelated model is found and implemented within the same portfolio, the combined portfolio could be very profitable. The dmthilo model's primary stock selection criterion is consistency of earnings; while the AG1 model's primary selection criteria are historical and project earnings growth. There are only 8 overlapping stocks, and these 2 models have potential for uncorrelated adverse move strategy buy signals. Because the back-test duration in the following is 175 weeks versus the previous table's 520 weeks, dmthilo model statistics are different.

	dmthilo Index	Original dmthilo Model	ag1 Index	Original ag1 model	dmthilo adverse moves	ag1 adverse moves	dmthilo ag1 merge
% Portfolio per trade	2%	33%	2%	33%	33%	33%	33%
Ave. Portfolio Utilization	100%	100%	100%	100%	39%	50%	71%
Max Portfolio Utilization	100%	100%	100%	100%	99%	99%	99%
Ending/Beginning Value	136%	347%	207%	553%	284%	801%	873%
% Winning Trades	??	56%	??	57%	70%	78%	75%
Maximum Drawdown	30%	15%	54%	27%	10%	5%	8%
TRiPS%	??	0.66%	??	1.28%	0.76%	2.15%	1.86%

The merits of combining adverse move strategies for different stock groups are borne out. The ratio of ending value to beginning value is greater for the combined strategy, as is portfolio utilization. The decline in TRiPS% and % Winning Trades from the AG1 adverse moves to merge strategy was not unexpected. This graph shows Portfolio value utilization, for part of the back-test period.

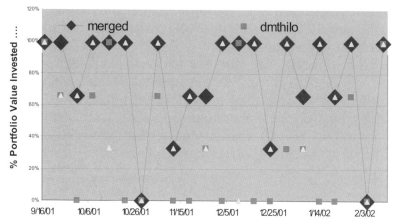

The graph shows considerable independence between the adverse move strategy buy timing for dmthilo and AG1 stock groups. The merge back-test had 4 portfolio value levels, 0%, 33%, 66%, and 99%. The merged portfolio value utilization was the lesser of dmthilo level plus AG1 level or 99%.

This adverse move strategy would be hard to implement in FOLIO*fn* accounts, with its window trades. This strategy would be easy to implement in a regular trading account with limit orders set 5% below the limit price. However, you would need to monitor totals invested to ensure that you stayed within margin rules set by your own money management or by your broker.

There is nothing particularly magic about using a 5% move to signal action. No effort was expended to optimize the amount of adverse move used to trigger an entry. Remember in the first MAE back-test, the 904 transactions that closed with a profit had an average MAE of 2.5%, and the 659 transactions that showed a loss had an average MAE of 5.8%. I originally picked 5% because it was close to the average MAE of losing trades.

The Adverse Move Strategy was looking good. The next step was to use NeuroShell trader to extend back-testing. A modified *Trend Regression Portfolio Strategy* model wrote OHLCV.csv files with buy signals replacing volume (OHLCV.csv files are individual stock price files with open, high, low, close prices and volume for each period). The buy signal stays on while the stock is in the top 10 buy positions of the *Trend Regression Portfo-lio Strategy* model. The modified OHLCV.csv files were read into NeuroShell Trader. Trading strategy #1 was to buy on buy signal in volume field. Trading strategy #2 bought on a 5% decline from the strategy #1 entry price. Both strategies sold when there was no buy sig-nal in the volume field.

NeuroShell Trader evalu-ates trading strategies on an equity by equity basis, versus *Trend Regression Portfolio Strategy* which looks at total portfolio performance. The NeuroShell results increased my interest in Adverse Move strategy, leading to construction of a new Adverse Move strategy testing Excel model. The new model uses the OHLCV.csv files created for NeuroShell to build a back-test with MAE, %p&l, days held then creates new trades based on Ad-verse Move from *Trend Regression Portfolio Strategy* model entry prices. The new model makes it easier to back-test Adverse Move strategy for different groups of equities. The performance statistics are a little different from earlier results. The biggest source of difference is that entries and exits occur at the close on the day of the entry or exit, whereas earlier tests assumed the en-

Switching from Excel to Neu-roShell Trader immediately pointed out the importance of trade size. Setting trade size at 100 shares yielded an average annual gain of 4.7% over a 10 year back-test with 50 dmthilo equities pulled into NeuroShell (66 trades, 40 winners). Setting trade size at $10,000 yielded an average annual gain of 7.8% (66 trades, 40 winners). Adding a $30 commission/slippage cost per transaction widened the gap; an average loss of 2.7% (66 trades, 18 winners) for 100 share trade size, an average annual gain of 4.5% (66 trades, 38 win-ners) for $10,000 trade size.

tries at limit order set at 5% from the *Trend Regression Portfolio Strategy* entry. The new model makes an entry at the close if the close is 5%, or more, below the *Trend Regression Portfolio Strategy* entry or 5%, or more, below a previous open entry.

When I started working on Adverse Move Strategy, 6 *Trend Regression Portfolio Strategy* models were maintained weekly; 3 of the 6 were actually funded. Three models were 10-year models and 3 were 3-year models. I back-tested Adverse Move Strategy for the 6 models, and merged within 10-year and 3-year groups.

	LEAP 50	dmthilo	HILO	LEAP dmthilo merge	10 LEAP, dmthilo, HILO merge	dmthilo Trend Reg Port Strategy Model	20 LEAP, dmthilo, HILO merge	33 LEAP, dmthilo, HILO merge
% Portfolio per trade	10%	10%	10%	10%	10%	33%	20%	33%
Ave. Portfolio in Trades	26%	28%	27%	39%	48%	100%	67%	76%
Max Portfolio in Trades	100%	100%	100%	100%	100%	100%	100%	99%
End/Begin Value	330%	354%	507%	500%	638%	799%	844%	1117%
% Winning Trades	69%	71%	70%	75%	74%	58%	73%	74%
Maximum Drawdown	6%	11%	8%	8%	7%	33%	6%	8%
TRiPS%	0.20%	0.22%	0.39%	0.49%	0.63%	0.62%	0.86%	1.22%
potentail # Trades	955	1000	964	1467	1573	1560	1573	1573
Trades made	889	937	881	1369	1339	1560	1006	775
wins	611	662	661	962	985	905	735	577

The preceding table shows Adverse Move Strategy for the 10-year models, LEAP 50, dmthilo, and HILO. TRiPS% are low, as are the average amount of account equity in trades and maximum drawdown. The preceding table shows Adverse Move Strategy for merged groups. Merged groups have higher TRiPS% than individual model groups, because more, on average, of the account equity is in trades. Merging model groups into one Adverse Move Strategy portfolio increases the number of trades available, and the more the models are independent (uncorrelated) the more trades can be made. The potential number of trades doesn't equal the sum of individual model trades, because of overlap between models. There are 50 equities in each of LEAP

50, dmthilo, and HILO, but only 75 equities in the LEAP/dmthilo merge, and 81 in the LEAP/dmthilo/HILO merge.

The preceding table shows a comparison between the LEAP/dmthilo/HILO Adverse Move Strategy and the dmthilo *Trend Regression Portfolio Strategy* model. TRiPS% is nearly identical. Maximum drawdown is much less for the Adverse Move Strategy, as is the average amount of the account equity in trades. Total gain for the Adverse Move Strategy is significantly less with ending value only 638% (after 10 years) of starting value versus 799% for the *Trend Regression Portfolio Strategy.*

The preceding table also shows the effect trade size can have on results. The LEAP/dmthilo/HILO Adverse Move Strategy with individual trade size set at 10% of account equity had TRiPS% of 0.63%, with individual trade size set at 20% of account equity had TRiPS% of 0.86%, with individual trade size set at 33% of account equity had TRiPS% of 1.22%. Back-tests with larger trade sizes have higher TRiPS%, because more, on average, of the account equity is in trades. As trade size increases the total number of trades made declines, meaning there is less trade diversification and probably meaning the lack of change in drawdown is not truly reflecting the change in risk.

The win rates for the Adverse Move Strategy back-tests range from 69% to 75% versus a 58% win rate for the dmthilo model. Assuming a 50% win rate marks a random situation, where a model has no predictive ability, the improvement in win/loss ratio from 58:42 to 70:30 is significant.

Adverse Move Strategy back-test results for the 3-year models generally confirmed those of the 10-year models, although there is more variability in the results.

	AG1	SG	corr qqq	AG1, SG, corr qqq
% Portfolio per trade	10%	10%	10%	10%
Ave. Portfolio Utilization	65%	53%	80%	91%
Max Portfolio Utilization	100%	100%	100%	100%
Ending/Beginning Value	404%	250%	223%	392%
% Winning Trades	78%	71%	58%	66%
Maximum Drawdown	7%	13%	33%	16%
TRiPS%	1.46%	0.27%	0.07%	0.41%
potentail trans	322	546	799	1583
trans	269	509	475	613
wins	209	363	277	407

Results cover a larger range because the duration is shorter, and because the equities pool is more diverse. The AG1 model is based on a screen for aggressive historic and projected growth. The SG model is based on a screen for stable, growing earnings. The corr qqq model is from a screen for price moves correlated with the price moves of QQQ. As expected, the amount of account equity used is greater for the merged back-test, but unexpectedly TRiPS% is not greater for the merged back-test than for the AG1 back-test. This unexpected result is most likely a result of the pseudo random way trades are added or rejected. All of the trades from the underlying model(s) are sorted by date, then by ticker symbol. When there is room by date for more trades, they are added in alphabetic order. If equities are not uniformly alphabetically distributed between models, then the equities of one model maybe overly represented in the merged back-test. I reran the merge test adding AG1 trades first, then SG, then corr qqq. TRiPS% climbed to 0.56%. Ending value over beginning value climbed to 445% and maximum drawdown fell to 12%. Other statistics were unchanged.

I like the Adverse Move Strategy enough to think about funding it. The table below is a control sheet set up to monitor day to day, or more frequently, which trades are on and *on deck*. This Excel spreadsheet uses MSN Stock Quote Functions to update model with 20 minute delayed prices. The table is for the 3-year model group. Notice that the three models are separated in the control sheet. The plan is to fund all the AG1 Adverse Move Trades as signaled with a trade size of 10% of account equity. SG and corr qqq trades to be entered with account equity left after AG1 trades are made. On the worksheet, " **hold** " marks trades entered, and " **BUY** " marks trades triggered but not yet entered. Buys can be trigged every time stock prices are updated.

	ticker	Trend Reg Port Strategy model 6/14/2002	Adverse Move 1 AM1 Trigger 5% off	Last Price	trigger	delta f/trigger	Adverse Move 2 bought	AM2 Trigger 5% off	Last Price	trigger	delta f/trigger	Adverse Move 3 bought	AM3 Trigger 5% off	Last Price	trigger	delta f/trigger	Adverse Move 4 bought	AM4 Trigger 5% off	Last Price	trigger	delta f/trigger
A	ACRT	$10.78	$10.24	11.10	hold	$0.86	$9.71	$9.22	11.10		$1.88		$0.00	11.10		$11.10		$0.00	11.10		$11.10
G	TYC	$13.40	$12.73	15.50	hold	$2.77	$8.91	$8.46	15.50		$7.04		$0.00	15.50		$15.50		$0.00	15.50		$15.50
1	SEIC	$29.77	$28.28	29.68	hold	$1.40	$33.49	$31.82	29.68	hold	($2.14)	$31.82	$30.22	29.68	BUY	($0.54)		$0.00	29.68		$29.68
	NTRS	$45.71	$43.42	47.49	hold	$4.07	$51.06	$48.51	47.49	hold	($1.02)	$48.51	$46.08	47.49		$1.41		$0.00	47.49		$47.49
	LUV	$15.63	$14.85	15.15	hold	$0.30	$17.25	$16.39	15.15	hold	($1.24)	$16.39	$15.57	15.15	hold	($0.42)	$15.48	$14.71	15.15		$0.44
	GE	$29.70	$28.22	27.55	hold	($0.67)	$32.16	$30.55	27.55	BUY	($3.00)		$0.00	27.55		$27.55		$0.00	27.55		$27.55
	CMVT	$10.14	$9.63	10.04	hold	$0.41	$12.36	$11.74	10.04	hold	($1.70)	$11.74	$11.15	10.04	hold	($1.11)	$10.14	$9.63	10.04		$0.41
	PAYX	$32.95	$31.30	33.15	hold	$1.85	$35.30	$33.54	33.15	BUY	($0.38)		$0.00	33.15		$33.15		$0.00	33.15		$33.15
	APH	$40.41	$38.39	41.88		$3.49		$0.00	41.88		$41.88		$0.00	41.88		$41.88		$0.00	41.88		$41.88
	NATI	$32.81	$31.17	32.60		$1.43		$0.00	32.60		$32.60		$0.00	32.60		$32.60		$0.00	32.60		$32.60
		6/14/2002																			
S	ALO	$17.45	$16.58	17.81	hold	$1.23	$17.29	$16.43	17.81		$1.38		$0.00	17.81		$17.81		$0.00	17.81		$17.81
G	ADBE	$31.37	$29.80	27.08	hold	($2.72)	$27.99	$26.59	27.08		$0.49		$0.00	27.08		$27.08		$0.00	27.08		$27.08
	KYO	$70.67	$67.14	66.22	hold	($0.92)	$74.01	$70.31	66.22	hold	($4.09)	$70.31	$66.79	66.22	BUY	($0.57)		$0.00	66.22		$66.22
	STD	$7.94	$7.54	7.95	hold	$0.41	$8.60	$8.17	7.95	BUY	($0.22)		$0.00	7.95		$7.95		$0.00	7.95		$7.95
	COF	$55.63	$52.85	58.72		$5.87		$0.00	58.72		$58.72		$0.00	58.72		$58.72		$0.00	58.72		$58.72
	DORL	$36.59	$34.76	36.37		$1.61		$0.00	36.37		$36.37		$0.00	36.37		$36.37		$0.00	36.37		$36.37
	KRB	$32.25	$30.64	15.89	BUY	######		$0.00	15.89		$15.89		$0.00	15.89		$15.89		$0.00	15.89		$15.89
	TYC	$13.40	$12.73	15.50	hold	$2.77	$10.91	$10.36	15.50		$5.14		$0.00	15.50		$15.50		$0.00	15.50		$15.50
	HAL	$16.80	$15.96	16.77		$0.81		$0.00	16.77		$16.77		$0.00	16.77		$16.77		$0.00	16.77		$16.77
	AGE	$35.74	$33.95	35.75		$1.80		$0.00	35.75		$35.75		$0.00	35.75		$35.75		$0.00	35.75		$35.75
		6/14/2002																			
c	RFMD	$9.00	$8.55	7.09	hold	($1.46)	$7.67	$7.29	7.09	BUY	($0.20)		$0.00	7.09		$7.09		$0.00	7.09		$7.09
o	TXCC	$0.70	$0.67	0.63	BUY	($0.04)		$0.00	0.63		$0.63		$0.00	0.63		$0.63		$0.00	0.63		$0.63
r	VIGN	$1.35	$1.28	1.50		$0.22		$0.00	1.50		$1.50		$0.00	1.50		$1.50		$0.00	1.50		$1.50
r	ITWO	$1.84	$1.75	1.83		$0.08		$0.00	1.83		$1.83		$0.00	1.83		$1.83		$0.00	1.83		$1.83
q	CNXT	$4.82	$4.58	3.78	hold	($0.80)	$4.42	$4.20	3.78	BUY	($0.42)		$0.00	3.78		$3.78		$0.00	3.78		$3.78
q	BIGT	$0.03	$0.03	0.01	BUY	($0.02)		$0.00	0.01		$0.01		$0.00	0.01		$0.01		$0.00	0.01		$0.01
q	TERN	$1.65	$1.57	1.59		$0.02		$0.00	1.59		$1.59		$0.00	1.59		$1.59		$0.00	1.59		$1.59
	VTSS	$3.93	$3.73	3.42	BUY	($0.31)		$0.00	3.42		$3.42		$0.00	3.42		$3.42		$0.00	3.42		$3.42
	JDSU	$2.75	$2.61	2.77		$0.16		$0.00	2.77		$2.77		$0.00	2.77		$2.77		$0.00	2.77		$2.77
	INSP	$0.70	$0.67	0.67		$0.01		$0.00	0.67		$0.67		$0.00	0.67		$0.67		$0.00	0.67		$0.67

I started moving to Adverse Move Strategy trading in late June, 2002. I traded the 10-year model in an IRA, FOLIO*fn* account and the 3-year model in a Scottrade account. Implementation was a little loose at first. There were distractions, and I couldn't devote all my concentration, time to trading Adverse Move Strategy. The 3-year model was traded sporadically through the day, and I tried to catch the FOLIO*fn* afternoon window but often ended up putting in overnight orders for the morning window.

Operationally the Adverse Move Strategy requires much more time and active involvement in the market. Normally the *Trend Regression Portfolio Strategy* requires weekly entries and exits. Adverse Move Strategy requires daily or more frequent maintenance.

Unhappy with the lack of precision in the execution, I move to end-of-day trading, placing entry orders, if closing price meets the 5% adverse move trigger points. Orders execute at next days' open or in next FOLIO*fn* window.

The proceeding Adverse Move Strategy analysis took place prior to reading *Maximum Adverse Excursion, Analyzing Price Fluctuations for Trading Management.* John Sweeny's book holds different conclusions than presented above, maybe because he was studying trend following rather than reversion systems.

John Sweeney's basic idea is that an analysis of post entry, price action shows that winning trades and losing trades act differently. The rule he suggests is "Generally, good trades don't go too far against you while bad ones do." He used the MAE concept to calculate the stop-loss levels that allowed winning trades to remain while getting out of losing trades before they become disasters. This seems consistent with a trend following strategy. If you are jumping on a trend, and it starts moving in the wrong direction, you are likely better off to find a new trend to follow. He believes if some degree of regularity doesn't exist in your post entry price action then you have little basis for trading your system.

Sweeney's chart of post entry action for typical loser trades has all samples closing out at the profit low.[47] Therefore, stop losses make a lot of sense.

Sweeney's discussion of post entry, price action leads to more analysis of price action for dmthilo weekly trades. Trades total 3285. Trades are classified by trading days in trade, and after eliminating series with few trades 3212 trades remain. Data is percent of closing price from day entry is triggered. Data covers period trade is on plus 3 days. The plotted series are day-by-day averages for each length of trade. Remember all trades are long, and the last three points in each series are post exit. Both 5-day and 6-day are 1-week, Thursday close to Thursday close. The 5-day series has one missing trading day, most likely because of a holiday. Similarly, the other series are 2-week, 3-week and 4-week. The series that were eliminated had more than 1 missing trading day, or were held longer than 5-weeks. There are 2040 1-week trades, 814 2-week trades, 264 3-week trades, and 94 4-week trades.

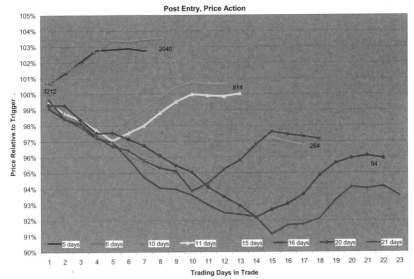

There is some regularity to post-entry, price action. Down-sloping lines are parallel, and up-sloping lines are parallel. Down-sloping lines precede up-sloping lines. The regularity is consistent with a reversal system. Sometimes the reversal takes longer to occur; you are early, the trend continues instead of reversing. The regularity of the post-entry, price action is confirmed by the high degree of correlation between the 2 series of each weeks-held category. The series with 1 day missing have the same shape as the larger series with more data points.

After eliminating trades with one missing day, 2379 trades remained. Classifying these trades by win/loss and weeks in trade produces 8 series.

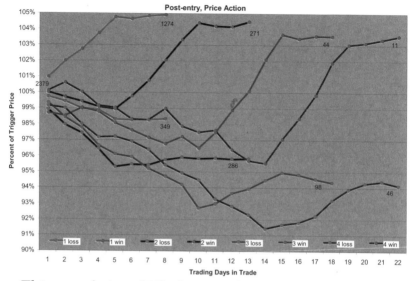

This graph is a little busier than the first, but there is still regularity in post-entry, price action. All but the 1-week series have a down-slope followed by an up-slope. Down-slope is steeper for losers than for winners. Magnitude of change between down-slope and up-slope is greater for winners than for losers. Spread between winners and losers increases with time in trade. Length of up-slope for all winners is 5 trading days. For winning trades, the spread between low (MAE) and exit increases with time in trade. For 1-week trades winners outnumber losers by 4 to 1. As trade length increases the win/loss ratio deteriorates and for 4-week trades losers outnumber winners by 4 to 1.

There seems to be some connection between first day action and outcome. As goes the first day, there goes the trade. Of these 2379 trades, 1600 closed with a gain (win ratio 1600/2379 = 67%). Closing all trades that didn't gain on the first day converts 649 winners to losers (win ratio (1600-649)/2379 = 40%). It also limits loss to first day loss, when first day has a loss. Winners are fewer and bigger. Losses are more numerous, but smaller. Exit value is exit price as a percent of trigger price.

First Day as Indicator

	dmthilo rules		1st day rules	
	count	exit value	count	exit value
wins	1,600	103.7%	951	105.4%
losses	779	97.2%	1,428	98.2%
total	2,379	101.6%	2,379	101.1%

It appears unprofitable to use first day loss as an indicator triggering trade exits for the dmthilo model. The reduction in average loss per losing trade and increase in average gain per winning trade don't combine to make up for the reduction in number of winners. *First Day Indicator* like MAE is part of a strategy to limit losses. Maybe these strategies work better for trend following systems.

The following is a more detailed look at post-entry, price action for 1-week trades. The chart is a colorized open-high-low-close bar. The high-low bar is green if today's close is greater than yesterday's close. The open-close bar is green if today's close is greater than today's open.

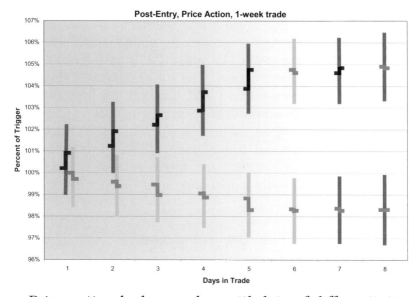

Price action looks regular, with lots of differentiation between action of winners and losers. First day closes are below 100% for losers, tested in side bar. First day close is below first day open for losers. Winners never close below previous closing price; exit is on close of fifth day. Losers never close above previous closing price. Daily ranges overlap from day to day. Winners have higher highs and higher lows each day, while losers have lower lows and lower highs each day. Most of the action is over in five days, and then the price goes sideways for both winners and losers. Remember, these are averages for 1,274 winning trades and 349 losing trades. Individual trades can behave much differently than the averages.

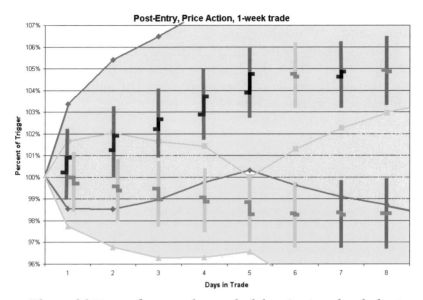

The addition of areas bounded by 1 standard deviation from the daily close for winners and losers gives a hint at the dispersion of actual trade post-entry, price action. The 2-color area is overlap between winners and losers. Notice there is no overlap on day-5, exit-day. Even at the 1 standard deviation, 68% confidence level lots of winners look like losers before day-5, and lots of winners go on to become losers after day-5. Also, lots of losers look like winners before day-5, and lots of losers go on to become winners after day-5. A lot of variation detail is hidden in the nice, regular price action of the averages.

The August 2002 issue of Technical Analysis of Stocks & Commodities had an article by Sergei Dobrovolsky about using MAE and MFE to set exit stops.[48] After studying this article, MAE and MFE for the dmthilo model were tested for optimal placement of stops. The following 2 charts show that any exit stop will decrease profit. The trades are the same 2,379 trades in the preceding charts. The vertical scale, y-axis, measures how much the exit stops add or subtract from profit. The horizontal scale, x-axis show the exit stop used. Calculations are based on closing prices triggering stops, and ignore transaction costs. Charts are constructed so the highest point on the gain line is the optimal gain from the stop, and the value immediately below on the x-axis is the optimal stop.

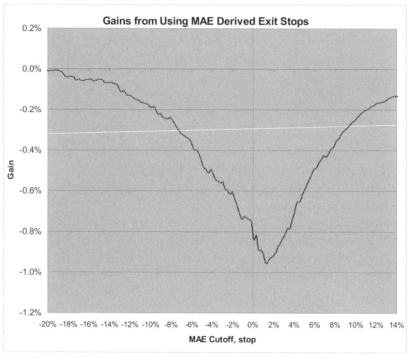

The MAE derived loss limiting exit has the least impact on portfolio profitability when it affects the fewest trades. The low and high stop levels are not visited by many trades. Worst results occur when exit stop is set 1.19% over entry price. With 1.23% stop (exit when trade falls below 101.23% of entry price), 434 trades have more profit because of the stop, 964 have less profit because of the stop, and 981 are unaffected.

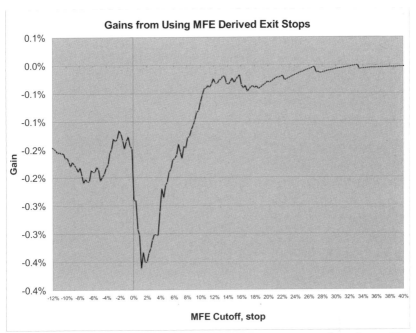

The MFE derived profit-protecting exit also has the least impact on portfolio profitability when it affects the fewest trades. Many trades do not visit the double-digit stop levels. Worst results occur when exit stop is set 1.19% over entry price. With 1.19% stop (exit when trade goes above 101.19% of entry price), 625 trades have more profit be-cause of the stop, 773 have less profit because of the stop, and 981 are unaffected.

Stop loss and profit protect stops don't work for the dmthilo model, but they do work for

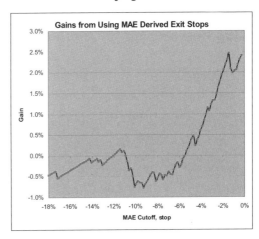

subsets of the dmthilo model.

Both stop loss and profit protection stops work for the 4-week trade subset, 57 trades. Stop loss stops would have in-creased profit over 2 percentage points and profit protection stops would have in-creased profit nearly 1%. The problem is identi-fying, in advance, which trades are go-ing to turn into 4-week trades.

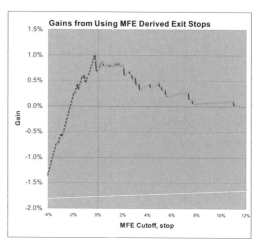

Trade Frequency

The increased maintenance of the Adverse Move Strategy prompted me to investigate trade frequency, determined by model run frequency. To this point, all successful models used weekly data, and weekly entries and exits. Monthly models would require less mainte-nance, and provide larger blocks of free time between trade calculation and entry. Daily models would require more maintenance, and more attention to daily detail.

The first back-test used monthly data from the dmthilo model dataset.

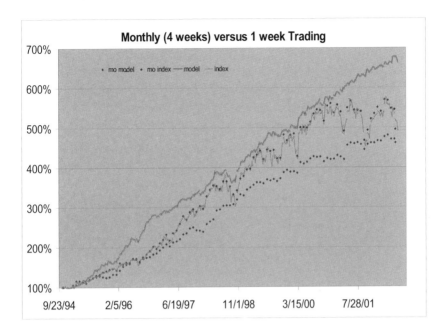

The monthly-trade model, dark green dots in graph above didn't perform as well as the weekly-trade model. The monthly-trade model didn't reach performance of "buy and hold" 50 equities of the model. Gain (ending over beginning value) for the period was 490% for the index, 660% for the weekly-trade model, and 460% for the monthly-trade model. The period covered is less than for the 10-year dmthilo model because of the data lost to initiating the 25 smoothing-months indicators.

The next back-test used daily data from the dmthilo model dataset.

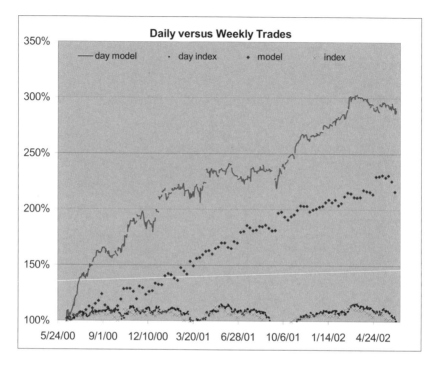

Both the daily-trade and weekly-trade models performed better than the dmthilo "buy and hold" index. The daily model performed better than the weekly model. The back-test period covered 2 years, from 6/13/2000 through 6/14/2002. Gain (ending over beginning value) for the period was 101% for the index, 215% for the weekly-trade model, and 290% for the daily-trade model.

In both the long and short trade duration tests, smoothing-weeks was kept at 3, with 100% of equity risked at all times. From the results of these back-tests it seems more frequent trading produces more gain. This wasn't expected. Further investigation is warranted as only one dataset was used and the back-test duration for the most interesting, daily trade back-test, was only 2 years.

Because the *Trend Regression Portfolio Strategy* model can handle only 520-bar back-tests, 10 random start 520 bar back-test were done using price data from the period 3/1/1991 through 6/14/2002. One bar is one data record (one open, high, low, close, volume). The record can be for any period appropriate for the model's goals (1 minute, 5 minute ... 1 day, 1 week, etc).

Daily versus Weekly Trades (2-yr back-tests within 10-yrs mid 1992 through mid 2002)

from	6/13/2000	8/7/1996	2/17/1992	5/22/1995	7/5/1993	1/20/1997	3/21/1994	7/13/1998	12/8/1997	7/12/1999	aver-
to	6/14/2002	6/5/1998	2/14/1994	5/19/1997	7/3/1995	1/18/1999	3/1/1996	7/10/2000	12/6/1999	7/9/2001	age
index	101%	202%	123%	202%	141%	187%	164%	139%	153%	119%	153%
daily-trade	292%	347%	324%	337%	281%	348%	301%	379%	297%	356%	326%
weekly-trade	217%	252%	197%	277%	197%	246%	221%	259%	251%	230%	235%

The chart shows not just that daily-trade portfolio is more profitable, but that it is also more independent of the index than the weekly-trade portfolio.

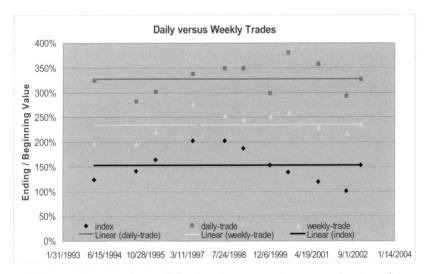

The index and weekly-trade seem to move in tandem. The table's correlation numbers confirm that the weekly-trade portfolio more closely tracks the index than the daily-trade portfolio.

	average	correlation with index
index	153%	1.00
daily-trade	326%	0.26
weekly-trade	235%	0.65

The next table compares results from 10 2-year back-test samples to the 10-year back-tests for the index and weekly-trade portfolios.

	average	standard deviation	average annual	
			10 2-yr	10-year
index	153%	35%	24%	20%
daily-trade	326%	32%	113%	
weekly-trade	235%	27%	67%	69%

For the index and weekly-trade model, the mean of averages from the 10 2-year back-tests are pretty close to the average for the 10-year back-test. The index mean of averages is a little higher than the 10-year back-test average, and the weekly-trade mean of averages is a little lower. Therefore, the daily-trade mean of averages is probably a reasonable estimate of what the average for a 10-year back-test might be if the model could handle 10 years of daily data.

The daily-trading strategy looks good. The next step is to move individual transactions from *Trend Regression Portfolio Strategy* daily-trade model to the adverse-trade strategy model. Remember the adverse-trade model came out of MAE (Maximum Adverse Excursion) discussed in the previous section. The adverse-trade model builds a worksheet with all roundtrip trade transactions from the daily-trade model.

Daily versus Weekly Trades

	dmthilo weekly-trade	dmthilo weekly-trade	dmthilo adverse move weekly-trade	dmthilo daily-trade	dmthilo adverse move daily-trade
% Portfolio per trade	33%	10%	10%	10%	10%
Ave. Portfolio in Trades	100%	100%	28%	100%	80%
Max Portfolio in Trades	100%	100%	100%	100%	100%
End/Begin Value	824%	576%	354%	921%	528%
% Winning Trades	58%	63%	71%	61%	71%
Maximum Drawdown	32%	25%	11%	51%	12%
TRiPS%	0.64%	0.87%	0.48%	0.39%	0.84%
potentail # Trades	1563	3289	1000	6437	2412
Trades made	1563	3289	937	6437	1302
wins	903	2080	662	3955	925

Based on ending over beginning value the best strategy is the Daily-trades. Based on TRiPS% the best strategy is the Adverse Move with Daily-trade. Daily-trades increase return and risk over weekly-trades strategies. The Adverse Move Strategy reduces return and risk from *Trend Regression Portfolio Strategy* models, by reducing average percent of portfolio equity in trades. The dmthilo weekly-trade column with 33% of the portfolio in each trade is straight from the *Trend Regression Portfolio Strategy* model. The dmthilo weekly-trade column with 10% of the portfolio in each trade uses the Adverse Trade Strategy model to compile trades from the *Trend Regression Portfolio Strategy* model output.

Predictably, the Daily-trades Strategy increases the number of trades and reduces the average profit per trade for trades entered off *Trend Regression Portfolio Strategy* model signals.

Daily versus Weekly Trades, Average Trade

	dmthilo weekly-trade	dmthilo weekly-trade	dmthilo adverse move weekly-trade	dmthilo daily-trade	dmthilo adverse move daily-trade
Trades made	1,563	3,289	937	6,437	1,302
average trade gain	440	145	271	128	329
standard deviation	1,814	597	771	645	887
RRR	0.34	0.34	0.49	0.28	0.52
average days in trade		8.7	7.5	11.2	9.4

Surprisingly, the average profit per trade for the Adverse Move Strategy is higher for daily-trades than weekly-trades. Another surprise was that the Daily-trades model kept trades open longer than the Weekly-trades model. Average days for Adverse Move Strategy is always less than for *Trend Regression Portfolio Strategy*, because after the buy signal, entry waits until stock price falls 5%.

None of the preceding includes commissions and slippage. Adding a $50 slippage/commission charge per round trip changes the rankings of the weekly-trade, daily-trade models.

	dmthilo weekly-trade	dmthilo weekly-trade	dmthilo adverse move weekly-trade	dmthilo daily-trade	dmthilo adverse move daily-trade
% Portfolio per trade	33%	10%	10%	10%	10%
Ave. Portfolio in Trades	100%	100%	28%	100%	80%
Max Portfolio in Trades	100%	100%	100%	100%	100%
End/Begin Value	746%	411%	304%	599%	427%
% Winning Trades	57%	59%	65%	58%	65%
Maximum Drawdown	34%	28%	12%	56%	13%
TRiPS%	0.56%	0.22%	0.36%	0.16%	0.62%
potentail # Trades	1563	3289	1000	6437	2412
Trades made	1563	3289	937	6437	2193
wins	896	2080	662	3955	1533

Predictably, the strategies with the highest average gain per trade are least affected by the slippage/commission charge. Based on ending over beginning portfolio value the best strategy is the *Trend Regression Portfolio Strategy* with 33% portfolio equity risked per trade. Based on TRiPS% the best strategy is adverse move, daily-trade, but the *Trend Regression Portfolio Strategy* is not far behind.

The slippage/commission charge reduces the percent winning trades, RRR, average trade gain, and TRiPS%. Maximum Drawdown increases.

Daily versus Weekly Trades, Average Trade

	33% dmthilo weekly-trade	10% dmthilo weekly-trade	dmthilo adverse move weekly-trade	dmthilo daily-trade	dmthilo adverse move daily-trade
Trades made	1,563	3,289	937	6,437	1,302
average trade gain	390	95	221	78	279
standard deviation	1,814	597	771	645	887
RRR	0.30	0.22	0.40	0.17	0.44
average days in trade		8.7	7.5	11.2	9.4

Average gain per trade is important to the robustness of a portfolio strategy, especially if your broker arrangements create high transaction costs (commissions and slippage). As for performance, it looks like the daily-trade Strategy has some advantages over the Weekly-trade Strategy, even with a $50 commission/slippage charge.

Operationally, the Daily-trade Strategy requires more work, more trades, and more attention. The Weekly-trade Strategy probably works best with model runs at the same time every week, with execution of trades as close as possible to time of stock price used in model run, and with no monitoring during the week. Between-model-run monitoring can be problematic, often leading to worry, and in extreme cases causing panic trades against the model. The Daily-trade Strategy probably works best with model runs at the same time every day, with execution of trades as close as possible to time of stock price used in model run, and with no monitoring during the day. Your time schedule, life-style might preclude the Daily-trade Strategy or even the Weekly-trade Strategy. Don't try to implement one of these strategies if you can't commit the time.

FOLIO*fn* advantages for implementing these strategies are lack of commission, easy set up of portfolio trades, and bias toward trading at specific times. However, slippage might be a problem, if model stock prices are not coordinated with current prices at time of FOLIO*fn*'s window trade.

The Daily-trade Strategy back-tests results were a surprise. Earlier daily-trade back-tests had been disappointing. In the earlier back-tests, 3 smoothing-weeks had been converted to 15 smoothing-days, without optimization. In these back-tests, 3 smoothing-weeks became 3 smoothing-days. Part of the reason the Daily-trade Strategy looks good could be that optimal smoothing-weeks, for dmthilo model, is detrimentally constrained to 3. In the weekly trade models, 3 is currently the minimum smoothing-weeks possible, because trend and slope indicators require 3 data points.

Optimization runs later confirmed that 3 smoothing-days is optimum for the dmthilo stock group. Remember dmthilo Weekly-trade had optimized at 3 smoothing-weeks, the minimum. It is not surprising that the Daily-trade Strategy optimal smoothing- days is less than 15 (3 weeks), but it is surprising that the smoothing-weeks is as low as 3 days.

A test of the AG1 stock group, which had optimized on 39 smoothing-weeks for the Weekly-trade Strategy, optimized on 35 smoothing-days (7 weeks) with a lower TRiPS% than the Weekly-trade Strategy. The 35-day,

daily-trade optimal corresponded to a 7-week intermediate optimal in the weekly-trade optimization. The
TRiPS% peak at 7 smoothing-weeks is second only to
the peak at 39 weeks. The AG1 and dmthilo daily-trade
back-tests indicate that the Daily-trade strategy probably provides the most potential for improving portfolio
results when optimal smoothing-weeks is at 3, the
minimum value.

Timing Trades

The *Trend Regression Portfolio Strategy* models assume trades are made at closing prices. Weekly-trade
models assume Friday close.

Day of Week

After switching to DownloaderXL it became as easy
to capture and save daily data as weekly data. Data is
open, high, low, close prices and volume. This facilitated testing the idea of changing the trade date. The
following graph resulted.

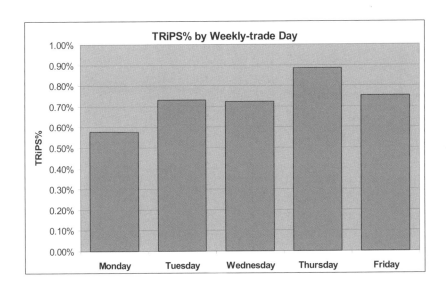

This graph resulted from running the dmthilo model using different trade days. Entries and exits were at the close on each day of the week. Positions changed every week on the same day. Thursday trading seems to have a significant performance advantage. Monday trading seems to have a significant performance disadvantage.

It is most likely if "day of week" trading is tested against enough data, say all the stock trades worldwide for the last 100 years, that there is no best day to buy or sell. It is also probable that for particular stocks or groups of stocks for specific time periods that there is a best day to buy or sell. The Thursday advantage for the dmthilo group of equities probably doesn't apply to the market in general, or other groups of equities.

Close/Open

In the earlier chapter, Trading History there is a section on Slippage and Commissions. My contention is that if the market is mostly random in the short-term, than the long-term slippage between model signal and purchase price should average Ø. As discovered earlier, in the short-term, average slippage isn't Ø. The table below is for the dmthilo model.

Entries, Exits at Open versus at Close

	dmthilo weekly-trade	dmthilo weekly-trade	dmthilo next open weekly-trade
% Portfolio per trade	33%	10%	10%
Ave. Portfolio in Trades	100%	100%	100%
Max Portfolio in Trades	100%	100%	100%
End/Begin Value	824%	576%	530%
% Winning Trades	58%	63%	62%
Maximum Drawdown	32%	25%	27%
TRiPS%	0.64%	0.87%	0.85%
potentail # Trades	1563	3289	3287
Trades made	1563	3289	3287
wins	903	2080	2039

With nearly 3,300 trades net slippage approaches Ø and the performance difference between trading at the close or the next day's open is small.

At Open versus At Close Trades, Average Trade

	dmthilo weekly-trade	dmthilo weekly-trade	dmthilo next open weekly-trade	slippage
Trades made	1,563	3,289	3,287	
average trade gain	440	145	131	
standard deviation	1,814	597	592	
RRR	0.34	0.34	0.31	
average days in trade		8.7	8.7	
average buy		$ 22.60	$ 22.79	$ (0.19)
average sell		$ 22.86	$ 23.03	$ 0.17

Although net slippage is close to Ø, purchases are made an average of $.19 more than the model trigger (daily close), and sales are made at an average of $.17 more than the model trigger. Notice the slippage is in the same direction, higher, for both purchases and sales. Maybe it is advantageous, in this stock group, to buy at the close and sell at the open. That is, speed up purchases and slow down sales. However, if you are 100% invested it may be hard to buy more until you sell.

That both buy and sell average slippage is in the same direction is consistent with a rising market. The dmthilo index was 632% of its starting value at the end of the back-test. The slippage does seem high.

The preceding slippage analysis looks at equities as they become involved in transactions. The next graph compares average stock price moves during a week.

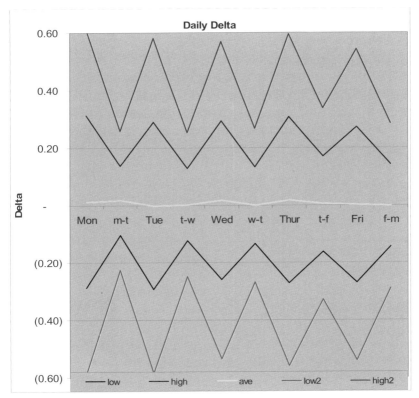

The Mon through Fri labels refer to market hours, open through close for each day. The m-t through f-m labels refer to overnight, close through next morning's open. Although some periods, during the week, have a higher average gain than others, the averages are small compared to the range of gains(losses). The centerline is the average; the saw-tooth lines next to the centerline are 1 standard deviation away from the centerline. The outer lines are 2 standard deviations away from the centerline. RRR is low (.01) to 0.13, *Trend Regression Portfolio Strategy* model runs are averaging 0.31 RRR. The saw-tooth pattern comes from the graph's alternating market hours and overnight moves. Overnight price moves are smaller than the moves made while the market is open. The variability of overnight moves is smaller than the variability from market open to market close.

The purpose of the above graph is to point out the potential problem of assuming slippage is not important because it will average out. Assuming updating models after hours and making trades on open, average slippage is the difference between market close (model trigger price) and market open (trade price). For the 10 years covered in the graph overnight slippage approaches Ø, $.0037 per trade per share. The problem is not the average, but the distribution. Standard deviation is $.1378; meaning 95% of overnight slippage per share should be between a low of ($.27) and a high of $.28. The actual average overnight slippage per share ranged between a low of ($1.19) and $.75. If you trade on an inflexible schedule for 10 years, your slippage should come close to zeroing out but in the meantime, you will suffer much volatility. Over a long period, slippage should average Ø. Short-term, slippage increases account equity volatility and drawdown.

Optimal f, Ralph Vince

Optimal f is about how much of your total stake you should invest in a trade. The basic premise is that the optimal percentage of your stake that you should have invested is dependent on the size of your largest loss. Optimal f, as explained by Ralph Vince, in *Portfolio Management Formulas*, is calculated as a step along the way toward determining optimal percent of stake to invest. I ran into problems trying to use Optimal f to improve the *Trend Regression Portfolio Strategy*.

I couldn't follow Vince's evolution from defining Holding Period Return (HPR) as trade gain divided by initial investment[49] to trade gain divided by largest loss.[50] I extended the basic *Trend Regression Portfolio Strategy* model to calculate Optimal Equity Risk (OER), the percent of account equity (stake) to put in equities. The calculation skips Optimal f and goes straight to OER. OER is found by creating a table with columns at 1% OER intervals from 1% to 100%, Holding Period Returns (HPR) are multiplied by each OER, geometric mean is found for each column, then max geometric mean (max TWR) determines best OER. Plotting Terminal Wealth Relative (TWR) against OER can produce curves similar to Vince's TWR versus Optimal f on page 80 of *Portfolio Management Formulas*. These Vince-like curves are created when largest loss is equal or close to the initial investment. Losses can be close to investment for derivative investments like options or futures. Losses could also be equal investment if you hold a short position in as a stock price doubles, or if you hold a long position in a company that goes bankrupt.

For *Trend Regression Portfolio Strategy* TWRs don't peak before 100% investment. The lowest peaks occur for models with the biggest percent losses. In the graph below, for the Corr **QQQ** model OER peaks at about 200%. This is the *Trend Regression Portfolio Strategy* model with the lowest OER at peak TWR. This implies that the highest TWR occurs when amount risked is twice amount of stake, using maximum possible margin. The slope of TWR-OER curves for current *Trend Regression Portfolio Strategy* models are positive, and still quite steep at 100% investment. Absent a market timing strategy, keeping funds invested maximizes TWR.

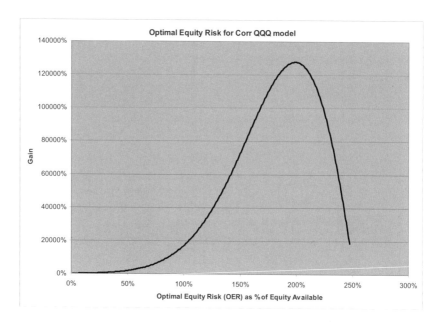

The gain versus OER curve is not linear below 100% in the graph above, or for any *Trend Regression Portfolio Strategy*. The slope at 100% OER is increasing for every *Trend Regression Portfolio Strategy* tested.

In *Portfolio Management Formulas*, Ralph Vince claims Optimal f is the big idea. About Chapter 4, Optimal Fixed Fractional Trading, he says, "It is the most important chapter in the entire book." He may be right for option and futures traders, but I found more interesting and useful information throughout the book. His rules for optimizing and de-optimizing led to improvements to some *Trend Regression Portfolio Strategy* models:

" 1. Optimize over as long a data set as possible.
  2. Use as few parameters as possible.
  3. Bias yourself to systems that show robustness across parameters.
  4. Forward test—preferably using the anchored technique of forward testing to be consistent with rule 1.

5. Identify the region of parameter values that appears to be the peak, and pick the parameter with lowest performance value therein that has higher performance values for the parameters on either side. Ideally you will have the same parameter values for all markets you are trading a given system on."

Rule 1 endorses what we saw earlier (page 96). No optimization on a small duration within a larger duration will yield better performance over the larger duration than an optimization over the larger duration. Often complicated systems with many optimized parameters fail to produce profitable trading results, in spite of good back-test results. Optimal values are usually not static; they drift over time, so it is helpful to look at performance with near optimal parameters. Rather than forward test, *Trend Regression Portfolio Strategy* models are set up to do short tests, with random start dates, within the larger duration. Rule 5 alludes to the value of plotting performance versus parameter values. The next graph shows TRiPS% versus Smoothing-weeks for the dmthilo model.

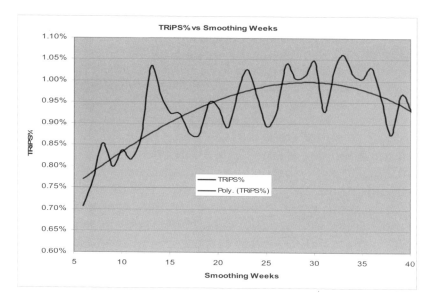

The peak TRiPS% is at 33 weeks, but a third order polynomial curve peaks at 29 weeks. The trader/investor has to chose how many weeks to use in the model he trades, but based on the data most would chose somewhere in the 29 to 33 range rather than 13 weeks where the earlier local optimum is.

Later on the same page 60, where Vince lists his rules, he discusses what to do with a system that looks good.

> "Finally, if you have de-optimized a system and it still looks good, then don't mess with it—just trade it. Leave the rules alone. Put them up on a shelf. The system is done. The problem with system traders is that they keep reworking their systems. When you get a good system don't change it. If you want to tinker, start on a new system—one you might use in conjunction with the one you have finished. As for the one you have just finished, although it may seem like a crude system, simple and hardly optimized, leave it alone. Its simplicity and crudeness are the very reason it works. Go to work on another system if the system-tinkering bug bites you."

This could/should be a rule. **Once you start trading a system, resist re-optimizing or retuning.** This hits home, I have been guilty of retuning too frequently and giving up on a system just before it produces a big run-up. Things do change, but trader/investors need to be extremely careful about the timing of changing or switching systems.

Ralph Vince states that mechanical systems go through cycles in performance because the stream of profits and losses from trading systems appears as non-stationary distributions.[51] He goes on to say that many people mistakenly believe that this cycling is caused primarily by optimal parameters changing when the real cause of most cycling is just the nature of profits and losses distribution in a trading system.

If the goal were getting optimal back-test results, a model that could solve for optimal parameter values that cycle through time would deliver higher return than a model that holds the parameters constant through the entire back-test. This is borne out by *Trend Regression Portfolio Strategy* back-tests. Random start date, short duration, back-tests within longer back-test duration will usually optimize on different parameters and show better performance than the long duration back-test. However, maybe Vince's idea about the source of trading system profits and losses cycling is overstated.

For the portfolio manager the goal is not optimal back-test but future performance. A system that relies on changing, cycling parameters is probably over-optimized, and most likely not a reliable generator of future profit. So, I think Vince underestimates the impact of drifting optimal parameters, but still believe he is right that investor/trader/portfolio managers should learn to live with non-stationary distribution of trading system stream of profits and loses. Vince says it best:

"… just as bear markets come and go in stocks, so do drawdowns come and go in … systems. If you are a trader, then you know that your account exists in one of 2 states. Either you are at equity highs, or you are in drawdown. Since equity highs are not sustainable forever, savor those moments when you are at them. Further, you should recognize that equity highs are followed by drawdowns just a night follows day, and should learn to be comfortable with this fact.

We must learn to be able to live in an environment that is characterized by being in a drawdown most of the time. We must learn to be able to live in a state of always wondering when the current drawdown will end and new equity highs be seen again."

Previously I suggested that buying and holding SPY is a good substitute for a system, if you don't have a system you know and trust. To give you an idea of what "in a drawdown most of the time" means, in the time period 1/29/1993 through 5/24/2002 SPY set new highs on 252 out of 2,349 market days (10.7%). That means SPY was in drawdown 89.3% of the time. Worse yet as of 3/28/2003 it has been in drawdown 755 market days (since 3/24/2000), and is 44% below the high. Get used to drawdown. If you invest in anything other than money market funds, you are going to experience drawdown.

Optimization

What is the verdict on optimization?

PRO	Con
• Optimization proves some mechanical systems with some parameters are capable of delivering market-beating performance.	• Past success of a particular mechanical system doesn't confirm its future profitability, let alone market beating performance.
• Optimization lets you know what worked best in the past.	• Best for past, probably not best for future.
• Optimization lets you know what didn't work in the past.	• Worst for past, may not be worst for future.
• Builds confidence in portfolio management, systematic trading.	• Dangerous, can lead to overconfidence in model.
• Provides time, to build expectations.	• Consumes time, requires work.
• Lets you try portfolio management and trading ideas without risking capital.	• What works in a model might not work when capital is at risk, when trading costs differ from model assumptions.
• Optimization can use any data you judge to be representative of future price moves.	• Optimization is sensitive to the time duration and time-period of the backtest.
• Can provide feel for robustness of system, feel for performance variance using different parameters, different markets.	• Robustness based on history is not future robustness.
• I love it as it helps increase portfolio equity.	• It can encourage sticking with obsolete values.

The pro and con columns for optimization have equal entries. There are about as many reasons for using optimization as avoiding it. Optimization is a very valuable tool, but it is important to keep its limitations in mind before committing money to optimized systems. Optimizations are determined by historic price patterns which when repeated in the future are always a little different. The market is always the same, but always different. The goal of optimizing is to produce a system that you have enough faith in that you are willing to fund and motivated to stick with. The goal of optimizing is not to produce a system that has the highest return in some historic period.

Once you have a model you like, how often should you re-optimize? Market dynamics do change, so you should re-optimize. However, the last rule in the previous section says don't re-optimize or retune. If you re-optimize every week you will likely cause excessive trading and deny the model time it needs to work. If your re-optimized model picks an entirely different set of buys and sells, the model is probably too unstable to trade. A stable model shouldn't change much when it re-optimizes. Before you start trading a model, you should re-optimize every week, assuming using weekly closes, and document how optimal input parameters and output results change.

Optimization is dangerous. It is easy to develop an over-fitted answer built on historic data. The awesome over-fitted back-test performance statistics produce high expectations that cannot be approached in actual portfolio management. The R-map (pages 99-102) helps keep perspective on relative performance of optimized parameters versus other parameters.

Future

The past is history and the future starts when you place a trade, invest. Strategies that test well in back-tests and paper-trading don't always deliver expected performance. Markets change. Sometimes the combination of commissions and slippage eats up the profit. There is no guarantee that what worked in the past will work in the future, and vice versa, there is no guarantee that what did not work in the past will work in the future. Actually, following our *Regression to the Mean* theme, there may be money in following a strategy that didn't work in the past.

You can benefit from my struggles, remember, "back-tests deal with the past, and we are looking for a strategy that will work in the future." However, there are 2 essential characteristics of successful portfolio trading and back-testing is important to both. The model has not only to produce winning trades, but also to be tradable. Tradability is the model's ability to keep trader/investor fear and greed in check. Psychologically it is easier to trade a strategy that has worked in the past than to trade one that doesn't have good back-test performance. It gets very hard to stick with a strategy that doesn't have a good back-test history when equity starts to draw down. As the drawdown gets larger and larger the trader gets more and more fearful, and often the trader abandons the strategy just before it turns. Therefore, to be a successful portfolio manager you need both a model that produces winning trades and the resolve to stick with the model. Resolve comes from the portfolio manager's belief that over time the model will recover from drawdowns.

The *Trend Regression Portfolio Strategy* models built on weekly data are not short-term; they are for those with a nest egg they want to grow over time. In the previous paragraph, I slipped in a re-labeling of the trader/investor to portfolio manager. It wasn't an accident, I think "portfolio manager" better describes what we are trying to accomplish by following a *Trend Regression Portfolio Strategy*. We are managing a portfolio of equity positions and the trades and investments we make are incidental to the performance of the portfolio. Whether individual trades are winners or losers is of less importance than whether the portfolio equity is climbing or falling.

"Portfolio manager" has a nice ring, but it still understates the responsibility. Portfolio responsibility also involves setting broader, strategic, policy for your nest egg. Maybe "portfolio entrepreneur" is a better label.

Participation in financial markets is gambling, trading, investing, and managing. Gambling is for those lucky people that don't need to do homework to develop an edge, and are okay with the house having the edge.[52] Trading is buying and selling. Systematic trading is buying and selling with an edge, based on homework. Investing is committing money with the expectation of a return. Managing is directing and controlling resources, including financial assets.

The portfolio manager shouldn't be a gambler. The portfolio manager is a trader because he/she trades equities. It can also be advantageous for a portfolio manager to be a trader for tax reasons. The portfolio manager is an investor in that he/she commits money to the portfolio and expects a profit. However, mostly the portfolio manager is a manager, controlling the portfolio's assets to balance return and risk.

Traders evolve. Most start as discretionary traders, buying on gut instinct. Discretionary traders sometimes get rich, sometimes go broke, and often evolve into technical traders. Technical traders buy and sell based on homework. They study, charts and/or news, and then place trades. Technical traders evolve into system traders. System traders are technical traders with money management rules. A few popular money management rules are:

- never commit more than 10% of your trading equity to one stock,
- never risk more than 2% of you trading equity on one trade,
- fund your trading account with risk capital, don't put rent money in your trading account,
- have a written plan for every trade,
- don't increase size in a losing trade,
- build pyramids from the base.

System traders focus beyond individual trades, looking at the utilization of their entire trading equity. The potential of individual trades is weighted against risk to entire trading equity.

I am still in awe of successful system traders. However, *Trend Regression Portfolio Strategy* may be useful to system traders for managing their non-trading accounts or for giving themselves a break from the stress of trading.

Left to Test

Because there are hundreds of indicators available from the price and volume histories of equities and markets, and thousands of equities, there are millions of ways to combine them. While this book documents some of the testing completed, I continue searching for the "Holy grail," and I hope that you will join in the search. I try to keep my testing objective, but sometimes it is hard to accept when models that should work, don't. I have spent countless hours trying to get acceptable *TRiPS%* for datasets that were carefully selected, before moving on to greener pastures.

Maybe the naysayers are right that the "Holy grail" doesn't exist, but let that not dampen our enthusiasm for its pursuit. Sometimes the journey is more important than the destination. There are always new stock selections, new stock indicators, and new market indicators to try.

The greatest potential may be in market timing. None of the market timing indicators I have tried has worked very well. Most of the best *Trend Regression Portfolio Strategy* models to-date optimized on staying 100% long, but coefficient of regression (R^2) for equities dependence on their market index can be high. For instance, R^2 for equities in the HILO model ranges from .00 to .92 with an average of .53, implying that 53% of individual equity price, opportunity for profit, comes from variability in the market. This leaves only 47% of profit opportunity in relative moves of individual equities. It seems that strategies that aren't in and out of the market (or long and short), based on market timing are leaving profit on the table. Drach "market times" with considerable success and warns about the impact of negative compounding, which hits your portfolio when the market is falling. I have faith in Drach's market timing, but continue to look for a simple, mechanical tradable market-timing indicator.

The Adverse Move Strategy has a market-timing component in that equity at risk varies. Equity at risk is increased as price of individual stocks drops below the *Trend Regression Portfolio Strategy* models' trigger prices. It may not be the same as a market-timing indicator, which applies to the total portfolio, but it has the desired effect of varying the amount of equity at risk per market conditions.

Break it Down

Each of the three steps to *Trend Regression Portfolio Strategy* model building should add value. I tried to break down the performance of different tests and portfolios to get an idea of how much each step contributes. Remember the three steps:

1. Pick equities that should increase in value.
2. Go long, or short, equities that are farthest from equilibrium.
3. Vary percent of equity risked with market cycle.

The HILO group of equities resulted from a screen done in December of 2000; by February 2002 the HILO index has fallen to 95.7% of its start value, while the S&P 500 index fell 84.5%. The Marketocracy HILO portfolio started 8/9/01, since then:

	8/9/2001	2/15/2002	Gain(Loss)
S&P 500	1,190	1,104	-7.2%
HILO Index	2,248	2,236	-0.5%
HILO Marketocracy Portfolio	10.00	11.35	13.5%

The index performance shows that stock picking had a positive effect, and the paper-trading Marketocracy Portfolio shows that entries and exits based on *Trend Regression Portfolio Strategy* had a positive effect. Because of the limited elapsed time and the fact that the data is for a single portfolio, the most positive statement possible so far is, probably, *Trend Regression Portfolio Strategy* can improve results in specific situations.

Unfortunately, I didn't have a funded portfolio lined up running with the HILO model during the 8/9/01 – 2/15/02 period. HILO optimized 100% long 100% of the time so there was no market-timing component.

EXCEL

Efficiency

I hadn't selected Excel because of its efficiency, over the years it just defaulted to my spreadsheet of choice. For a long time I was concentrating on trying to build tradable models, and happy with the speed of Excel. However, as the *Trend Regression Portfolio Strategy* models became larger, optimization times grew, and I wondered if I could speed up Excel. A complete optimization for 3 to 50 smoothing-weeks and 0% to 100% timed, with 10 years of price history, was taking days to solve

Optimization Duration

> = ((48 smoothing-week possibilities times 11 %-timed possibilities) divided by 6 iterations per hour)

> = 88 hours

I wanted to get the optimization back to where it could optimize overnight, within 8 hours. First I upgraded from a 733mhz P3 to an Athlon 2100XP with bigger, faster RAM and disk drive. I hoped for a threefold increase in throughput, but got a doubling. It turns out that Excel doesn't use the extra memory, and the disk drive only comes into play when loading and saving models.

Next, I searched the Internet for ideas and found FastExcel.[53] The website has many suggestions for making Excel go faster, and the FastExcel program is excellent for finding what is eating up time. FastExcel helped me understand how Excel works in a way that a reorganization of the *Trend Regression Portfolio Strategy* model was quickly able to produce another doubling of performance.

The model is an Excel—VBA (Visual Basic for Applications) model. Therefore, opportunities for performance improvements exist in both the structure of the Excel Workbooks/Worksheets, and in the VBA code. After working with FastExcel for a few weeks, I noticed that model performance wasn't linear with back-test size. Model performance deteriorated more with the addition of one week of back-test size than the average time per back-test week to that point. In the longer back-tests, I observed that the time for each iteration was increasing with each iteration. I reasoned that the number of calculations performed, in each iteration, was growing with each iteration. This discovery led to a breakthrough in model performance. Changing the VBA code to move these calculations to the end of a cycle led to a four-fold increase in performance.

Before I started working on improving model speed, throughput for a 520-week back-test was 6 cycles per hour. Now with the fast Athlon processor, FastExcel insights, and restructured code, throughput is 55 cycles per hour, a nine-fold increase. The model shrank in size from over 12 megabytes to 3 megabytes. Big models kill Excel performance and the new smaller models still slow down when other sizeable Excel worksheets are open.

The Athlon processor is good, and FastExcel is excellent. I am happy with both purchases. However, I found Excel/VBA performance in places that required no out-of-pocket expenditures. Remember, any out-of-pocket expenditure reduces the capital available for investing. I was lazy, spending money before thinking through the performance problem and researching solutions. If the Athlon processor had increased performance to 55 cycles per hour, I would probably have missed learning more about how Excel and the *Trend Regression Portfolio Strategy* models work.

Building faster Excel models is good, but faster models are not the main goal. Tradable, profitable models are the goal. Therefore, you should concentrate on the finance, indicator, entry, exit logic (your trading/investing logic) until duration of optimizations becomes a problem. Faster model optimization will not save a model with negative expectations.

Once your model is tradable, you can work on improving your Excel models and VBA code. The biggest opportunity for me came from re-sequencing VBA posting of Excel formulas into Excel cells. Posting new formulas that use inputs from other formula cells causes all other cells referenced to recalculate. For instance, if you have a trend formula cell that calculates the trend of an equity curve from its origin, and you add weeks from most recent to oldest, the trend cell for most recent weeks will be recalculated each time you add a new week. I didn't need the trend calculation answer until all weeks were added and was able to postpone adding the trend calculation cells until after all weeks were added. Other improvements came from reorganizing the Excel worksheets according to recommendations from FastExcel. I found that FastExcel also helped identify opportunities for improving the VBA code part of the *Trend Regression Portfolio Strategy* models.

Once your model is tradable, be careful how you change it. It is very easy to get excited about making changes to speed up optimization. Don't go too far without checking the answers to make sure the new improved fast model is giving the same answers as your *tried and true* model. If you go too far, make too many changes, before you check, it may take a long time to audit source differences between answers of old and new models.

Tracking

It is important to keep track of how you are doing, what your equity curve looks like. It is important to keep track of what is working and of what is not. It is important to keep track of details that you can use to determine what is causing strategies to fail. The more accounts you maintain and the more equities you are holding at any time the more you need a tracking system.

There are many ways to keep track. Online brokers provide some portfolio tracking capabilities. Quite a few web sites have portfolio-tracking modules. There are commercial and shareware programs that keep track for you. Over the years, I've tried a few including Microsoft Money and Quicken. The program I stuck with the longest was MSN Moneycentral Portfolio. I still sometimes use it for paper-trading new strategies. Moneycentral is easy to use and powerful, although I have had some problems with MSN availability and with reconciliations.

While using other programs, I often supplemented my routine tracking with Excel spreadsheets to capture certain aspects of my trading. Finally, I pulled the plug on other tracking systems and built an Excel workbook to track my portfolios. This switch to Excel is greatly facilitated by MSN Stock Quote Functions. Stock prices, 20-minute delay, can update you portfolio equity anytime. If you like Excel, and know or want to know VBA (Visual Basic for Applications), please consider using Excel to track your trading. Using Excel has the following advantages:

- You build it so you understand how it works.
- You build it so it fits your needs.
- Data is open so you can modify anything.
- The portfolio-tracking workbook can link to other Excel workbooks.

- The portfolio-tracking workbook can evolve with your needs.
- Code developed for special situations is easily integrated into your routine tracking.
- Output summaries, reports, and graphics are limited only by your imagination.
- Current prices, 20-minute delayed, are easily updated.

FREE

A sample MS Excel portfolio tracking worksheet is available for downloading from this website:

www.diyportfoliomanagement.com.

Part III — Portfolio Management Issues

There is more to Portfolio Management than building *Trend Regression Portfolio Strategy* models.

10. Risk

Risk and Uncertainty

The concepts of risk and uncertainty although related are not synonymous. Risk can be quantified, as the probability of something bad happening, i.e. suffering a financial loss. Uncertainty on the other hand, is unquantifiable, the unknown.

Risk implies that the investor has objective knowledge from which to predict the probability of possible outcomes of his investment strategies. Uncertainty implies that the investor has no objective knowledge from which to predict the probability of possible outcomes. Risk is an objective phenomenon, while uncertainty is a subjective phenomenon.

The risk of losing at a single toss of "heads or tails" is 50%. The risk of picking the shortest straw from a group of 3 is 1/3, 33%. The risk of not pulling a heart, from a full deck is 75%, 39/52. The risk of not pulling the Queen of Hearts from a full deck is 98%, 51/52.

The uncertainty of what is lurking around the next corner, or of whether the product design superiority of Apple will hold off the marketing superiority of Windows/Intel/PC cannot be objectively stated. It is simply unknown.

Risk, the possibility of loss, is bad. Uncertainty can be good or bad, but it is often more scary than risk. It can be scarier simply because our imaginations conjure up and exaggerate negative possibilities when we don't know.

In the short-term, financial markets are more uncertain than risky, and in the long-term financial markets are more risky than uncertain. In the long-term, the fate of individual companies may be more uncertain than risky.

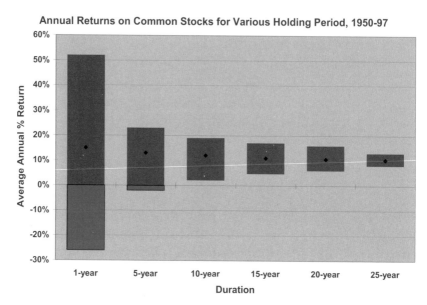

Annual Returns on Common Stocks for Various Holding Period, 1950-97

The preceding graph shows the dispersion of percent returns for various holding period durations during the 47-year period 1950 through 1997. The graph very dramatically shows that although the average return for various holding periods does not vary much, the range of average annual returns shrinks as the holding period increases. Returns for any one year have risk, more risk than the returns for longer holding periods. It is highly probable that the return for one year will be better than -27% and worse than 53%. Returns for any one year have a lot of uncertainty. It is likely that events within the next 12 months will move the market, but it is not certain what the events will be, and even less certain what impact those events will have on the market. Returns for any 25-year period are risky. It is highly probable that the return for 25 years will be better than 7% and worse than 13%. Returns for any 25-year period have some uncertainty. It is certain that events within the next 25 years will move the market, and it is uncertain what the events will be, but it is likely that the impact of those events on the market will average out over time. For instance, Black Monday in October of 1987 marked the biggest one-day drop (20.5%) in the S&P 500 in the 1950-1997 time-period, but 10 years later the 25 year return was 8.5% per year and Black Monday was just a blip on the graph.

There are risks in the market and there is uncertainty in the details.

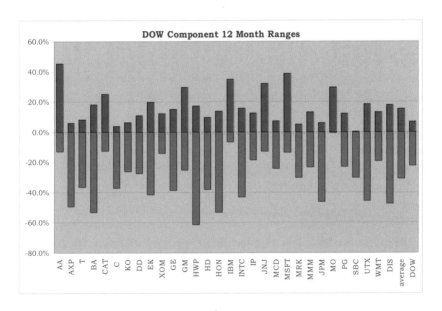

Remember earlier we discussed turnover in Dow components, company life cycles, as part of the reason there is more risk in individual equities than in indexes. There is more to it. The preceding graph shows percent price range of Dow components over the last 12 months, with 0% being the price at the start of the period. The average column is the weighted average of percent price ranges of the Dow components. The Dow index, last column, has a smaller range than the average of the components. An index always has a smaller percent range than the average range of its components, because the components' price moves are not perfectly correlated. The average person buying and holding any one stock had more risk than a person buying and holding the index.

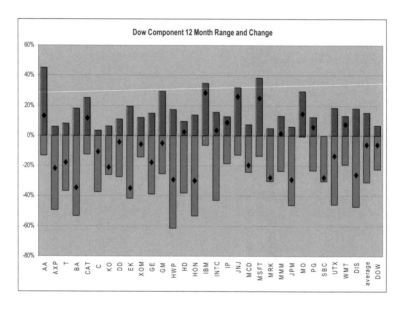

The second Dow component graph adds a black • to mark the closing price after 12 months. It is uncertain what the range and closing price for any equity will be. However, it is certain that the range of the index will be smaller than the range of the components, and that the average of the 12-month percent gains of components will equal the 12-month percent gain of the index.

Looking at the graph, it is easy to see how one could have made money. Go long the equities that have the highest gain, IBM, JNJ, and MSFT. Go short the equities that have the biggest loss (BA, EK, HWP, HON, MRK, JPM, SBC, DIS). The uncertainty of knowing which events will cause which equities to move in which direction creates the market. The market continues to exist because:

- some people think they can pick the next period's IBM, JNJ, and MSFT,

- some people think because the market was down in the last 12 months it will be up soon,

- some people think because IBM, JNJ, and MSFT are up they will continue going up,

- some people think because BA, EK, and HWP are down they will be up soon, and

- some people think the market is still overvalued based on their estimates of future earnings.

Without all these opinions and uncertainty, investors wouldn't have an incentive to trade, and the market would cease to exist. Uncertainty of detail is an essential element of a complex market.

The easy, conservative, John Bogle thing to do is to buy the index. The more aggressive will want to try to beat the index. If you threw one dart at a list of Dow stocks 12 months ago and held the stock there is a 10% (3/30) probability that you are up more than 20%, and a 33% (10/30) probability that you are down more than 20%.

"...it is in the market's interest to make itself as complex as possible. ...the end result is always the same: rising and falling prices. ...global structure and local randomness.

...paradox of capitalism and free markets: opportunity for everyone, but the advantage to no one. No one investment approach will work all of the time, at least in the short term. Many approaches will work some of the time. ... Uncertainty is the market's main source of stability and

> innovation. It needs uncertainty to perpetuate the competitive nature that is its lifeblood."[54]

The uncertainty of the short-term and of details begets risk. The certainty of the long-term and the complex mitigates risk.

Risk and Reward

Risk and Reward are positively correlated. Ask any finance professor, he will say, "The less risky your investments the less you are rewarded." The risk baseline, the least risky investment, is USA Treasuries. If you hold these securities to maturity you will be returned all your capital plus enjoy interest payments at the coupon rate. The USA government has never defaulted on its treasury commitments, and USA Treasuries are sometimes referred to as riskless investments. However, the "buy and hold" return is never more than initial investment plus interest. Investing in USA equities is more risky, investing in foreign equities is even more risky (because foreign exchange risk is added). On average, investing in equities has a greater return than holding USA Treasuries. The relative risk/rewards for six popular USA investment vehicles are ranked in the following table.

Relative Risk of Popular USA *Investments*

Investment Vehicle	Return Highest =1, Lowest =6	Risk Most =1, Least =6
Small Capitalization Stocks	1	1
Large Capitalization Stocks	2	2
Long-term Corporate Bonds	3	3
Long-term Government Bonds	4	4
Intermediate-term Gov. Bonds	5	5
USA Treasury Bills	6	6

Application is straightforward. If you need a risk-less investment, you buy USA Treasury Bills. If you need a high return, you buy small company common stock. If you need a high return but can't accept much risk, you buy long-term bonds, or build a portfolio of stocks and treasuries.

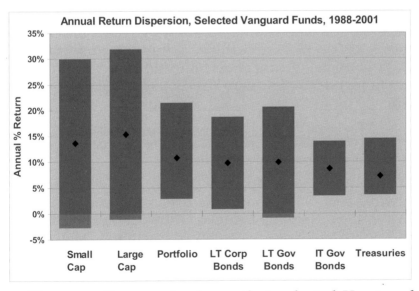

The preceding graph shows that selected Vanguard funds performed pretty much as predicted by the preceding table. Vertical bars show 65% confidence range around means. The portfolio bar assumes an equally weighted portfolio of the six Vanguard funds (remember John Bogle). The portfolio has less risk than all but the short-term and intermediate-term bond funds and a higher return than all but the common stock funds. The portfolio has less risk than the average of the risks of the 6 funds, (the average standard deviation is 10.3% and the portfolio standard deviation is 7.9%). The portfolio lost money in 1994 and only beat the large capitalization fund 5 out of 14 years, but it has less risk. Remember, in the opening paragraphs of *Trend Regression Portfolio Strategy*, I stated that my retirement accounts were spread evenly among 10 available options. The risk reduction shown in this graph is why. I had learned a little about MPT while getting my MBA.

Harry M. Markowitz invented Modern Portfolio Theory (MPT) during the 1950s, it became widely adopted in the 70s, and he won a Nobel Prize for it in 1990. For individual investors, financial planners use MPT as the basis for recommending diversifying your investment assets between fixed income securities and equities. Most financial planners recommend more equities for young investors and more fixed income for older investors.

> "The longer the time-period over which you can hold on to your investments, the greater should be the share of common stocks in your portfolio."[55]

This quote is supported by the opening graph for Part III, page 224 (Annual Returns on Common Stocks for Various Holding Periods, 1950-1997), both quote and graph are from page 355 of Burton G. Malkiel's *A Random Walk Down Wall Street*. Assuming future market action is not unlike patterns of time-period covered by this graph, someone with 25 years left until retirement would want to be 100% in equities. Low risk fixed income investments haven't yielded as much as the 7%

expected range bottom for 25-year return of holding common stocks.

In the Malkiel graph on page 224, the reduction of return-range with longer duration holding periods is as expected, same phenomenon as the graph on page 92 (TRiPS% Distribution by # of Weeks in Back-test). The decline in average return with longer duration was not expected. The decline in averages is most likely because individual years are not contained in equal proportions in all holding period duration samples. For instance, for one-year duration, 48 one-year samples are possible and all years have the same impact on the average. However, for 25-year duration, only 24 contiguous 25-year samples are possible and the years 1950 and 1997 are each in only one sample while 1973 and 1974 are in all 24 samples. Thus, 1973 and 1974 have 24 times the impact on the 25-year average as 1950 and 1997.

The following graph is a takeoff from the Malkiel graph. It uses Dow data back to 1929 adjusted for inflation and is adjusted for the unequal weighting of years in the contiguous samples.

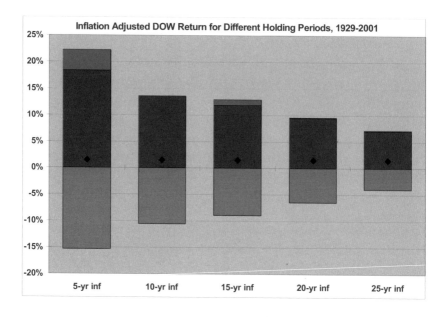

The mean return, black diamond, is 1.5% for each holding period. The 95% confidence levels are the top of the dark green and bottom of the red bars. The tops of the light green bars are outliers, holding period average annual gains that were greater then the 95% upper confidence limit. There were no downside outliers in this series of back-tests. The confidence limits narrow with longer holding periods, as expected. The 1.5% average annual gain is much less than the more than 10% in Malkiel's graph, because the years before 1950 had lower gains, these returns are inflation adjusted, and because these returns are based on geometric not arithmetic means. Adjusting for inflation measures the change in real wealth, the change in ability to buy things.

Geometric Mean

Geometric mean is an important concept in calculating future value for assets priced by a free market. The following table shows a few comparisons of geometric and arithmetic means.

GEOMETRIC MEAN

	% Change for Year	Year End Value as % Year Start	Balance		% Change for Year	Year End Value as % Year Start	Balance
Start	**A**		$1,000	**B**			$1,000
1st year	90%	190%	$1,900		-90%	10%	$ 100
2nd year	-90%	10%	$ 190		90%	190%	$ 190
	Arithmetic	Geometric			Arithmetic	Geometric	
mean	0.0%	-56.4%			0.0%	-56.4%	
Start	**C**		$1,000	**D**			$1,000
1st year	10%	110%	$1,100		-10%	90%	$ 900
2nd year	10%	110%	$1,210		-10%	90%	$ 810
	Arithmetic	Geometric			Arithmetic	Geometric	
mean	10.0%	10.0%			-10.0%	-10.0%	
Start	**E**		$1,000	**F**			$1,000
1st year	20%	120%	$1,200		40%	140%	$1,400
2nd year	40%	140%	$1,680		20%	120%	$1,680
	Arithmetic	Geometric			Arithmetic	Geometric	
mean	30.0%	29.6%			30.0%	29.6%	
Start	**G**		$1,000	**H**			$1,000
1st year	-20%	80%	$ 800		-40%	60%	$ 600
2nd year	-40%	60%	$ 480		-20%	80%	$ 480
	Arithmetic	Geometric			Arithmetic	Geometric	
mean	-30.0%	-30.7%			-30.0%	-30.7%	

In example A, starting with $1,000 account balance, the 1st year increases 90% to $1,900, and the 2nd year decreases by 90% from $1,900 to $190. The arithmetic average of plus 90% and minus 90% is 0%, but the account balance drops from $1,000 to $190. The $190 ending value is 19% of the starting value (100%+90%)*(100%-90%) or using the geometric average (100%-56.4%)*(100%-56.4%). Example B shows the final value doesn't depend on the order of the annual returns, only on the direction and magnitude. Examples C and D show that the geometric and arithmetic means are the same when return per year is constant. Examples E, F, G, and H show that geometric and arithmetic means are different as long as returns vary between years, regardless of the sign or timing of the returns.

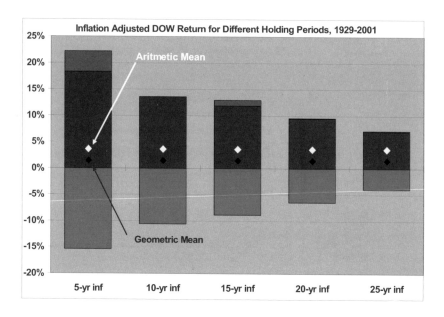

This is the same Inflation Adjusted Dow Return graph with the addition of arithmetic mean. The arithmetic mean is 3.6% compared to geometric mean of 1.5%, a big difference. Remember from the geometric mean table that the difference between geometric and arithmetic means flows from variability in annual returns. The more variability in annual returns the greater the difference between geometric and arithmetic means. Geometric means are always lower. If you believe the historical period being analyzed is a good basis from which to project into the future, use the geometric mean return to calculate future value.

The green and red bars should contain 95% of average annual return for each holding period. The upper and lower bounds of the 95% range are much farther apart than the arithmetic and geometric mean. This implies that selection of the time-period from which to project is important. If a 25-year, contiguous sample was pulled from the 1929-2001 period as being representative of what to expect for the next 25 years, then the range of means is 11.0% points compared to the difference between arithmetic and geometric means of 2.1% points.

Markowitz discovered that risk could be reduced by building a portfolio of investments as long as price movements of the investments do not have a high correlation. That means the Vanguard funds graph portfolio works (portfolio has reduced risk), because of the relative lack of correlation among the six funds, not because funds have different places on the risk/reward continuum.

Correlation between equities of a *Trend Regression Portfolio Strategy* group seems to be a predictive characteristic of a model's success. Generally, the higher the correlation between equities in the model, the better the performance of the model. Diversification will have to come from having multiple models with different group selection screens, or having some accounts using strategies other than *Trend Regression Portfolio Strategy*.

Risk, Reward, Systematic, Specific, Profit

I know, I know, you've heard it before, no pain–no gain, no guts–no glory, no risk–no reward.

Reward, the geometric mean of % return per period, is proportional to risk. In an efficient, rational world, investors are compensated for the increased risk, or they move their money into less risky investments. Systematic risk is market risk, the risk that the overall market price (index) will be volatile, will drop in price. Specific risk, unsystematic risk, is individual security price risk, the risk that the individual equity or debt instrument price will be volatile, will drop in price.

RISK MATRIX

	Systematic	Specific
Reduce Risk	Hedge	Diversify
Profit	Timing	Stock Picking

Systematic risk can be hedged away. Hedging involves taking opposing positions in a market. For instance if you are long $100,000 a portfolio of individual stocks you might short $100,000 of some market index. The market index chosen should be highly correlated with the individual stocks. The hedge dollar amount might be increased or decreased depending on the relationship of beta for your portfolio to beta for the market. For instance if your portfolio stocks are Dow stocks, the portfolio beta is 1.2, and the Dow beta is 0.95, then you should short the Dow index or Diamonds $ 126,316 (1.2 / 0.95 *$100,000) . The hedge dollar amount might be increased or decreased depending on the amount of risk you want to hedge away. If you hedge away all the market risk, you limit yourself to profiting from only specific risk. The success of hedging depends on the correlation of the instruments between the long and the short side.

Specific risk can be diversified away. Diversifying involves taking multiple positions, positions in uncorrelated or weakly correlated instruments. Portfolios of instruments with weak correlation provide some of the benefits of diversification. However, the more uncorrelated the price movements of component instruments the greater the risk reduction. The more instruments in your portfolio the greater the risk reduction. However, the more instruments in your portfolio the more effort it takes to manage it. USA Mutual Funds have diversification guidelines; no equity can be more than 25% of portfolio value, at least half of the portfolio value has to be composed of equities that are each less than 5% of portfolio value. Many trader/investors use a rule of thumb that they will never have any more than 10% of the trading capital in a single trade.

Systematic risk converts to profit through timing entries and exits. "Buy low–sell high," "Short high–cover low," "Buy high–sell higher." The timing strategy championed by the conservatives is "buy and hold," which works because of the long-term upward bias of the market. "Buy and hold" works better for indexes and for diversified portfolios, than for individual equities. "Buy and hold" works better for longer holding periods. Over time, the market moves higher, it has an inherent bias toward increasing prices. Time mitigates systematic risk. A few have mastered timing that is more aggressive. Many more have tried and continue to try. The masses are encouraged to try aggressive timing, as it looks so easy on historical charts with easy to see bottoms (buy) and tops (sell), and because we have all heard or read stories about people who are making money in the market.

Specific risk converts to profit through picking the right stocks. Microsoft rose from $1.285 in January 1990 to close 2001 at $66.25. General Electric rose from $5.188 in January 1990 to close 2001 at $40.08. Much analyst research and financial news is about individual companies and their expected performance. Much of Wall Street is commission based; Account Executives' pay often depends on how many companies you buy, how many transactions you make. Wall Street professionals' have an incentive to keep you buying and selling, but your trading of specific equities won't often have the underlying RRR of owning the market. Time won't mitigate the specific risk, as individual companies have shorter life cycles than economies. Even though "stock picking" strategies don't have the inherent upward bias of the market as a whole, some individual stocks can be saved by the rising market. "A rising tide floats all boats."

The overall economy has its up bias because growing world population and increasing individual productivity are combining to expand the economy. Within this overall expansion context, individuals and companies come and go. Committing to the market long term has risk, return can be predicted within probable ranges. Committing to individual companies long term is uncertain, returns cannot be predicted within useful probability ranges. The evolution of the Dow index has been mentioned earlier. Another example of the permanence of the market versus the impermanence of the individual companies is that, the Dow Industrial average was expanded to 30 companies on October 1, 1928 and by the end of 2001 only 4 remained. General Electric, General Motors, Allied Signal (descended from Allied Chemical & Dye), and Exxon (descended from Standard Oil of New Jersey) were among the 30 Dow companies on October 1, 1928 and survive as part of the Dow today. Some former Dow companies disappeared in reorganizations, and others are no longer benefiting from Dow status (Sears).

The number of births goes up more than the number of deaths goes up, and the population goes up. The upward march of population is only momentarily deterred by natural and man-made disasters. Product and service markets are born, grow, mature and die. The number of new companies goes up, the number of dissolutions goes up, and the economy grows. The upward march of gross world product is only briefly deterred by natural and man-made disasters. The complex world economic system is more robust than its components.

Diversification and hedging can be mixed in your portfolio to line up with your return objectives and risk tolerance. If you are a timer, you might want to trade index futures, or index-tracking stocks, as most specific risk is diversified out and profits and losses come from systematic risk. Since DIA, SPY, and QQQ are amalgams of a broad list of stocks, they reduce company and industry risk, leaving only market risk/opportunity. If you are a stock picker, you might want to consider correlation between your present and future holdings as you build and maintain your portfolio.

Hedging and diversifying can work to limit risk, and usually limit the opportunity for profit in the process, because of the link between return and risk. However, because price movements between equities are not perfectly correlated, diversification can provide the economist's dream, "free lunch."

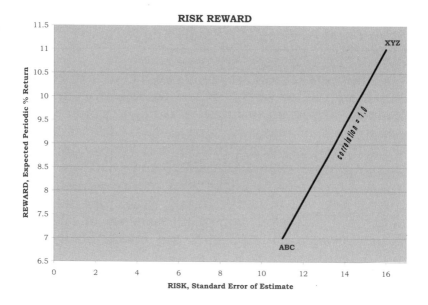

When the equities in your portfolio are perfectly correlated, there is no advantage to purchasing more than 1 equity. In the chart above, ABC is an equity with low risk and low return, and XYZ is an equity with higher risk and higher return. With equities ABC and XYZ having perfect positive price correlation, no combination will reduce risk from that of holding 100% of either. If every point along the line connecting risk/reward coordinates of individual equities has the same risk reward ratio (RRR) there is no gain from diversifying.

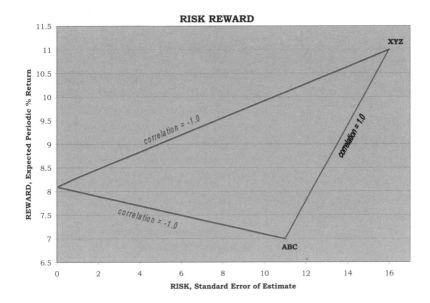

Maximum benefit from diversification is attained when there is perfect negative correlation between equities. If the prices of ABC and XYZ move exactly opposite to each other, holding any combination of the 2 equities will have less risk than holding either. An ideal combination with Ø risk exists with a return greater than ABC and lower than XYZ. In the above graph, this point is on the y-axis where the magenta lines meet the axis.

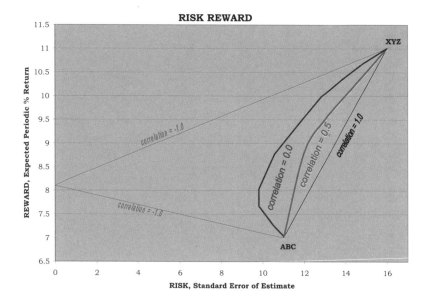

Most often, the correlation of 2 equities will be less than 1 and greater than -1. Every correlation will have a curved risk reward line existing in the space bounded by perfect positive and perfect negative correlation. As correlation drops the curved correlation moves left toward lower risk. At some point the correlation curve moves far enough left that it's left-most point is left of ABC's risk/reward coordinates. That point left of ABC has a higher return and lower risk than ABC. At that point, at that specific combination of holdings, holding a combination of ABC and XYZ has not only lower risk but also a higher return than holding ABC alone.

Because not many pairs of equities are perfectly correlated, most diversification results in a reduction of risk. As pairs of equities move from perfect positive correlation through imperfect correlation toward perfect negative correlation, there are situations where replacing some ABC with XYZ will provide "free lunch," greater return and lower risk simultaneously. The preceding graphs were theoretical constructs. The following is based on 10-year Treasury bond yield and S&P 500 index gains, 1979 through 2001.

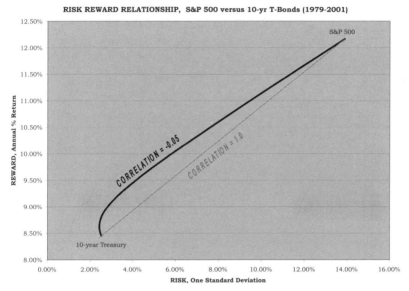

RISK REWARD RELATIONSHIP, S&P 500 versus 10-yr T-Bonds (1979-2001)

Source: Yardeni.com

Based on the above, adding some S&P 500 equity to a portfolio of bonds reduces risk while increasing average annual return. At least, it reduced risk during the time-period of the sample, 1979 through 2001. The correlation of -0.05, very close to Ø, implies that interest rates and stock market returns are uncorrelated. It's all about risk, diversifying can reduce risk below the risk of holding the single least risky investment, or it can increase return while holding risk at that of the single least risky investment, but it can't increase reward above that of the most risky investment. The lowest risk point and best Reward Risk Ratio (RRR) are at a mix of 6% S&P 500 and 94% T-Bonds. The y-axis return for 10-year bonds is interest only ignoring price change, assuming bonds bought and held to maturity.

The y-axis return for S&P 500 is index gain only ignoring dividends. The x-axis risk is the amount of annual return equal to 1 standard deviation. So, from the graph the mean 10-year treasury return is 8.5% and there is 67% probability that any year has 8.5% ± 2.6% return.

The above graph is for 1-year average returns, but what about longer holding periods.

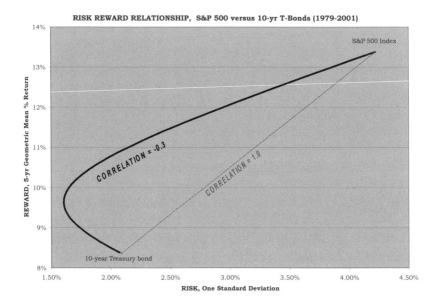

The longer holding period decreases risk and increases the effect of diversification on risk reduction. The above graph assumes a 5-year holding period. The lowest risk point is at a mix of 25% S&P 500 and 75% T-Bonds, and best Reward Risk Ratio (RRR) is at a mix of 30% S&P 500 and 70% T-Bonds. A mix of 70% S&P 500 and 30% T-Bonds has a higher RRR than a 100% T-Bonds portfolio. Notice that correlation starts to move beyond uncorrelated to negative correlation. This seems to imply that interest rate reductions take years to affect stock price appreciation. The change in risk shown by the lower values on the x-axis, compared to the previous 1-year graph, is the result of the beneficial effect of the longer time-period. The change in reward at the 100% bonds and 100% S&P 500 ends of the curves is due to the 5-year averaging processes' bias toward middle years. As long as all of the data in the 1979-2001 period are weighted equally, average returns should stay the same regardless of the holding period.

RISK REWARD RELATIONSHIP, S&P 500 versus 10-yr T-Bonds (1979-2001)

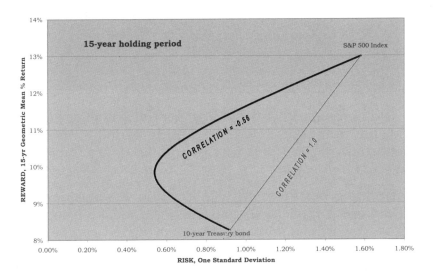

The longer the holding period the bigger the decrease in risk, and the greater the effect of diversification on risk reduction. The above graph assumes a 15-year holding period. The lowest risk point is at a mix of 33% S&P 500 and 67% T-Bonds, and best Reward Risk Ratio (RRR) is at a mix of 36% S&P 500 and 64% T-Bonds. A mix of 90% S&P 500 and 10% T-Bonds has a higher RRR than a 100% T-Bonds portfolio. Notice that correlation moves farther toward negative correlation. This seems to imply that low interest rates have a lasting effect on stock price appreciation. The change in risk shown by the lower values on the x-axis, compared to the previous 1-year and 5-year graphs, is the result of the beneficial effect of the longer time-period.

RRR varies with holding period and mix.

RRR and Holding Period

RRR	HOLDING PERIOD		
Reward Risk Ratio	1-year	5-year	15-year
10-YR T-Bonds	333%	401%	900%
Optimized Mix	355%	608%	1841%
S&P 500	88%	317%	822%
S&P 500 in Optimized Mix	6%	30%	36%

RRR increases with holding period, the effect of optimizing increases with holding period, and the proportion of S&P 500 in the optimized mix increases with holding period.

Building portfolios with more than 2 securities is a little more complicated, but the basic ideas of populating your portfolio with the least correlated components and holding your portfolio for a long time persist. Remember though, you are building a portfolio for future reward; rewards and correlations that existed in the past, are history.

11. Cycles

Yield Curve

If risk decreases with holding period, why does the normal yield curve look the way it does?

YIELD CURVES

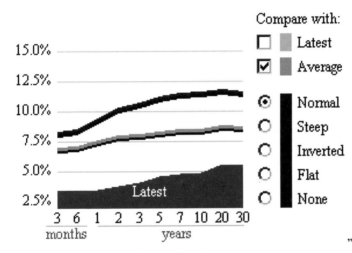

source = http://www.smartmoney.com/onebond/index.cfm?story=yieldcurve#menu

In the graphic above, the latest (blue area), average (green line), and normal yield curves all show lowest rates at shortest maturities increasing gradually to highest rates at longest maturities. Lower rates are normal for shorter maturities because there is greater likelihood of default for longer maturities, greater likelihood of inflation for longer maturities, and greater likelihood of lost investment opportunities for longer maturities. Lenders like the feel of cash in their pockets and want to charge more the longer it is out of pocket.

The www.smartmoney.com site contains lots of interesting free information plus a subscription service. Smartmoney's yield curve page is especially interesting and useful. The animated yield curve runs as a "yieldcurve movie" showing the evolution of the yield-curve over the last 18 years. The mini movie is entertaining and with the surrounding text very educational.

Do longer loans being perceived as more risky contradict the earlier RRR calculations that show less risk with longer holding periods? No! That would be comparing apples and oranges. Holding a portfolio of priced equities is different from holding a fixed return instrument. Say you need $20,000 for a deal coming up in 90 days, you would accept a lower interest rate with a guaranteed return of your principal, rather than invest in something that pays a higher return but doesn't protect your principal. Or say you have $100,000 you don't need until you retire in 10 years, 10-year bond rates have to be higher for you to consider bonds an alternative to common stock.

Life-Cycle

Malkiel and most investment advisor/financial planners advise the life cycle approach to portfolio building. Malkiel is referring to the human life cycle, not the company life cycle discussed earlier. The human life cycle approach generally recommends more common stocks than bonds for the young and more bonds than common stocks for those approaching retirement. The basic underlying idea is that time mitigates risk, and those approaching retirement have less time. Let's see!

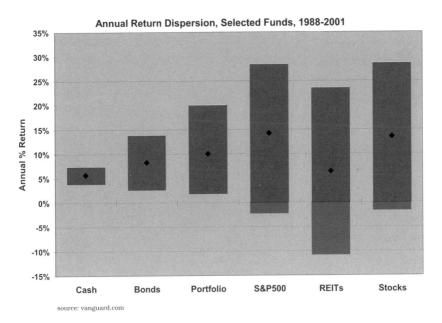

source: vanguard.com

This is the graph with Malkiel's recommended allocation for those in their fifties. It seems to work for the
14-year test period, return is greater than for holding
cash only, and risk is less than for holding common
stocks only. The Vanguard REIT fund recommend by
Malkiel didn't start until 1995 so early years data came
from REIT-Diversified Index available on **moneycen-
tral.msn.com.**

Malkiel Life-Cycle Allocation Guide

Years to Retirement	Cash	Bonds	REIT	Stocks
More than 30	5	20	10	65
15 to 30	5	30	10	55
5 to 15	5	37.5	12.5	45
Less than 5	10	50	15	25

The next graph compares portfolio risk/reward for
the different age groups.

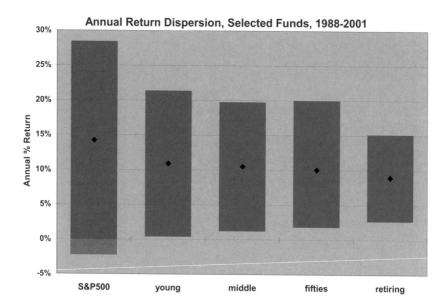

For the 14-year period 1988 – 2001, life-cycle alloca-tion changes would have achieved their objective of reducing risk as retirement got closer. How much did this reduction in risk cost, assuming starting with $100,000 at the end of 1987?

Life-Cycle Portfolio End Values

	12/31/1987	1/1/2002	B(W) S&P500
S&P500	$ 100,000	$739,604	
young	$ 100,000	$452,115	$(287,489.14)
middle	$ 100,000	$424,122	$(315,482.04)
fifties	$ 100,000	$395,198	$(344,406.56)
retiring	$ 100,000	$339,001	$(400,603.04)

The cost of mitigating risk seems steep. The Annual Dispersion graph shows the 65% confidence range for any 1 year. The end values are calculated from the means for the 14-year period. A confidence range for the mean can also be calculated. The graph below analyses the 4 life-cycle portfolios a little more.

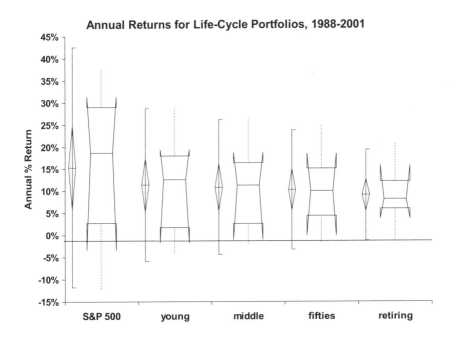

This graph shows that if you kept your life-cycle portfolio through the 1988-2001 period, diversification did little to diminish downside risk while limiting upside potential greatly. The graph is from Analyse-it. The blue diamond shows the mean and the 95% confidence interval around the mean. The horizontal line at the widest part of the diamond is the mean. The vertical high and low points of the diamond are the 95% confidence limits for the mean of annual average returns. The blue lines show 95% confidence range for annual average returns. The notched box shows the median, lower and upper quartiles, and 95% confidence interval around the median. The middle horizontal line at the narrowest point of the notched box is the median. The upper and lower ends of the notch mark the 95% confidence limits of the median. The upper and lower horizontal lines mark the upper and lower quartiles. The table below compares mean 95% confidence levels and their effect on ending balances for the life-cycle portfolios.

	Geometric Mean	95% CI of Mean		End Value 95 low	End Value Mean	End Value 95 High
S&P 500	14.2%	5.4%	23.0%	209	643	1,822
young	10.9%	5.1%	16.7%	200	426	872
middle	10.5%	5.3%	15.7%	207	405	769
fifties	10.0%	5.4%	14.6%	209	381	677
retiring	8.9%	5.4%	12.5%	209	332	520

End values are in thousands of dollars. The 95% confidence lower limit calculates to the same dollar end value for the S&P 500 as for any of the life-cycle portfolios. The following graph uses end value data from the table above.

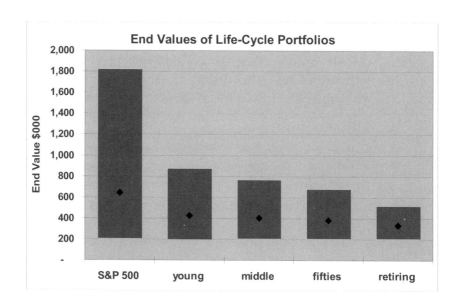

The graph immediately points out the power of compounding. The end values calculated from mean returns are not centered between end values calculated from the high and low 95% confidence limits, even though the 95% confidence limits are equidistant from the mean. The mean annual return for the S&P 500 is only 3.3 percentage points (14.2% versus 10.9%) greater than the mean annual return for the young portfolio, however the mean end value for the S&P 500 is 51% greater than the end value for the young portfolio.

There is nothing magic about the 14 years 1988-2001. I used that range because when I started looking at Vanguard Funds it seemed that a lot of them had data back to 1988. There is no guarantee that what happened in this period will happen in the future.

The graph should make you think about the applicability of life-cycle portfolios for you. The graph should make you think about your concept of risk. Is risk the range of annual returns? Is risk the range of end values? Is risk the minimum end value? Is risk the probability that the end value will be lower than the start value?

Another consideration on compounding is the effect of inflation. Inflation during this period averaged 3.25% with a standard deviation of 1.05%. Investment return builds your real wealth while inflation eats away at it. Reducing all returns by the inflation rate increases the percent advantage of the S&P 500 over the young portfolio from 51% to 53%.

What if you want to retire now? Say your MD thinks you are in reasonably good health, and your life insurance actuary table says you will live another 14 years. Say the market is improving, and we expect the next 14 years to be statistically the same as the 1988-2001 period and the IRS thinks it will be okay if you use the "term certain" method and distribute the reciprocal of your years to live each year.   If you have $1,000 left in your IRA and a life expectancy of 14 years, you take out $1,000 times 1/14 equals $71 to spend.   If you have $1,000 left in your IRA and a life expectancy of 5 years, you take out $1,000 times 1/5 equals $200 to spend.

Say you have $100,000 in your IRA. You read *Die Broke*[56] and you want to die with only enough money to pay for your burial. How much do you have to spend per year?

Annual Return Assumptions

Portfolio	**Cash**	**Bonds**	**Retiring**	**S&P 500**
mean annual Return	5.67%	8.28%	8.95%	14.22%

The tables on the next two pages show how much you can spend each year if you realize the above returns and leave 100% of the remaining nest egg in Cash, Bonds, Retiring portfolio or S&P 500, All options leave you with $0 at the end of 14 years.

Annual Distribution from Retirement Portfolio (constant annual return)

Start $ 100,000

Year	Reciprocal	Balance before Distribution				Annual Distribution			
		Cash	Bonds	Retiring	S&P 500	Cash	Bonds	Retiring	S&P 500
1	7.1%	105673	108282	108945	114222	$ 7,548	$ 7,734	$ 7,782	$ 8,159
2	7.7%	103692	108875	110213	121147	$ 7,976	$ 8,375	$ 8,478	$ 9,319
3	8.3%	101146	108824	110835	127732	$ 8,429	$ 9,069	$ 9,236	$ 10,644
4	9.1%	97977	108017	110687	133739	$ 8,907	$ 9,820	$ 10,062	$ 12,158
5	10.0%	94124	106331	109626	138872	$ 9,412	$ 10,633	$ 10,963	$ 13,887
6	11.1%	89517	103624	107489	142759	$ 9,946	$ 11,514	$ 11,943	$ 15,862
7	12.5%	84085	99739	104093	144944	$ 10,511	$ 12,467	$ 13,012	$ 18,118
8	14.3%	77749	94499	99229	144863	$ 11,107	$ 13,500	$ 14,176	$ 20,695
9	16.7%	70422	87708	92661	141827	$ 11,737	$ 14,618	$ 15,444	$ 23,638
10	20.0%	62015	79143	84125	134998	$ 12,403	$ 15,829	$ 16,825	$ 27,000
11	25.0%	52426	68559	73320	123357	$ 13,107	$ 17,140	$ 18,330	$ 30,839
12	33.3%	41551	55678	59909	105675	$ 13,850	$ 18,559	$ 19,970	$ 35,225
13	50.0%	29272	40193	43512	80470	$ 14,636	$ 20,096	$ 21,756	$ 40,235
14	100.0%	15466	21761	23702	45957	$ 15,466	$ 21,761	$ 23,702	$ 45,957
	Total			14-year	Dist.	$ 155,036	$ 191,115	$ 201,678	$ 311,736

The table above assumes mean annual return is earned through the year and distribution is made at the end of the year. This table is a good argument for leaving your retirement nest egg in common stock after you retire. However, in this table every year gets the same percent return, what about the risk, what about the variability between years? We can simulate future possibilities assuming the future is like the 1988-2001 period and that future variances are distributed normally.

Annual Distribution from Retirement Portfolio (variable annual return)

Start	$ 100,000	Balance before Draw				Annual Draw			
Year	Reciprocal	Cash	Bonds	Retiring	S&P 500	Cash	Bonds	Retiring	S&P 500
1	7.1%	106207	124082	112077	119170	$ 7,586	$ 8,863	$ 8,005	$ 8,512
2	7.7%	104216	127362	110774	161078	$ 8,017	$ 9,797	$ 8,521	$ 12,391
3	8.3%	103712	116025	98590	204171	$ 8,643	$ 9,669	$ 8,216	$ 17,014
4	9.1%	101310	118165	96761	195250	$ 9,210	$ 10,742	$ 8,796	$ 17,750
5	10.0%	97161	115108	93078	229095	$ 9,716	$ 11,511	$ 9,308	$ 22,909
6	11.1%	91472	115100	84443	259317	$ 10,164	$ 12,789	$ 9,383	$ 28,813
7	12.5%	84473	106744	74723	225262	$ 10,559	$ 13,343	$ 9,340	$ 28,158
8	14.3%	78502	102190	79831	221884	$ 11,215	$ 14,599	$ 11,404	$ 31,698
9	16.7%	72543	96823	83119	204685	$ 12,090	$ 16,137	$ 13,853	$ 34,114
10	20.0%	64312	92832	71557	203270	$ 12,862	$ 18,566	$ 14,311	$ 40,654
11	25.0%	52995	84188	62366	145506	$ 13,249	$ 21,047	$ 15,592	$ 36,376
12	33.3%	42638	64808	51545	142651	$ 14,213	$ 21,603	$ 17,182	$ 47,550
13	50.0%	30190	45321	38944	108625	$ 15,095	$ 22,660	$ 19,472	$ 54,313
14	100.0%	16032	23642	19506	62933	$ 16,032	$ 23,642	$ 19,506	$ 62,933
						$ 158,650	$ 214,968	$ 172,890	$ 443,185

This table shows more variability in the annual distribution. All but the cash portfolio column has at least 1 year when the distribution is less than an earlier year. Simulation is based on normal distribution and random number generation. Once you set up an Excel model to do the simulation, it just takes a keystroke to do another simulation run. Each new simulation run is interesting and unique.

Even more interesting is the dispersion of total distributions obtained from multiple simulation runs. This graph is a summary of 100 simulation runs.

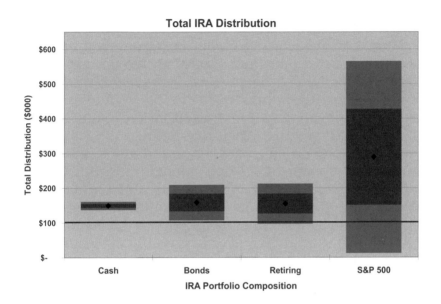

The black diamonds are the mean total distribution for each IRA portfolio strategy. The dark green bar contains the 65% confidence interval for mean total distribution, and the light green bars extend the confidence interval to 95%. If you invest all your retirement nest egg in an S&P 500 index fund, there is a chance you will be able to draw out less than the amount you start with. The simulation started with $100,000, blue horizontal line. This seems a very clear picture of the relationship between risk and reward. If you are able to accept the risk of putting you nest egg in the S&P 500 you can potentially enjoy a much greater return. From the graph, the probability of the S&P 500 paying out more than the Retiring portfolio is more than 70%, the probability of the S&P 500 paying out more than the cash portfolio is more than 80%. The probability of the

S&P 500 paying out less than the starting amount is less than 10%. Variability between simulation runs is great, but variability between the means and standard deviations of means for sets of 100 simulation runs is not great.

I am not alone in my belief that commonly recommended asset allocations are far too conservative. Lowell Miller in *The Single Best Investment*[57] says "Except for short-term parking of funds and to preserve fixed amounts that you may need in five years or less, all investors, whether they are retirees on corporate pension plans or churches or foundations must say goodbye to bonds, bills, CDs, money market funds..." and other fixed income investments. Miller has concluded that fixed income investments never yield as much as stock investments except in the short term. He points out that short-term investments sometimes fail even to match inflation.

How you choose to invest your retirement nest egg will depend on your desire and ability to accept risk. If you set up your retirement with a lot of fixed expense, mortgage, rent, utilities, insurance, health care, club dues, grandchildren's education, you may not be able to accept much risk. If you can reduce your fixed expense and be more flexible, you may be able to accept more risk. Being flexible means spending more when you have it and less when you don't. Some categories invite flexibility; gifts to relatives and other charities, travel, new cars, new TVs and other appliances, and your education. Other categories require creativity, work, or sacrifice to reduce expenditure: housing, food, health care. Living in a tent on the beach might be fun for a night, but it will start to drag as your eightieth birthday approaches and the temperature drops below freezing.

Volatility, risk, is the enemy of spending. Your spending plans determine your ability to accept volatility. You don't want your peak spending to coincide with a bear market. Gains are pay for accepting fluctuation in price, for accepting the chance that price will be low when you need cash.

Wait a minute! On page 245 15-year RRR is maximized when the stocks are only 36% of our portfolio, now we want to be 100% stocks because chances are we will make more money. Part of the problem with RRR, in this situation, is that it is based on standard deviation, which measures volatility, not risk of loss in terminal value. Remember standard deviation measures both positive and negative deviation from expected.

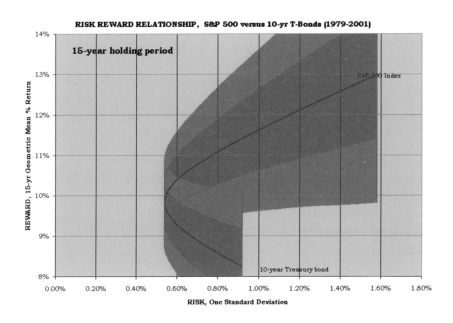

This above graph uses the same data as the 15-year graph on page 245. The dark blue line is the same Reward Risk Ratio (RRR) line as on page 245. The blue band is RRR plus and minus one standard deviation. The green band is RRR plus and minus 2 standard deviations. RRR peaks where the dark blue line reaches its lowest x-axis value, standard deviation (risk) is .54, return is 9.8%, RRR is 1826%, and the mix is 36% S&P 500 and 64% T-Bonds. For 100% S&P 500 portfolio, risk is 1.58, return is 13.0%, and RRR is 822%. If RRR is our sole criteria, the 36/64 diversification is much better than 100% equities. However, there is only 2.5% probability that the 100% S&P 500 portfolio has annual return less than 9.8%. It is coincidental that the 36/64 portfolio mean and the 100% S&P 500 mean minus 2 standard deviations both equal 9.8%. The ignoring of bond price changes and equity dividends is questionable and the 13% S&P 500 annual return is greater than normally quoted 11% long term common stock returns. Different historical sampling would create different RRR curves, and projecting future expectations from historical data is not foolproof. In spite of the aforementioned concerns, long-term investors who concentrate on maximizing RRR will probably end up with less money than those who focus on maximizing return. Return is the reward for taking on risk.

Lowell Miller is a proponent of allocating portfolios entirely to common stock. He worries that bond investments might not beat inflation. He recognizes that stock prices fluctuate, but feels "greater return... is a kind of payment for tolerating the fact that the value of your principal may bounce up and down."[58]

Reverse Mortgage

The basic ideas behind a reverse mortgage are that you want to live in your house, your house is paid for (or at least you have a lot of equity in it), you need a source of living expense. You get a monthly payment stream, or a lump sum, and the bank gets paid off when you die or sell. The bank doesn't usually end up owning your house, you or your heirs pay off the bank by selling or refinancing. What reverses is the direction the loan principal balance moves. With a regular mortgage, the balance owed is reduced with each payment, in a reverse mortgage the principal balance increases as payments flow to you or as interest accrues.

Instead of a rising debt reverse mortgage, consider a new bigger cash out mortgage, with all excess proceeds going into an investment account. The basic idea is you pay the mortgage and other fixed essentials every month from the account. If the account balance is greater than the mortgage balance, you splurge, and if the account balance is less than the mortgage, you scrimp.

It is probably best to invest conservatively, everything in SPY, follow Drach's newsletter, or follow a *Trend Regression Portfolio Strategy*. Remember the RRR curves between bonds and S&P 500, interest rates and S&P 500 yield are uncorrelated using annual data. A portfolio of debt and equity securities is less risky than a portfolio of either. Therefore, a portfolio of equity securities financed with variable rate debt is more risky than a portfolio built with cash. You can reduce the risk by locking in a fixed rate when long rates are low and taking advantage of knowing that for longer periods fixed investment yields tend to be inversely correlated with common stock yields, and knowing that your interest rate won't increase.

I built new bigger mortgage models in February 2002, but didn't close my new mortgage until July 29, 2002. The delay was mostly waiting for my conservative gut to catch up with my aggressive head. I knew in my head that it was financially the right thing to do, but I just kept dragging my feet. I closed a 15-year fixed rate mortgage at 5.918% APR as the S&P 500 closed at 898.96.

I had created a new FOLIO*fn* account for my mortgage strategy. Originally, I planned to use this account as my living account, running all my checking through it, to improve efficiency over multiple accounts. Ultimately, I decided to keep this a pure mortgage strategy account with the only checks out, mortgage payments and excess withdrawals. Excess equals account balance minus mortgage balance. I funded the account with the net amount of the mortgage, mortgage less points and closing expenses. My plan was to follow Drach's market timing letter. I had missed Drach's move from 6% equities to 100% equities by a few weeks, but decided to go slow, bringing equities to 100% over 3 weeks rather than all at once. When the account reached 100% equities, average cost was 99% of account that matched Drach's timing. So, the delay in closing the mortgage had actually helped get better prices. Drach had been a little early.

August, 2002, was a pretty good month, the S&P climbed ½% and my mortgage account climbed 6%. After making the first mortgage payment, the account still held $5,000 more than the mortgage balance. I transferred the excess $5,000 to my living account. The plan was to transfer excesses out, but not to fund shortfalls unless account balance fell below next due mortgage payment amount.

Performance since taking out the $5,000 excess hasn't been as good. No further excesses have been withdrawn and after making 7 payments account equity is at 96.8% of principal balance. I'm still convinced long-term financially it is the right thing to do.

12. Issues

Love

Love is best when it is reciprocal. One-way love can be dangerous. Try not to fall in love with the equities in your portfolio; they don't love you.[59] Love your kin, your neighbor, not your equities.

Proponents of buy and hold sometimes say that you should know as much as possible about the equities you own, or want to own. You should know the companies' fundamentals, know the products, know the management, know the financial statements, and know the competition. You should consider yourself part of the company, a stakeholder. You should buy companies you understand and trust. I think the proponents of buy and hold are entitled to their opinions.

I also think spending that much time with your equities puts you emotionally at risk of getting too familiar with them. Please read "Confused about Earnings?" Page 77, of Business Week's November 26, 2001 issue. If you are a fundamentalist, this Business Week article should wake you up.

Trend Regression Portfolio Strategy is mechanical, no emotion, and no love.

Okay! okay! If you just can't stop loving your stock picks, find 50 stocks that you love, put them in a *Trend Regression Portfolio Strategy* model and go long the 3 that are most oversold. However, don't forget to update the model weekly and follow the trades generated.

News

News affects price. News increases volatility. News can be good or bad or neutral. Price reaction can be up or down, or sideways. Price move and news, cause and effect is usually much clearer in hindsight. News can drive the market or move a single equity. Traders make money trading news or rumors about news. "Buy the rumor, sell the news" is popular trader gospel.

Trend Regression Portfolio Strategy is not a news system. News is a source of volatility, uncertainty. To limit individual equity news risk the portfolio manager should limit exposure by keeping investment in any company to 10% of holdings. Limiting market news risk is harder. Market news risk might be mitigated by having multiple strategies in multiple markets, but it will depend on the news. Market news risk might be mitigated by reducing equity to cash ratio, but most backtests optimized on 100% long.

Fundamental and Technical Analysis

Drach:

> "Fundamental vs. Technical: There seems to be some sort of ongoing competition among market pundits as to the relative merits of fundamental or technical analyses as though each must be considered separately and we are repeatedly asked our opinion. The fact is that credible data is a blend. In our theory/application, Master List construction is purely fundamental (attempting to isolate corporations of superior fundamental quality). From there, it can be considered to shift to technical by concentrating on credible data (standard accounting, structural, psychological, professional positioning) that can be relegated to probability distributions. However, all credible data has a logical base, i.e., the printouts of raw numbers are from what are effectively measurements of fundamental and/or behavioral factors translated to pure numerical form."

Drach is right on, it isn't an either/or thing. Fundamental analysis and technical analysis are tools portfolio managers use. Just like carpenters have both hammers and saws in their house building toolbox, and just like tailors use both scissors and sewing machines to make clothes; portfolio managers use fundamental and technical analysis.

Fundamental analysis is determination of a company's theoretical value based on analysis of internal company information, industry information, and macro political and economic information. Input data includes company reports, company financials, industry outlook, news, economic reports, etc. All the information collected about the company and its environment supports projected future earnings calculations, which are then discounted back to a present day theoretical value. Most of the professionals on Wall Street rely on fundamental analysis.

When Wall Street thinks stocks are priced below their theoretical value they issue buy recommendations and when they think stocks are priced above their theoretical value they issue sell recommendations. An easy, interesting paper-trading experiment for you is to buy on Wall Street recommendations and sell on Wall Street recommendations. Wall Street Analyst recommendations are available on the internet at moneycentral.msn.com, Zacks.com, and probably other sites. This paper-trading test has never produced well for me. Professor Burton G. Malkiel[60] has a good explanation of why stock analysts' records are poor. Calculating theoretical value from future earnings is not a big deal. The problem is future earnings.[61] Who knows the future? For self-directed investors, another problem is that analyst ratings provide no edge, as everybody gets the information at the same time.

Fundamental analysis is also the determination of the market's direction based on analysis of economic data. Check out http://205.232.165.149/stocklab.asp. Dr. Ed Yardeni is Chief Investment Strategist, and a Managing Director of Prudential Securities Incorporated, in New York. The site has a lot of interesting and useful information. I particularly like the weekly valuation which calculates how over or under valued the S&P 500 is based on.

$$FVP = \frac{E}{CBY - b * LTEG}$$

$$FairValue\,Price = \frac{ExpectedEarnings}{CorporateBondYield - b * LongTermEarningsGrowth}$$

That is, the Fair Value Price of the S&P 500 index equals Expected operating Earnings divided by [Moody's A-rated Corporate Bond Yield minus an earnings growth coefficient times Long-Term Expected Earnings Growth]. Expected operating earnings uses the 12-month forward consensus earnings estimates compiled by Thomson Financial First Call. Long term expected earnings growth uses consensus five-year earnings growth projections from I/B/E/S International. The earnings growth factor "b" adjusts long term earnings projections for weight market has given long-term earnings growth in past.

Dr. Yardeni's valuation analysis and explanation are very thorough, very convincing, and he carries his analysis through to a recommendation of a stocks/bond allocation ratio. I've tried to use his valuations as market timing indicators, without success. His weekly valuation letter recommends appropriate Common Stock/Bond allocations based on how much the S&P 500 is currently over or under valued. This graph shows the progress of a $10,000 investment made in January 1988, buy and hold versus *Yardeni timed*.

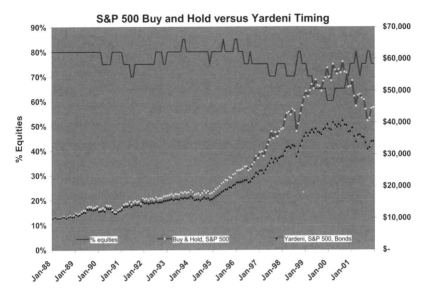

Ignoring stock dividends, bond interest, commissions and slippage, buy and hold was ahead by nearly $10,000 after 14 years 1/88 through 12/01. Buy and hold has more risk. R^2 is .86 for buy and hold and .89 for *Yardeni timed*. Maximum drawdown is 30% for buy and hold and 20% for *Yardeni timed*. Bond yield is usually higher than dividend yield. A 3% premium for bond yield would only reduce the buy and hold advantage by $2,478 to $7,516 for the 14 year period. Dr. Yardeni's fundamental analysis driven market timing didn't work (that is, didn't beat buy and hold return) for the period tested. Out of 156 12-month holding periods possible, *Yardeni timing* beat buy and hold only 22 times. In this test Vanguard GNMA (VFIIX) was used as a proxy for bonds, and the S&P 500 ($INX) index was used as a proxy for common stocks.

The stock/bond allocations on the graph look timely, but it didn't work. A simple manual optimization attempt of changing the stock allocation range to 80 to 100 instead of the original 60 to 90, made Yardeni timed better than buy and hold by $195. A subsequent delaying of the timing effect increased the Yardeni timed advantage to $591. These improvements are interesting, but may have no applicability to the future. All these changes really prove is that it is relatively easy to look at a historical chart and come up with a scheme that beats buy and hold.

Technical analysis is the determination of a company's perceived value based on price movement. Input comes from price and volume data and includes calculated indicators and price graphs. Technical analysis is also the determination of the economy's position in economic cycle based on price action. Technical analysis is used on Wall Street less than fundamental analysis. The cynical claim full service brokers invented technical analysis to increases broker commissions by increasing trading volume.

Fundamental analysis is how things should be (what the price should be), based on business fundamentals. Technical analysis is, given historic price action what should happen next. Fundamental analysis is, 'this is a good company, with strong management, a strong balance sheet, a lower PEG than its peers, a growing market, great products; therefore the price should go up.' Technical analysis is, 'the price is trending up; therefore the price should go up.' Technical analysis is, 'the price is down so far, it has to go up.'

Fundamental analysis tries to make a *cause and effect* relationship. For instance, price climbs on news of increased earnings because price moves with the theoretical value of a stock, which is a function of its future earnings. Technical analysis tries to assess the changing market perception of the equities value. Fundamental analysis is about business while Technical analysis is about emotion, psychology. For instance, the reason a previous high becomes a resistance point for a climbing price, is that many who bought at the previous high will sell when they can eliminate their loser by getting out at breakeven. For instance, the reason a previous low becomes a support point for a falling price, is that many who missed a buying opportunity at the previous low will buy when they can get a bargain, because they are afraid of missing the next advance.

Trend Regression Portfolio Strategy can be all technical analysis. For instance picking 50 equities based on price correlation to an index, placing trades based on relative price, and varying equities/cash ratio by number of equities with price lower than "X" weeks ago. I have used fundamental analysis in *Trend Regression Portfolio Strategy* models for stock selection, to build the group of 50. Fundamental analysis could also, maybe, be used for entries and exits, and for market timing, if a source of historic fundamental data was available.

Leverage

The 2 most popular ways to leverage equity investments are margin and options. Leveraging can increase returns, but it also often increases risk dramatically. Without leverage, losses are limited to equity, you only stand to lose your life savings. With leverage, losses can exceed equity, you can lose more than your life savings and end up owing.

Margin

Margin is the use of broker capital to increase purchase power. Margin is a terrific idea if the percent gain on trading is greater than margin interest. Margin can possibly increase return while always exposing you to more risk. If you limit equity positions to your account equity, all you risk is your account equity. When you borrow from your broker you risk your account equity plus the amount you have borrowed. If your positions go against you, you can lose more than you have, and find yourself owing your broker and worrying about how to climb back to Ø.

To operate on margin you need a strategy with which you are very comfortable.

Options

Using options to increase leverage is pretty straight-forward; you can capture a portion of the change in equity prices with the purchase of an option for less than the cost of taking a position in the underlying security. Using options to reduce risk can be a little more complicated[62] A simple risk control is that when purchasing calls or puts instead of buying or shorting equities the loss is limited to the cost of the option. This is similar to taking a position in a stock then putting in a stop loss order to minimize loss. A slightly more complicated way of reducing risk is buying puts to insure a minimum sale price for a long position, or buying calls to insure a maximum purchase price for a short position.

There is lots of objective information about options available, in the *Characteristics and Risks of Standardized Options*[63] at option broker websites, and at the Options Industry Council website www.888options.com. I haven't found an option strategy that enhances *Trend Regression Portfolio Strategy* performance.

Leverage, Diversification and Risk

Using leverage to diversify will probably not reduce risk. The risk taken on by leveraging will often over-shadow the risk reduction from diversification. Diversification by spreading your equity over more positions reduces risk. However, diversification by establishing new positions with leverage adds new risk to existing risk.

Remember standard deviation (s) = the square root of the sum of deviation squared divided by the number of samples.

$$s = \sqrt{s^2} = \sqrt{\frac{\sum (d)^2}{N}}$$

Starting with a portfolio of 100 shares of equity A with a price per share standard deviation of 2, the standard deviation (s_p) of the portfolio is 200.

$$s_p = 100 * s$$

$$s_p = 100 * 2 = 200$$

If A and B are independent, then the variance of sum is equal to the sum of the variances

$$s^2(A+B) = s^2(A) + s^2(B)$$

and the standard deviation of the sum is equal to the square root of the sums of the variances

$$s_{A+B} = \sqrt{s^2(A) + s^2(B)}$$

If you sell 50 shares of A to purchase 50 shares of equity B, which has the same price and price per share standard deviation as A, but has price moves uncorrelated with price moves of A, the standard deviation of the portfolio is less than 200.

$$s_p = \sqrt{(50 * s)^2 + (50 * s)^2}$$

$$s_p = \sqrt{(50*2)^2 + (50*2)^2} = 141.4$$

If you keep 100 shares of A and purchase 100 shares of equity B, which has the same price and price per share standard deviation as A, but has price moves uncorrelated with price moves of A, the standard deviation of the portfolio is more than 200.

$$s_p = \sqrt{(100*s)^2 + (100*s)^2}$$

$$s_p = \sqrt{(100*2)^2 + (100*2)^2} = 282.8$$

So, 282.8 is to 200 the same as 141.4 is to 100, relative risk hasn't really changed.

Say the share price of A and B is $20, your cost of margin is 6% and average return matches long-term S&P, 11%. The RRR for the un-leveraged portfolio is 11% of $2000, $220, divided by 141 = 1.56. The RRR for the leveraged portfolio is $220 + $100 ((11%-6%) of the second $2000), $320 divided by 282 = 1.13. The Return Risk Ratio (RRR) falls; the expected return falls relative to the risk taken on.

Glyn Holton has assembled an informative, well organized, presentation on risk at www.contingencyanalysis.com. There is a lot of information available free at Contingency Analysis itself, plus recommendations for sources of more detailed, more technical, coverage of risk.

Taxes

Taxes, like commissions and slippage, are unavoidable expenses, of active account management. You can and should work on reducing them, but probably shouldn't dwell on the tax impact of individual round-trips. You should concentrate on trading systems that create profit, generally that means you will have to pay taxes, but you don't want to pay more than your fair share. Your goal is to minimize taxes now, so your account, and your trading size will grow, thus increasing your future taxes.

One-way to reduce trading taxes is to trade within IRAs. This has the added advantage of reducing workload at tax filing time. Another way to reduce taxes is to trade enough to be able to file as a trader. Trader status increases expense deductions, increases the deductibility of loses, and allows mark to market adjustments at year-end. Investors' ability to deduct home office expense, subscription expense, computer expense, and seminar expense is more restricted than traders'. Another way to reduce taxes is to create an entity to contain trading, a corporation, or a partnership. The trader as employee of the new entity receives tax-free benefits, such medical plans and savings plans. *The Trader's Tax Solution* is a good resource.[64] However, depending on how big your accounts are and how sophisticated you want to be, you should consult with accountants and lawyers familiar with the tax consequences of trading, before making big changes.

Shortcut

I am not wholeheartedly endorsing shortcuts. Shortcuts weren't in my specific recommendations early in this book. Maybe I am being too puritan, sticking to my belief that return is proportional to work done or effort expended, because some regression to the mean strategies requiring no models, seem to work.

Remember, the three basic steps in *Trend Regression Portfolio Strategy*, and in Drach's High Return Low Risk Investment, are:

1. Select a group of stocks to track (master list).
2. Determine market emotion (market timing).

3. Determine relative emotion of individual equities (entries and exits).

It is possible to do three steps, or reduce the need for a step without building an elaborate model. There are internet web sites that allow selection of companies based on your selection criteria. Use selection criteria that you feel is a predictor of future stock price moves. Hedging can reduce the need for market timing. Entries and exits for longs and shorts can be based on the relative rank of individual companies in the selection screen, or on a single indicator in the selection screen.

Therefore, rather than build an elaborate Excel model, you screen for equities that best meet your criteria. You go long the top 3 to 5 positions and go short the bottom 3 to 5 positions. You size positions so 1/6 of your account is in each position. If this were your only strategy, you would want to diversify more by trading the top and bottom 5 to 20 positions, putting 1/10 to 1/40 of your account in each position.

A problem with *Trend Regression Portfolio Strategy* is in knowing when to replace equities in the model or switch models. The Shortcut eliminates this problem by re-screening every week and trading the top and bottom positions, regardless of whether they were on the list last week.

The one problem with the shortcut is I'm not sure it works. I have paper-traded 8 screens over the last 6 months, or so. Four have been abandoned, because they clearly didn't work. The remaining 4 have mixed results:

Screen	Percent Gain(Loss)
Growth (buy high historic and projected growth)	28%
Price Sales Rank (buy lowest price to sales ratio)	10%
Relative PE (buy lowest PE current relative to projected)	(9%)
S&P High Cap (buy largest capitalization, lowest PE S&P)	(3%)

The percent gain(loss) is from inception, 4 to 6 months. The Growth and Price Sales Rank look good, so far, but I haven't started trading either. Remember out of 8 schemes started 6 are underwater.

If you can find a scheme that you trust enough to trade, it might save a lot of time and effort. *Trend Regression Portfolio Strategy* models do take much time and effort to construct and maintain. After 6 months I haven't found a shortcut scheme I trust enough to trade. I'm still watching Growth and Price Sales Rank.

FREE

The MS Excel portfolio tracking worksheet available for downloading from www.diyportfoliomanagement.com comes loaded with paper-testing for a long/short hedging strategy based on two screens. The long screen finds stocks whose prices have potential to go up. The short screen finds stocks whose prices have potential to go down. Long and short positions offset to reduce market risk.

This shortcut approach eliminates step 2 (market timing), and uses screens to select groups of equities and determine relative emotion of individual equities within the groups.

13. Action Plan

This book's subtitle implies that if you read the book you should be able to learn how to manage your portfolio. Okay! You read the specific recommendations early in the book and decided you want more than a quick fix, you want to be more intimately involved with the management of your portfolio. You have decided to do the work needed to manage your portfolio, your sleeves are rolled up and your spreadsheet has a blank worksheet.

The graphic and following table highlight the steps of the standard business or entrepreneurial feedback loop. Portfolio Management requires the same attention.

Entrepreneurial Feedback Loop

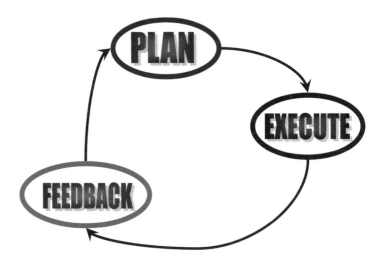

1) Develop Model (PLAN)
    A) Build Model
        a. **Pick a group of equities**
        b. **Build method to sort equities from most oversold to most overbought.**
        c. **Structure model to buy equities that are oversold, and maybe, short equities that are most overbought**
        d. **Structure model to adjust equity level appropriate for position of market in its cycle.**
        e. **Fill model with price, and/or indicator history.**
    B) Test the Model
    C) Tune the Model
    D) Repeat A through C Until 'Ready to Trade'

2) Trade the Model (EXECUTE)

3) Monitor Portfolio Performance (FEEDBACK)

4) Repeat 1 through 3 Until all your money is working.

5) Switch Models, evolve with market

Picking the equities you want to consider is important. You might want to start with equities you own, or with equities, you are tracking. My models all have 50 equities, but I am sure there is nothing magic about 50. In fact, I think more is probably better for hedging strategies.

There are many methods/indicators for determining what is oversold and overbought. I have covered some of the indicators in Part II of *DIY Portfolio Management.*

For back-testing, your model needs to track buy and sell decisions, or at least the results of buy/sell decisions.

Your model will most likely show better results if you incorporate some way of determining position in market cycle.

You should back-test your model. If your strategy can't be back-tested, or if you are not completely comfortable with the back-test, paper-trade.

If the back-test doesn't meet your performance objectives, change equities, change indicators, change something and then back-test again. It is usually good to change only one variable at a time. It is always good to document input and output variables for each back-test. Without documentation, you can waste time re-testing ideas that don't work.

Keep building, testing and tuning until you get a model you like enough to trade. Having a model you like, and trust to work in the future, will help you stick with it. This is a mechanical system; mechanical systems don't work without discipline.

Trade the Model! Trade the Model! Trade the Model! Once you build a model you trust, trade it. You need discipline. Regression to the Mean usually requires you to buy when/what others are selling and requires you to sell when/what others are buying.

Keep track of your portfolio. At least maintain an equity curve. If you are into details keep a p&l by trade. If you are really into it keep track of commissions, slippage, and maybe even maximum excursion. It's okay to get into the details but as portfolio managers our focus is the portfolio equity curve. Don't let the forest get out of focus while you concentrate on a few trees.

Don't stop with one working model. Don't put all your equity into one model. If you build 3 models, divide your equity equally, always go 100% long, and go long 3 positions, you will have 11% of your equity in each stock. Eleven percent is pretty close to the small trader rule of thumb that no more than 10% of your equity should be in any single stock. Another advantage of maintaining 3 models is that FOLIO*fn* provides 3 portfolios with commission free window trades for $295 per year. If you use FOLIO*fn* there is no reason to stick to 3 positions per portfolio, as they allow 50 positions per portfolio.

Once you are trading 3 models that work, take a day off. Take a couple of days off. When you get tired of relaxing, start building new models. Once you develop a superior model, start trading it by allocating equity to it. You can add another portfolio or switch a portfolio from the old model to a new model. If you decide to switch, you should probably time the switch to occur as the old model produces sell signals. This will probably delay switches, which is probably a good thing. *Trend Regression Portfolio Strategy* is not a short term strategy. Too many switches between models will probably hurt your results.

This book may come across to some as a sales pitch for *Trend Regression Portfolio Strategy*. That is an unfortunate byproduct of my limited communication skills. *Trend Regression Portfolio Strategy* is interesting, but what I champion is that the independent self-directed investor/trader conservatively balance risk with expected reward while taking over active management of his/her portfolio. The financial life of a trader/investor should ideally follow this cycle.

Stage 1. Take responsibility for your financial life. Pay off credit cards and other consumer debt. Save religiously; remember giving up your daily Starbucks coffee or pack of cigarettes at say $4 per day invested at a compounded 11% reaches $100,000 in less than 20 years. Internalize:

PERSONAL WEALTH = ACCUMULATED (INCOME MINUS EXPENSE)

If you don't spend less than you earn, it doesn't matter how much you make, or how terrific an investment scheme you have, you will never create your own financial independence.

Stage 2. Conserve your capital. Put your life savings in a secure place, savings account, CD, index funds, or a Drach following account. Shift more of your current income into savings. Don't use intuition to trade, don't trade on news. Skip the high tuition of working you way up through discretionary, fundamental, technical, and system trading. Going through these phases cost money and diverts your attention from building a portfolio management system.

Start reading some investment books. If you are not living beneath your means to build your nest egg, read *Rich Dad Poor Dad* or *Die Broke*. If you still believe beating the market is going to be easy, read *A Random Walk Down Wall Street*. However, if you believe beating the market is not just difficult, but impossible, read *New Market Wizards* or *High-Return Low-Risk Investment*. Remember, it is less expensive to learn from books, from teachers, than from the market.

Stage 3. Build your portfolio management system. Build models to test your trading/investing theories. Paper-trade your ideas. Refine your strategies. Be patient, work hard at building a method you trust. Document the results of your research. Remember, it is less expensive to learn from back-testing, from paper-trading, than from the market.

Stage 4. Fund your portfolio management system. Start small, shift more equity as your confidence grows. Keep working on your portfolio management system. Document the results of your trading. Remember, reading and planning are only prerequisites to learning from the market.

Stage 5. Share your research, your story. Give financial advice. Give money to charity.
Remember, there is more to life than the market.
Remember, money only buys happiness if you
spend it on the right things.

The preceding stages reflect life stages. First we are
dependent on others, then we grow to independence,
later others can depend on us. Unfortunately, still later
most of us regress and become dependent again.

Financial life has some advantages over real life. In
stage 1, we can pick who we are going to be dependent
on to conserve our capital. Unlike real life where children don't pick their parents. In stage 2, we can control
timing. Unlike real life where parents decide when they
cut off support. "Happy Graduation, congratulations on
your new job, we changed the locks, don't come home,
we've rented out your room." In stage 3, you should get
to see your wealth grow, which should help you progress in life to a position where others can depend on
you. In stage 4 you are comfortable with your financial
life, which makes it easier to be comfortable with your
real life. If your financial life is your real life, you need
a new book, not this book.

This whole process may seem like a lot of work. Yes.
Self directed investment can be a lot of work. The process of becoming a successful self-directed portfolio
entrepreneur can also be enjoyable, challenging, ab-
sorbing, and potentially profitable.

"The force be with you."[65] The lone investigator,
working at home with Excel and internet access, can do
research teams of programmers with million dollar
computers dreamed about 20 years ago.

Do you remember the IBM commercial about the
internet/IT opportunity where the business CEO is trying to get advice because his staff says the consultant's

brilliant plan is not implement-able? The advisor says they are both right. The consultant is right; it is a brilliant plan. The employees are right; the plan cannot be implemented. IBM's point – there is not much value in brilliant plans that cannot be implemented. For you to be a successful portfolio entrepreneur you need a good plan that you can implement. To be implement-able, you need enough capital to implement, you need a personal schedule that allows you to implement on time, you need account flexibility to implement specific trades, and you need enough faith in your strategy that your loss aversion adjusts to weather drawdowns. It's like auto-racing or horse racing. It's not the car or the driver, it's the combination. It's not the horse or the rider, it's the combination. For your portfolio, it's not the manager or the plan, it's the combination. Your plan has to fit you, your capability and personality. If you try to trade a plan, which is beyond your risk tolerance you will fall apart when your account equity swings below your pain threshold.

Specific Recommendations, Revisited

The specific recommendations discussed early in the book present valid investment alternatives to the regression to the mean strategies. They are valid not only if you reject *Trend Regression Portfolio Strategy*, but also for timing (where to put your money while getting ready to use *Trend Regression Portfolio Strategy*), or for risk management (where to put your money that is not in *Trend Regression Portfolio Strategy* portfolios). *Trend Regression Portfolio Strategy* is not something you can or should put all of your wealth in immediately. You need time to build, test, and gain confidence in your models. However, you can buy DIA, SPY, or QQQ and match the performance of the market you choose, immediately. You can also read High-Return Low-Risk Investment, subscribe to the Drach Market Newsletter, and have a Drach portfolio funded within a couple weeks.

> Not everyone is as big a fan of the S&P 500, as Vanguard's John Bogle.
>
> John Markman says "**The S&P 500 is a mutual fund – and a bad one.** Countless individual investors have tied some three-quarters of a trillion dollars to the "passive" index. In truth, the index is a poorly managed fund with the recent track record to prove it." His main argument against the S&P is that it is not a passive reflection of the economy, but rather a portfolio of equities built by non-professionals. That is, people that are not regulated professional money mangers. He believes the decline in the S&P 500, relative the Dow Industrials Index since 2000, is due largely to those non-professionals who at the peak replaced value equities with equities that were peaking. He goes on to say that an eight-person committee of S&P bureaucrats -- editors, business managers, quantitative analysts and an economist -- … adds and subtracts stocks frequently in accordance with a largely subjective list of criteria that includes market capitalization, liquidity and their representation of industrial sectors."
>
> **Supermodels column 6/26/2002, Jon D. Markman** is managing editor at CNBC on MSN Money. Author of the site's weekly "Supermodels" column as well as the best-selling book "Online Investing,"

DIA, SPY, and QQQ are unit investment trusts designed to track the performance of popular indexes. The Diamonds Trust, Series 1 (DIA) is designed to track the Dow. This tracking stock for the 30 corporations of the Dow Jones Industrial Average is worth about $1/100^{th}$ of the Dow Jones' value. If the Dow Industrial

Index is at 10,000, DIA should be at $100. The price of DIA generally corresponds to daily fluctuations in the Industrial Average. The SPDR Trust, Series 1 (SPY) issues Standard & Poor's Depositary Receipts (SPDRs or "spiders"), designed to track the S&P 500, is worth about one-tenth of the index, and is designed to mirror its daily undulations. The USA's largest companies are included in Standard & Poor's 500 Composite Stock Price Index (the S&P 500). Including 500 companies makes the S&P 500 a much broader measure of how the USA economy is doing, than the narrower Dow with 30 companies. The Nasdaq-100 Trust, Series 1 (QQQ), is designed to track the 100 largest companies listed on the NASDAQ exchange. The price of the tracking stock corresponds to the performance of its component equities and is about one-fortieth of the Index's value.

The three unit investment trusts described above are similar to, but have some advantages over, mutual funds. DIAs, SPYs and QQQs can be traded throughout the trading day like equities, with stop and limit prices. Generally, unit investment trusts have lower management fees than mutual funds. Commission on buy and sell transactions are the same as for equities; there are no 'trail commissions' or 12b-1 fees.

If you are in a hurry to bring order to you portfolio, start by allocating you equity between short-term bonds, DIA, SPY, and QQQ. Then read High-Return Low-Risk Investment, subscribe to Drach's newsletter, and start building a Drach portfolio. Then, start building *Trend Regression Portfolio Strategy* models. Of course, if you are already reasonably comfortable with your portfolio you can just start building *Trend Regression Portfolio Strategy* models.

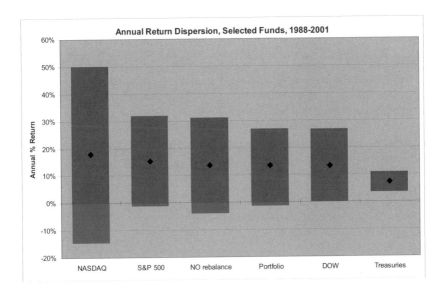

Annual Return Dispersion, Selected Funds, 1988-2001

The graph shows how a hypothetical unit trust index portfolio would have done over the last 14 years. This portfolio assumes rebalancing so each fund starts the new year with the same equity. Risk increases a little, if there is no rebalancing. For this 14 year period there was little advantage to holding the four-component portfolio, over putting everything in the S&P index (or SPY).

So, you could use unit investment trusts and Drach portfolios instead of *Trend Regression Portfolio Strategy*, or as stabilizing steps prior to funding *Trend Regression Portfolio Strategy*. You should exercise patience while building, back-testing, and paper-trading *Trend Regression Portfolio Strategy* models or models of your own creation.

Creativity, Discretion, and Discipline

One last note. Try not to use creativity and discretion when placing trades. Your edge is the synergy of your model and your discipline. If you trade against your model, you lose your edge. In the casino, the house has the edge and if you play long enough you will lose all your money. If you want to make money, use your edge.

Use your creativity to come up with strategies to test. Use your discretion to decide which models to trade. Use self-discipline to stick with your model until you have a better model ready to move out of development into production.

Appendix

Trend Regression Portfolio Strategy **Runs**

As my back-testing progressed, I became more organized and started keeping a summary of performance
data for instances that I optimized or update prices in a
model. The large table on the next page shows detailed
records of model runs.

The graph below shows return (gain%) plotted
against risk (drawdown) for 313 model runs.

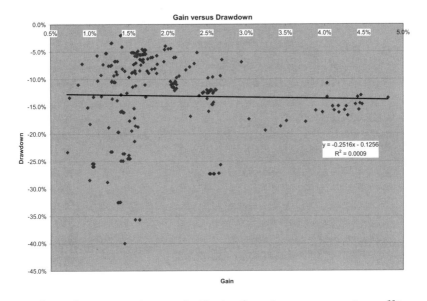

The data-points and their least squares trendline
don't show the expected relationship between reward
and risk. Risk does appear to increase with return, but
R^2 is less than .001. That is, risk accounts for less than
.1% of the variability in return. For *Trend Regression
Portfolio Strategy* models risk seems independent of return. This graph includes 313 runs made between
7/13/2001 and 6/23/2002.

Trend Regression Portfolio Strategy Model Runs

313	INPUT	Optimized OUTPUT													
model	Run Date	TRiPS %	MAX Drawdown	RRR	Gain%	Gain$	Relative Gain	Index Gain	Optimized Smoothing Weeks	Optimized Proportion Timed	Long Optimized Indicator	Short Optimized Indicator	Trade % Win	Week % Win	% LONG
LEAP 50 NT d.xls	6/21/02	0.5%	25.4%	26.9%	1.0%	$ 1,029	133%	474%	3	0	comp	price %	57.1%	61.6%	100%
HILO 052202 NT.xls	6/21/02	0.9%	23.9%	35.0%	1.5%	$ 1,498	149%	595%	4	0	comp	price %	59.2%	65.0%	100%
corr qqq 052202 NT.xls	6/21/02	0.4%	58.4%	21.0%	3.0%	$ 3,034	1625%	34%	4	30	slope	price %	50.1%	54.3%	80%
ag1 052202 NT.xls	6/21/02	1.4%	25.7%	35.9%	2.7%	$ 2,666	291%	196%	35	0	comp	price %	58.0%	61.4%	100%
SG 052202 NT.xls	6/21/02	0.5%	40.0%	26.9%	1.4%	$ 1,443	238%	149%	8	0	rel price	price %	59.3%	63.6%	100%
LEAP 50 NT d.xls	6/21/02	0.4%	26.0%	28.2%	1.0%	$ 1,034	134%	474%	3	0	comp	price %	57.9%	60.7%	100%
HILO 052202 NT.xls	6/18/02	0.9%	23.9%	35.0%	1.5%	$ 1,497	147%	603%	4	0	comp	price %	59.2%	65.0%	100%
dmthilo NT.xls	6/18/02	0.6%	32.5%	34.8%	1.4%	$ 1,357	118%	677%	3	0	comp	price %	57.8%	63.0%	100%
LEAP 50 NT d.xls	6/17/02	0.5%	26.0%	28.5%	1.0%	$ 1,043	130%	493%	3	0	comp	price %	58.0%	60.8%	100%
corr qqq 052202 NT.xls	6/17/02	0.4%	58.4%	20.4%	3.0%	$ 3,044	1879%	28%	4	30	slope	price %	48.7%	53.9%	80%
LEAP 50 NT d.xls	6/14/02	0.5%	26.0%	28.5%	1.0%	$ 1,043	130%	493%	3	0	comp	price %	58.0%	60.8%	100%
SG 052202 NT.xls	6/14/02	0.7%	35.7%	31.4%	1.6%	$ 1,633	270%	142%	8	0	rel price	price %	60.2%	64.2%	100%
corr qqq 052202 NT.xls	6/14/02	0.5%	58.5%	24.3%	3.1%	$ 3,075	1407%	46%	4	30	slope	price %	50.8%	55.7%	79%
HILO 052202 NT.xls	6/14/02	0.8%	24.5%	34.4%	1.5%	$ 1,484	171%	516%	4	0	comp	price %	58.8%	65.0%	100%
ag1 052202 NT.xls	6/14/02	1.2%	27.3%	34.4%	2.5%	$ 2,539	290%	189%	35	0	comp	price %	56.6%	61.4%	100%
dmthilo NT.xls	6/11/02	0.6%	32.5%	35.3%	1.4%	$ 1,370	117%	693%	3	0	comp	price %	57.8%	63.1%	100%
LEAP 50 NT d.xls	6/9/02	0.5%	26.0%	28.7%	1.0%	$ 1,048	130%	499%	3	0	comp	price %	57.9%	60.8%	100%
LEAP 50 NT a.xls	6/8/02	0.5%	25.4%	27.5%	1.0%	$ 1,047	130%	499%	3	0	comp	price %	57.3%	61.8%	100%
dmthilo NT.xls	6/7/02	0.6%	32.4%	35.2%	1.4%	$ 1,387	119%	691%	3	0	comp	price %	57.8%	63.5%	100%
corr qqq 052202 NT.xls	6/7/02	0.5%	58.5%	24.9%	3.1%	$ 3,137	1387%	47%	4	30	slope	price %	50.9%	56.3%	79%
ag1 052202 NT.xls	6/7/02	0.7%	35.7%	30.3%	1.6%	$ 1,578	257%	148%	8	0	rel price	price %	60.2%	63.6%	100%
HILO 052202 NT.xls	6/7/02	0.9%	24.5%	35.1%	1.5%	$ 1,500	164%	543%	4	0	comp	price %	58.9%	65.0%	100%
ag1 052202 NT.xls	6/7/02	1.2%	27.3%	34.2%	2.5%	$ 2,527	283%	192%	35	0	comp	price %	56.6%	61.4%	100%
LEAP 50 NT a.xls	6/7/02	0.4%	25.4%	25.4%	1.0%	$ 993	122%	508%	9	0	comp	price %	56.3%	61.0%	100%
LEAP 50 NT.xls	6/5/02	0.3%	23.3%	22.7%	0.7%	$ 710	136%	342%	12	30	comp	comp	52.8%	62.2%	76%
LEAP 50 rsi long 050302 NT.xls	5/31/02	0.6%	23.6%	28.1%	1.4%	$ 1,376	229%	230%	4	0	comp	price %	55.8%	60.5%	100%
ag1 052202 NT.xls	5/31/02	1.3%	27.3%	35.1%	2.6%	$ 2,577	267%	207%	35	0	comp	price %	56.8%	61.9%	100%
HILO 052202 NT.xls	5/31/02	0.9%	24.5%	35.4%	1.5%	$ 1,511	159%	564%	4	0	comp	price %	59.0%	65.2%	100%
r 10 peg 1 NT.xls	5/26/02	1.0%	21.6%	37.5%	1.5%	$ 1,523	145%	197%	8	0	comp	price %	60.3%	62.7%	100%
LEAP 50 rsi long 050302 (ver 1) 5/25/02	5/25/02	0.6%	23.6%	28.5%	1.4%	$ 1,394	224%	238%	4	0	RSI	RSI	56.3%	60.8%	100%
HILO 052202 NT.xls	5/24/02	0.9%	24.5%	35.4%	1.5%	$ 1,511	156%	572%	4	0	comp	price %	59.1%	65.2%	100%
ag1 052202 NT.xls	5/24/02	1.3%	27.3%	35.2%	2.6%	$ 2,587	271%	205%	35	0	comp	price %	56.6%	62.5%	100%
ag1 052202 NT.xls	5/24/02	0.7%	13.1%	35.4%	1.1%	$ 1,147	149%	201%	35	0	comp	s/see	52.0%	64.2%	50%
HILO 052202 NT.xls	5/22/02	0.9%	24.5%	35.3%	1.5%	$ 1,508	153%	584%	4	0	comp	price %	59.0%	65.2%	100%
ag1 052202 NT.xls	5/22/02	1.3%	27.2%	35.9%	2.6%	$ 2,645	281%	201%	34	0	comp	price %	58.0%	64.2%	100%
dmthilo 050702 c.xls	5/22/02	0.8%	17.6%	34.1%	1.5%	$ 717	67%	702%	3	70	comp	price %	58.0%	64.1%	49%
dmthilo 050702.xls	5/21/02	0.9%	16.1%	34.3%	1.4%	$ 1,389	115%	711%	13	0	rel price	price %	57.5%	61.8%	100%
LEAP 50 rsi long 050302 (ver 5/17/02	5/17/02	0.6%	24.9%	28.4%	1.4%	$ 1,376	215%	249%	4	0	RSI*%T	RSI	57.2%	60.5%	100%
HILO long 10yr (version 1) 13	5/17/02	0.7%	23.2%	29.5%	1.3%	$ 1,241	127%	583%	15	0	rel price	price %	57.9%	64.5%	100%
SG1 051602.xls	5/17/02	0.4%	28.8%	22.3%	1.2%	$ 892	181%	156%	8	50	rel price	price %	58.1%	60.3%	75%
AG1 012102.xls	5/17/02	0.9%	17.1%	38.2%	1.6%	$ 2,050	168%	208%	12	50	price %	s/see	52.6%	59.6%	43%
dmthilo 050702.xls	5/14/02	0.9%	16.1%	34.0%	1.4%	$ 1,379	112%	731%	13	0	rel price	price %	57.4%	61.6%	100%
LEAP 50 rsi long 050302 (ver 5/10/02	5/10/02	0.6%	24.9%	28.1%	1.4%	$ 1,352	218%	239%	4	0	RSI*%T	RSI	57.2%	60.5%	100%
HILO long 10yr (version 1) 13	5/10/02	0.7%	23.2%	29.2%	1.3%	$ 1,225	130%	566%	15	0	rel price	price %	57.9%	64.5%	100%
SG1 042002.xls	5/10/02	0.7%	21.4%	27.2%	1.6%	$ 1,093	200%	150%	8	50	rel price	price %	58.5%	60.9%	72%
AG1 012102.xls	5/10/02	0.8%	18.6%	38.3%	1.6%	$ 2,062	175%	200%	12	50	price %	s/see	52.6%	61.6%	43%
dmthilo 050702.xls	5/7/02	0.9%	16.0%	33.9%	1.4%	$ 1,366	115%	704%	13	0	rel price	price %	57.3%	61.4%	100%
dmthilo small.xls	5/6/02	0.9%	12.6%	33.6%	1.5%	$ 1,086	94%	711%	13	40	rel price	price %	57.3%	61.2%	78%
dmthilo small short.xls	5/6/02	1.0%	9.6%	32.8%	1.5%	$ 863	141%	101%	12	70	rel price	price %	58.2%	62.7%	62%
LEAP 50 rsi long 050302 (ver 5/4/02	5/4/02	0.6%	18.8%	28.5%	1.2%	$ 1,199	213%	222%	4	0	RSI*%T	RSI	57.2%	60.8%	100%
HILO long 10yr (version 1) 13	5/3/02	0.7%	23.2%	29.3%	1.3%	$ 1,227	127%	582%	15	0	rel price	price %	58.0%	64.5%	100%
SG1 042002.xls	5/3/02	0.7%	15.4%	27.4%	1.6%	$ 1,087	196%	154%	8	50	rel price	price %	58.5%	60.3%	72%
AG1 012102.xls	5/3/02	0.9%	18.7%	40.2%	1.6%	$ 2,109	178%	199%	12	50	price %	s/see	52.5%	62.3%	43%
dmthilo0.xls	5/1/02	0.7%	19.7%	32.5%	1.4%	$ 1,323	111%	711%	15	0	rel price	price %	57.6%	61.4%	100%
dmthilo50.xls	5/1/02	0.8%	15.8%	32.4%	1.4%	$ 956	84%	711%	25	50	rel price	price %	57.2%	61.2%	64%
dmthilo.xls	4/30/02	0.8%	16.0%	34.1%	1.4%	$ 1,349	113%	711%	29	0	rel price	price %	57.4%	61.2%	100%
dmthilo.xls	4/30/02	0.8%	19.7%	32.9%	1.4%	$ 1,315	112%	704%	29	0	rel price	price %	57.3%	60.8%	100%
AG1 012102.xls	4/28/02	1.1%	5.2%	39.6%	1.6%	$ 2,083	173%	204%	12	50	price %	s/see	52.3%	61.6%	43%
LEAP 50 rsi long.xls	4/26/02	0.6%	7.6%	24.3%	1.2%	$ 1,199	214%	222%	9	0	RSI*%T	RSI	55.0%	61.7%	100%
corr qqq a.xls	4/26/02	1.7%	13.3%	26.2%	4.4%	$ 4,280	1335%	60%	4	0	slope	price %	51.4%	58.3%	100%
HILO long 10yr (version 1) 13	4/26/02	0.8%	3.4%	29.3%	1.3%	$ 1,231	129%	574%	15	0	rel price	price %	57.9%	64.5%	100%
DMT 010802.xls	4/26/02	1.4%	12.5%	29.7%	2.4%	$ 6,503	226%	204%	29	0	rel price	price %	58.3%	58.3%	100%
SG1 042002.xls	4/26/02	0.8%	5.8%	27.6%	1.6%	$ 1,095	194%	154%	8	50	rel price	price %	58.5%	60.3%	72%
dmthilo.xls	4/23/02	1.1%	1.9%	34.6%	1.4%	$ 1,384	112%	723%	30	0	rel price	price %	57.7%	61.2%	100%
HILO long 10yr (version 1) 13	4/22/02	0.9%	3.4%	29.6%	1.3%	$ 1,239	125%	597%	15	0	rel price	price %	58.0%	64.7%	100%

The next graph results from filtering run data to concentrate on the 5 models with the most frequency. These are also the 5 models that are being maintained weekly as of June 2002.

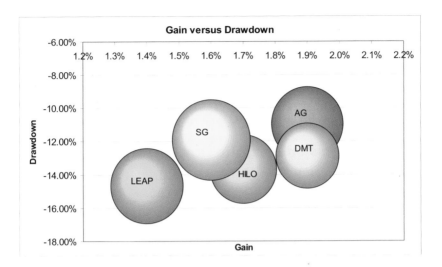

Drawdown is plotted as a negative number on the y-axis, gain is on the x-axis, bubble size is standard deviation of drawdown. Return appears to increase with reduced drawdown. This implies that finding models having both higher return and lower drawdown is possible.

Summary information for these five models shows some convergence.

INPUT			Optimized OUTPUT									
			TRiPS	MAX Drawdow			Gain	Optimized Smoothing	Optimized Proportio	Long Optimized	Short Optimized		%
model	Run Date	Weeks	%	n	RRR		%	Weeks	n Timed	Indicator	Indicator	% LONG	SHORT
LEAP 50	6/22/02	520	0.5%	25.4%	26.9%		1.0%	3	0	comp	price %	100%	0%
HILO	6/21/02	520	0.9%	23.9%	35.0%		1.5%	4	0	comp	price %	100%	0%
AG	6/21/02	150	1.4%	25.7%	35.9%		2.7%	35	0	comp	price %	100%	0%
SG	6/21/02	150	0.5%	40.0%	26.9%		1.4%	8	0	rel price	price %	100%	0%
dmthilo	6/18/02	520	0.6%	32.5%	34.8%		1.4%	3	0	comp	price %	100%	0%

All models optimized going 100% long, none employs market timing or shorting. The 10-year models optimized with few (3 or 4) smoothing-weeks and composite indicator. The composite indicator in all cases results from ranking equities based on their Price%, Relative Price, and Slope indicators. The 3-year models optimized with more smoothing-weeks (8 and 35), and used composite and relative price indicators. TRiPS% range is broad, from 0.5% to 1.4%.

These models are setting norms for back-testing; results outside of these ranges would be cause for enthusiastic greeting of a breakthrough, or increased auditing of model logic and stock price history.

Trend Regression Portfolio Strategy Back-test **Norms**

Performance Measure	Worst	Best
TRiPS%	0.5%	1.4%
Max Drawdown	-40%	-24%
Risk Reward Ratio	27%	36%
Gain%	1%	2.7%

When I get results outside these norms, the first thing I look for is inconsistencies in the stock price histories. The most frequent problem is stock splits, sometimes it is delisting or name changes. The second thing I look for is logic problems. I check the most recent logic changes to ensure that current results are meaningful. Now, the last thing I do is start trading a new system/model that has unusually good results.

The graph below compares results for seven indicators that were the optimal indicator in at least 6 runs.

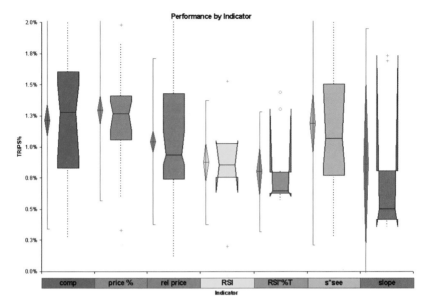

Relative price showed up as the optimal indicator the most frequently, followed by composite, then price%. The best average TRiPS% was recorded for price%, followed by comp, then s*see.

Performance by Stock Indicator
(frequent models)

Indicator	n	Mean TRiPS%	Std Dev
Composite	63	1.21%	0.532%
Price%	57	1.29%	0.442%
relative price	83	1.04%	0.406%
RSI	16	0.88%	0.302%
RSI*%T	11	0.80%	0.292%
s*see	25	1.19%	0.595%
slope	6	0.86%	0.660%

The chart and table below are from 10-year model runs. For these longer runs only the comp and relative price indicators have been optimal indicators.

There are three models with 10-years of price data, dmthilo, LEAP 50, and HILO. Between the three 50 equity models, there are only 82 equities in total. LEAP 50 has always optimized on the composite

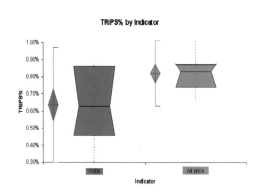

indicator. HILO and dmthilo have optimized on relative price, but currently optimize on a composite indicator. As of 6/22/2002, all three optimize on a composite indicator composed of price%, relative price, and slope components.

Performance by Stock Indicator
(10-year model subset)

Indicator	n	Mean TRiPS%	Std Dev
Composite	20	0.64%	0.204%
Relative price	19	0.82%	0.117%

As back-testing evolved the winning percent of trades and of weeks was recorded for each run. This chart summarizes results from 228 back-tests that had both winning percent trades and winning percent weeks re-corded.

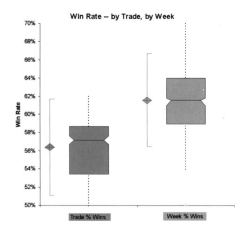

The mean for weekly win rate is much higher than the trade win rate. Given the win rate for a random trade should be 50% (50/50, 50 wins for each 50 losses, 1:1), then 56% (56/44, 1.27:1) trade win rate is quite an improvement over random, and the 61% (61/39, 1.56:1) weekly win rate is much better than the trade win rate.

Win Rate – by Trade, by Week

	n	Mean Win Rate	Standard Deviation	Standard Error of Estimate
Trade % Win	228	56.4%	3.2%	0.2%
Week % Win	228	61.5%	3.2%	0.2%

The average weekly win rate is greater than trade win rate because the average win amount is greater than average loss amount. All these models buy and track three positions per week. There are more weeks were one win is larger than the sum of 2 losses than there are weeks were one loss is greater than sum of 2 wins.

The next graph illustrates the distribution of optimal smoothing-weeks for the 228 runs in the previous table. The histogram shows a heavy concentration in bars that cover the 0-4 and 5-9 smoothing-week

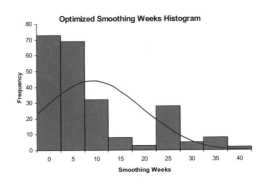

Optimized Smoothing Weeks Histogram

ranges. This means the most important cycle to the *Trend Regression Portfolio Strategy* is a relatively short one, somewhere in the 3 to 9 week range.

The next graph was a surprise.

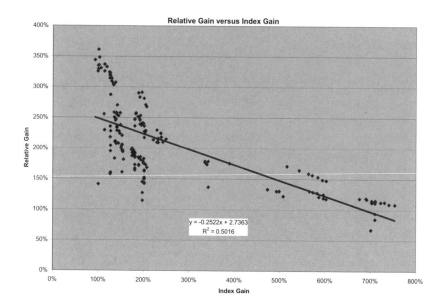

I expected little correlation between relative gain and index gain. Index gain is the amount a buy and hold portfolio of 50 equities appreciated over the back-test duration. Relative gain is the amount the model portfolio increased over the index gain. I am surprised that 50% of the variation in relative value is explained by the variation in index value. I am more surprised that the relationship is inverse. Relative gain declines as index gain increases. This may mean that *Trend Regression Portfolio Strategy* will work best, relative to 'buy and hold,' for stock groups that have flat to moderate growth price trends.

The graph below, Drawdown versus RRR, was also a bit of a surprise.

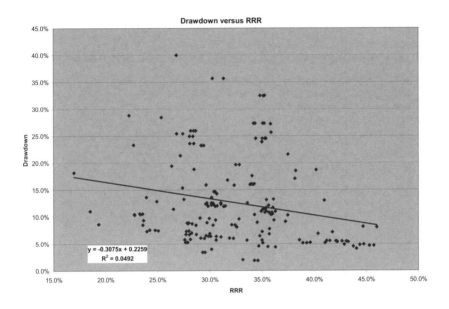

I expected more of a relationship between drawdown and Reward/Risk Ratio (RRR). Drawdown, like RRR, is a function of the standard deviation of trades' gain (loss). I expected drawdown to decline as RRR climbed, and it seems to, but not to the extent anticipated. The drawdown trendline declines nearly a third of a percentage point per percentage point increase in RRR, quite a bit. However, R^2 is less than 5%. RRR explains only 5% of the variability in drawdown. RRR is calculated directly from standard deviation of trades' gain (loss). Drawdown depends not only on standard deviation, but also on sequence of trades.

Index

NOTES

[1] An automotive example of a black box is an automatic transmission. The transmission processes data about engine speed, ground speed and accelerator pedal placement to select appropriate gears for the current situation. The driver only has to regulate placement of the accelerator pedal and the transmission figures out the details. An electronic example of a black box is a telephone. The user doesn't need to worry about how voice is converted to electric signals that can be conveyed over wires and converted back to voice by another telephone at the other end. The trading black box issues trades for traders.

[2] Schwager, Jack D., 1992, *The New Market Wizards,* .

[3] In introduction to *The New Market Wizards.*

[4] Bernstein, Peter L., 1996, *Against the Gods (The Remarkable Story of Risk),* John Wiley & sons, Inc. p. 284, quoting Daniel Kahneman coinventor of Prospect Theory.

[5] For contrast, in the Woody Allen movie *Deconstructing Harry,* the devil (Billy Crystal) says something like 'Sure the house always wins, but at least you're having fun.'

[6] *Against the Gods,* p. 297.

[7] Carter, Jack, 1999, *The 7 Habits of Highly Successful Online Stock Traders.*

[8] Goldberg, Steven T., "He Never Saw The Sun," *Kiplinger's Personal Finance,* August 2001, Vol.55, No.8, pp. 40-45.

[9] *Against the Gods,* pp. 166-171.

[10] *Against the Gods,* pp 168-169.

[11] Thomas J. Herzfeld, Robert F. Drach, 1981,*HIGH-RETURN LOW-RISK INVESTMENT, (Combining Market Timing, stock Selection, and Closed-End Funds),*

[12] As of 3/28/2003 the same account is up 28%from its January 2001 inception.

[13] Peter Juhl, *Does a mean reversion strategy really work?* February 2000, Robert Fleming & Co. Limited, 25 Copthall Avenue, London, www.flemingsresearch.com

[14] Charles D. Ellis, *The Investment Setting,* in Peter L. Bernstein, *The Portable MBA in Investment,* 1995, John Wiley & Sons, Inc. p 11. According to Ellis Tversky and Kahneman also pointed out 3 other phenomenon important to investors. 1) People's fear of loss often prevents them from taking risk even when they could "in all probability" profit by taking certain risks. 2) People's fear of regret or shame restrains the way most investment managers do their work. 3) People

exaggerate the importance of very unusual events. 4) People overreact to recent information (causing eventual regression to the mean).

[15] Ronald J. Balvers and Yangru Wu, *Momentum And Mean Reversion Across National Equity Markets*, December 2001

[16] Momentum   - Jegadeesh and Titman (1993)
                - Chan, Jegadeesh, and Lakonishok (1996)
                - Rouwenhorst (1998)
                - Chan, Hameed and Tong (2000)
                - Grundy and Martin (2001)
                - Jegadeesh and Titman (2001)
  Reversion   - DeBondt and Thaler (1985, 1987)
                - Chopra, Lakonishok, and Ritter (1992)
                - Richards (1997)

[17] Dr. Clayton M. Christensen, author of *The Innovator's Dilemma: When New Technologies Cause Great Firms to Fail*, interviewed in *Strategy + Business,* issue 25 December, 2001, by Lawrence M. Fisher.

[18] Encarta Pocket Dictionary, number 4 of 5 definitions.

[19] American Heritage Talking Dictionary, number 4 of 5 definitions.

[20] *Against the Gods*, p. 182.

[21] Tushar S. Chande, PhD, 1997, *Beyond Technical Analysis*, p. 41

[22] Hill, Arthur, <u>StockCharts.com</u>, <u>http://www.stockcharts.com/education/resources/glossary/AROON.ht ml</u>

[23] Turner, Michael P., *DayTrading into the Millennium*, 1998, p. 69

[24] *DayTrading into the Millennium*, 1998, p. 123

[25] DownLoaderXL available for download from <u>www.analyzerxl.com</u> -- $34.95 registration after 10 day free trial, runs as a VBA package within Excel, only end-of-day (EOD) data.

[26] HQuote available for download from <u>www.hquote.com</u> $49 registration after 30 day free trial, can automate download of up to 1000 securities. Both intraday and EOD data are available.

[27] AIQ Trading Expert Pro is available from AIQ Systems, PO Box 7530, Incline Village, NV 89452 <u>www.aiqsystems.com</u> -- $59/month for software and data feed.

[28] If detailed www address doesn't work start at root address and look for screen page. Most sites have pre-built screens and the ability to customized or build from scratch.

[29] <u>http://www.e-analytics.com/dowchang.htm</u> Equity Analytics, Ltd. has a detailed history of the evolution of the Dow indexes and other useful investor information. One of the best things about the site is their tag

line. **"Invest Your Time Before You Invest Your Money**
Test Your Strategy Before You Risk Your Money"

[30] NeuroShell Trader is available from Ward Systems Group, Inc., Executive Park West, 5 Hillcrest Drive, Frederick, MD 21703 , Phone: (301) 662-7950, Fax: (301) 663-9920 Email: sales@wardsystems.com. In addition to NeuroShell's 800+ indicators, it also provides tools for creating custom indicators.

[31] The reversal of sign comes about because of my organizing the model with most recent weeks above later weeks. To get Excel to plot time proceeding left to right x-axis has to be reversed causing sign to be switched in linear regression formulas.

[32] *Beyond Technical Analysis,* p. 179.

[33] A. A. Groppelli, and Ehsan Nikbakht, *FINANCE*, 1995, Barron's Educational Series, Inc.

[34] RRR is similar to Sharpe Ratio or Information Ratio. Sharpe and Information Ratios use return compared to riskless return or return compared to benchmark return.

[35] Martin J. Pring, *Martin Pring on Market Momentum*, 1993, McGraw-Hill

[36] Annis, Charles, P.E. www.statisticalengineering.com
"The distribution of an average tends to be Normal, even when the distribution from which the average is computed is decidedly non-Normal. ...Furthermore, *this normal distribution will have the **same mean** as the parent distribution*, and, variance equal to the variance of the parent divided by the sample size."

[37] David and Tom Gardner are financial authors and founders of the www.fool.com, the Motley Fool web site. The web site has a clean design, and lots of interesting and useful information. Their 13-steps is an interesting read, especially for investor newbies or wannabees. Tom and David are 'buy and hold fundamentalists,' and their 13-steps have evolved more in that direction, since I first came across them 2 or 3 years ago.

[38] Fredston, Jill, *Rowing to Latitude, Journeys Along the Arctic's Edge*, 2001, North Point Press, pp 242 & 258.

[39] www.diyportfoliomanagement.com has current Marketocracy results.

[40] Independent studies by Burton G. Malkiel, Mark Carhart, and the trio of Jenke ter Horst, Theo Nijman and Marno Verbeek show that mutual fund performance statistics are overstated by a significant amount, when average performance is reported for existing funds without including poor performing funds that have disappeared.

[41] Anonymous. Okay, maybe it was my full service broker charging me $200 a round trip for slow manual executions. What a difference a decade makes.

[42] Slippage is the difference between the trigger price, from a model or system, and the actual trade price. Slippage can also be the difference between the price you think your broker will get for you and the actual trade price. Sometimes its not the broker's fault; the market is moving too fast or is too slow to get the execution you want.

[43] FOLIO*fn* allows 500 commission-free window trades a month.

[44] Ginold, Richard C. and Kahn, Ronald N., *Active Portfolio Management, A quantitative Approach for Producing Superior Returns and Controlling Risk*, 1999 p. 446

[45] Enron when it filed for bankruptcy on 12/2/2001 was the largest bankruptcy in USA corporate history. It effected other oil companies, its suppliers and its banks. It pulled down stock prices of other companies with aggressive accounting, probably delayed the end of the bear market that started in March 2000, and spurred congressional action on pension security, accounting, and financial disclosure.

[46] Sweeney, John, *Maximum Adverse Excursion, Analyzing Price Fluctuations for Trading Management*, 1997, John Wiley & Sons, Inc.

[47] *Maximum Adverse Excursion, Analyzing Price Fluctuations for Trading Management*, p10.

[48] Dobrovolsky, Sergei, *Setting Stops And Taking Profits With Maximum Excursion*, Technical Analysis of Stocks & Commodities, August 2002, pp. 70-74.

[49] Vince, Ralph, *Portfolio Management Formulas*, 1990 p.68.

[50] *Portfolio Management Formulas*, p.85.

[51] Vince, Ralph, *Portfolio Management Formulas*, 1990 p.183.

[52] Turner, Michael P., *DayTrading into the Millennium*, 1998 p. 13 "If you do not have a statistical advantage, and you are guessing at price movements, then you truly are gambling."

[53] Charles Williams, http://www.decisionmodels.com/, Decision Models Ltd, FastExcel about USD$ 50.

[54] Edgar E. Peters, *Complexity, Risk, and Financial Markets*, John Wiley & Sons, Inc. 1999, pp. 5-6.

[55] Burton G. Malkiel, *A Random Walk Down Wall Street* (The Best Investment Advice for the New Century), 1999, W. W. Norton & Company Ltd. p. 355.

[56] Stephen M. Pollan, *Die Broke*, 1997, Harper Business.

[57] Lowell Miller, *The Single Best Investment*, 1999, Adams Media Corporation, p. 5.

[58] *The Single Best Investment,* p. 9.

[59] When I wrote this Love thing, I thought it was clever and original. However a few days later I read, "**Don't let emotions rule your actions**. ... Invest thoughtfully and rationally. Stocks don't love you, so don't fall in love with them." 11/27/2001, Brian Lund, The Motely Fool, Investing Strategies newsletter.

[60] *A Random Walk Down Wall Street.*

[61] Dr. Malkiel said it best, "...the mathematical precision of the firm-foundation value formulas is based on treacherous ground: forcasting the future."

[62] Bittman, James B., Chicago Board Options Exchange,1995, *Options, Essential Concepts and Trading Strategies,* McGraw Hill

[63] Characteristics and Risks of Standardized Options is produced by USA stock exchanges and your broker must deliver it to you when your option account is opened.

[64] Ted Tesser, *The trader's Tax Solution (Money-saving Strategies for the Serious Investor),* 2000, John Wiley & Sons, Inc.

[65] Obe Wan Kenobi in Star Wars.

About the Author

Lyle Wilkinson was born and raised in Canada. He has a Diploma of Technology from the British Columbia Institute of Technology, and both BBA and MBA from the University of Hawaii. His employee career included administrative and management positions in Hawaii sugar and coffee agribusinesses.

In the mid 70s, Lyle discovered that brokers' incentives weren't always aligned with increasing Lyle's wealth. He backed off his discretionary trading when his broker bragged about his record commission based earnings, while Lyle was risking equity and barely breaking even. His MBA Finance classes, performance of average mutual funds, and lack of correlation between financial analyst recommendations and subsequent price movement had him leaning toward the random walk theory of price movement. The fact that his business education and work experience didn't lead to stellar investment returns also helped him rationalize that equity price movements were random. Still his belief in the randomness of price movements was dogged by lingering doubt. Always a fan of data driven decisions he began researching disciplined, mechanical, system approaches to the stock market in 1999. His email address is

lyle@diyportfoliomanagement.com

Quick Order Form

www.diyportfoliomanagement.com

email orders: orders@diyportfoliomanagement.com

Postal orders: Selact Publishing
PO Box 3182-304
Wailuku, HI 96793, USA

Please send ____ copies of DIY Portfolio Management. I understand that I may return for a full refund—for any reason, no questions asked.

Name: _____

Address: _____

City: _____ State: _____ Zip: _____

Telephone: _____

Email address: _____

Sales tax: Please add 4% for books shipped to Hawaii.

Shipping by Air:
USA: $4.50 first book, $2.00 for each additional
International: $9.00 first book, $5.00 for each additional

Payment: ___ Check   ___ Credit Card
___Visa

Card number: _____

Name on card: _____ Exp. Date: _____